A Village Called Trinity

A Headmaster's Reflections through the First Twenty Years

Peter T. Denton, Jr.

Trinity School of Durham and Chapel Hill

© 2015 by Peter T. Denton, Jr.

Published by Lulu Press
www.lulu.com

Printed in the United States of America

All rights reserved. No part of this publication may be reproduced, stored in a retrieval system, or transmitted in any form or by any means—for example, electronic, photocopy, or recording—without the prior written permission of the publisher. The only exception is brief quotations in printed reviews.

All scripture quotations, unless otherwise indicated, are taken from the Holy Bible, New International Version®, NIV®. Copyright ©1973, 1978, 1984, 2011 by Biblica, Inc.™ Used by permission of Zondervan. All rights reserved worldwide. www.zondervan.com The "NIV" and "New International Version" are trademarks registered in the United States Patent and Trademark Office by Biblica, Inc.™

Nothing worth doing is completed in our lifetime; therefore we must be saved by hope. Nothing true or beautiful makes complete sense in any immediate context of history; therefore we must be saved by faith. Nothing we do, however virtuous, can be accomplished alone; therefore, we are saved by love.

REINHOLD NIEBUHR, *THE IRONY OF AMERICAN HISTORY*

Contents

- v   Contents
- ix   Preface
- xiii   Introduction
- xvii   The Trinity Story

1   Section 1 – Vision
- 3   A Village Called Trinity
- 6   Why Go to School?
- 9   Experimenting on Our Children
- 12   Positively Countercultural
- 15   The End of Education
- 18   Why Trinity?
- 22   One Nation Under God?
- 27   Self Education
- 31   What Good Is an Education?
- 35   What I Saw When I Looked Up
- 39   Truth, Goodness, and Beauty

45   Section 2 – Christian
- 47   A School That Changes Lives
- 50   Where Is the Christian in Christian Education?
- 53   The Dilemma of Faith and Learning
- 57   Science and Religion at Trinity School
- 61   All Truth Is God's Truth

- 65 Section 3 – Classical Learning
  - 67 A Liberal Education
  - 70 *Paideia*
  - 74 The Education of Abraham Lincoln
  - 77 Math Matters
  - 81 The Genius of a Classical Education
  - 85 Teaching Students to Think for Themselves
  - 89 The Classical Ideal
  - 93 Fishing for Answers or Fishing for Men?

- 97 Section 4 – Rich Learning
  - 99 Why Trinity Reads
  - 103 Beyond Educational Tourism
  - 107 The Developmental Approach to Learning
  - 111 On the Sacredness of Personhood
  - 114 Education from the Inside Out
  - 118 Mind Food

- 125 Section 5 – Unhurried Learning
  - 127 An Education of Classical Proportions
  - 131 On Dealing with Problomes
  - 135 Homework: Friend or Foe?
  - 140 On Being Bored
  - 143 The Art of Teaching
  - 147 The Myth of Multitasking
  - 151 Unhurried Generosity
  - 155 Homework 2.0

- 161 Section 6 – Moral Education
  - 163 A Steep Good
  - 167 Some Thoughts on Moral Education
  - 171 A Jewish Book for a Christian School
  - 174 The Gift of *Non Nobis*
  - 178 True Grit
  - 182 On Habit and Character

187 Section 7 – The Arts
    189 *De Gustibus*
    192 Strange Artists
    195 Struggling Toward Originality
    198 The Aristocracy of Art

203 Section 8 – Diversity
    205 Everybody's Doing Diversity—But Not Like This
    208 Trinity's Diversity Policy
    211 Do We Still Have a Dream?
    215 Picture Trinity School
    220 The Birthright of Freedom

223 Section 9 – Technology
    225 The Once and Future School
    229 It's Complicated
    232 What Technology Affords
    234 Our Digital *Minhag*

239 Section 10 – Athletics
    241 The Race That Three Girls Won
    244 Speaking of Sports
    248 Respect the Game
    251 Sportsmanship

255 Section 11 – Occasional Pieces
    257 A Second Year of Growth
    259 A Second Year of Growth (Revisited)
    261 A School for Our Community
    264 My Chronicle of Narnia
    266 Boundary Lines in Pleasant Places
    269 What I Learned in Africa
    273 Our Given Christmas Story

277 Bibliography
287 Index

Preface

We take care of Trinity, and Trinity takes care of us. I have said that many times, and I have seen that the school has been a good place for many. Certainly I am one of those. I have so much to be thankful for, and I am glad that so much of my adult life and calling have been lived in the shade of the community that is Trinity School.

On the occasion of our twentieth year of school (2014–2015), it seemed good to collect a number of *Parent News* columns into one volume. My hope is that this might secure some of the memories of Trinity's beginnings, memories that fade every year the school grows. I also want to perpetuate the school's founding mission and pass along to new generations of parents and school leaders what we have been aiming for in these first two decades. I hope that these pieces show a strong continuity, and I know that they show growth and development, too. Both are essential to any healthy institution.

It would be futile to try to thank everyone here. Over twenty years, there have been so many allies, friends, supporters, and partners that the list would look like a compendium of the school's directories. Along the way, in essays and introductions, I give some credit where credit is due. This is not the place to chalk up all my debts, and I ask the forbearance of many special people whose names are not mentioned in this volume. I hope that before I go I may have a better chance to acknowledge their importance in my life and the work of the school.

PREFACE

But there are a few whom I must thank publicly now. The first is my wife Desirée, who first had the notion of a new school along with founding board member Nancy Brooks. Desirée believed that I could be a headmaster before I did, and she has endured the many sacrifices that this job has imposed on us. Desirée was the first to select essays for this volume. I want also to thank my children, whose father was too often preoccupied with school and not present enough with them as they grew—may God grant them grace to love me and the school in spite of it. A special thanks to my daughter, Jenny, who helped me to put these essays into some sort of order and to design the book. My parents, Pete and Bobbie Denton, have been a great inspiration, support, and encouragement to me over the years, visiting the school often and always asking about the school. My father died in late 2013, and I will miss his predictable questions: How's enrollment? When's the last time you talked to your banker? Who's on the board? My friend and cofounder Jim Lamont was the first to sit me down and ask me to consider taking this job—thanks, Jim. I would never have made it past the first couple of years if it hadn't been for two wise men whom the Lord gave to Trinity: Bill Cobey and Fred Brooks. In the first twenty years of the school, they have served at different times as board chairs for all but one or two years. Their mentorship, guidance, and support have been a Godsend for me and for the school. I am also deeply indebted to Rita Davis, our first hire as fourth grade teacher, and to Kathy Tyndall (founding board member and then teacher) and Jane Adams, who together shaped the seminal curriculum of Trinity. Thanks also go to those who have served as my loyal administrative assistants over the years: Laura Sanders Sayre, Cindy Metzger Phillips, and now Molly Pasca. The long line of *Parent News* editors have put up with my missing deadlines and late revisions through the years: Laura Sanders Sayre, Doreen Hostetler, Daniele Berman, Gretchen Kelly, Leslie Brookman, Ashlyn Clary, Andrew Needham, Adrian Mack, Holley Broughton, and now Virgilla Gist. Finally, Lynn Hand's generous, careful, and expert editing and

PREFACE

proofing have saved me from many gaffes over the years and whipped this volume into shape.

Three people have volunteered countless hours to this project, and I want to thank them in a special way: my daughter, Jenny, who entered all the text and made revision upon revision; Kristen Blair, who read the book twice, giving thoughtful substantive critique and painstaking stylistic comments; and the amazingly selfless and talented Lynn Hand, who edited the entire book and created the impressive index. I am most grateful, also, to Fred Brooks for his introduction.

I don't really expect anyone to read this book from cover to cover. Some folks may browse through it; others may dip into it for an essay or two of topical interest. One of my readers suggested that I select a group of essays that might serve as an introduction to Trinity for anyone who wanted a quick but substantial sampling of the school's mission and culture. The following list includes most of the general topics covered by this volume:

- "A Village Called Trinity" (p. 3)
- "Truth, Goodness, and Beauty" (p. 39)
- "A School That Changes Lives" (p. 47)
- "The Classical Ideal" (p. 89)
- "On the Sacredness of Personhood" (p. 111)
- "The Art of Teaching" (p. 143)
- "Unhurried Generosity" (p. 151)
- "The Gift of *Non Nobis*" (p. 174)
- "On Habit and Character" (p. 182)
- "*De Gustibus*" (p. 189)
- "Everybody's Doing Diversity—But Not Like This" (p. 205)
- "The Once and Future School" (p. 225)
- "Boundary Lines in Pleasant Places" (p. 266)

May God use this volume to further his purposes for Trinity School. *Non nobis, Domine.*

Chip Denton
January 2015

Introduction

In 1996, the Trinity board sent parents a newsletter called "A Second Year of Growth" (p. 257 herein). Trustee committees were searching for land, and for a head of school: "Our Director will embody and articulate the school's vision...."

We got one. The embodying of the vision is indeed in the flesh; the articulation is eloquently set forth in this book of essays from the *Parent News*.

A living saint once told me, "I continually pray to understand what a man's life should be from His point of view." Chip Denton's essays reflect a twenty-year progressive understanding of what a school's life should be, from His point of view. They are remarkable for the broad sweep of topics explored and for a striking consistency of theme: Many things are excellent, many are important, many are praiseworthy, but the Gospel of our Lord Jesus Christ is the most excellent, most important, most praiseworthy, most central. Every stanza culminates in that refrain. Trinity belongs to the triune God.

In the first few sections, Chip explores and elaborates on Trinity's fourfold mission—distinctive, perhaps unique, in its combination of commitments.

Trinity is foremost a *Christian* school, utterly committed to teaching and living out what C. S. Lewis called "mere Christianity." It is not a denominational school, but we share a commitment to historic, evangelical, scriptural Christianity. We insist our teachers share this faith; we do not require it of our students or their families. It is a happy outcome that our families represent some fourscore churches. The school has become in some ways a nexus for evangelical families.

Trinity is a *classical school*, not slavishly, but respecting the judgment of generations as to what of our intellectual heritage is gold and what is dross. We aim to emphasize the gold, along with the mixed metals of current thinking. At the same time, Trinity teachers are designing learning experiences in which students apply the wisdom of the past to today's ever-fresh quandaries.

Trinity is committed to a *rich* curriculum and methodology. We follow the Christian educational philosophies and methods of groundbreaking British educator Charlotte Mason (1842–1923). These emphasize the worth of each child as a full person. They demand that each be fed meat and not twaddle. Mason pioneered active-learning techniques that emphasize intense attending on each of stories, tunes, pictures, plants, critters. Mason's principles, formulated originally for elementary school students, turn out to apply even to high schoolers. I often wish my university students, who study a discipline in which every detail is crucial, would enroll having already mastered the skill of close attending.

Most distinctively, Trinity is explicitly committed to an *unhurried* education. We deliberately swim against the tide of our culture—too much, too soon, too frantic, and all of a student's life filled and fulfilled by school. Hymnwriter Cecil Frances Alexander (1818–1895) had a deep insight into our temptations: "Days of toil and hours of ease,… Christian, love me more than these." Toil, even learning, even more than recreation for some of us, often deflects our love from Christ.

There is, of course, an inherent tension between a rich education and an unhurried one. This tension is amplified in the Upper School, where we prepare students for competitive college admissions. Trinity attacks this tension by emphasizing the most important and fruitful

INTRODUCTION

learning skills and materials. We strongly favor enrichment over acceleration for the eager learner. We constrain our schedules to enable and respect formal education outside our school, and, more important, family-led informal education. Chip puts it well: we aim to be "positively countercultural." (So far, the college-admissions record affirms our approach.)

Later chapters explore a wide range of important education topics, always asking why more than how, and all from a deeply Christian perspective. A sample: not a sports fan, I found myself more instructed by the thoughtful pieces on athletics than by any others. They honestly face the inherent emphasis problems. They address how a *Christian* school's athletic program should therefore be different.

Several rich themes run as colored threads through these essays. Humanities education is about being *human*. Trinity is a *community*, traveling together the royal road of learning, and the common life of the village is essential to our journey. *Many people* in this community have contributed to what Trinity is today; Chip is generous with acknowledgements. A privileged school, we have a larger responsibility to the embedding *society*. Education is crucial to America's *democratic experiment*. Trinity must teach those civic ideals, which indeed flow from our country's Christian foundations.

In all the chapters we have a gifted essayist himself exemplifying the fruits of a liberal education. The arguments are clear, the metaphors rich, the diction precise, the illustrations imaginative. The quotations range widely over the Western heritage. The allusions reflect a broad, appreciative, but suspicious awareness of current American culture. These essays are also enjoyable; read on.

Fred Brooks
Chapel Hill, North Carolina
May 2015

The Trinity Story

November 21, 2003

Originally entitled "Telling the Trinity Story"

I wish we had brought a tape recorder. Even a video camera. Or at least a scribe, who could have chronicled that half hour of remembrances, anecdotes, and snippets of Trinity history. It was one of those unplanned discussions that bore so much more fruit than anything we could have planned.

Ten board members and five staff and faculty were sitting in the sunroom at the home of Fred and Nancy Brooks. We had gathered on the first Saturday of November 2003, for our annual fall retreat. Our agenda? To review the school's strategic plan and to revisit, as we do each fall, this question: How well is Trinity fulfilling its mission? Late in the morning, our newest board member, Terry Ervin, asked a simple question. "What was it that had really moved the original leaders of the school? What had brought them to their knees?"

That's when somebody told the story about Jim Lamont finding Hope Creek Church as Trinity's first home. Then Jim answered with a story about hiring our first teachers. Which reminded Fred Brooks of how we hired our first (and only so far) headmaster. Then followed the saga of our search for land, replete with false starts and cul-de-sacs, recounted by Jim, Rick Adams, and Janice McAdams.

I've thought a lot about that conversation over the last three weeks, and not a few board and staff have made it clear that it was a rare gift to have been privy to that storytelling. I want to offer a few reflections on that conversation now, for the larger Trinity community.

First, I was surprised how many people didn't know the story. I should have realized, but it kind of sneaked up on me: Only Kathy Tyndall and Rita Davis, among our employees, were there in the beginning; only Jim Lamont remained of the charter board members; others were there as parents (Tom Kawula) or spouses of original board members (Fred Brooks). Janice McAdams came along in the second year of the school. So in that sunroom with key leaders of the school, more than half could only sit and listen to the stories that these half dozen told. If this is true of the leaders, how much more do the new parents and teachers at Trinity need to know the history of the school?

I also missed some key folks. We've already "graduated" not only several classes of eighth graders, but also some original leaders of the school. Bob Byrd should have been there to tell his stories. (I remember vividly a picnic lunch on the back lawn of the Church of the Good Shepherd office on East Lake View, when Bob and I dreamed together of a new Christian school.) Dave English is a name that maybe only a dozen of us still know—Dave was a charter board member and also played a key role in founding the school. Nancy Brooks was not in that room either, and her husband Fred would never have presumed to be her proxy. It was after a homeschool gathering in that same sunroom at Nancy's house that my wife came home and said, "They talked about needing an alternative to the schools in our community. I wondered if you could think about that and help." Jane Adams, too, should have been there, recalling with Kathy Tyndall the story of how the original curriculum was written. I came away from that morning full of joy at what God had done, but also concerned that the history of Trinity may be slipping through our fingers.

I had forgotten some things. We need each other to tell the story; no one of us can be the school historian. Jim Lamont reminded us of an open house at the home of Kim and Matt Dealy which I had completely forgotten about. An oral history of Trinity, interviewing as many of the original principals, would be an interesting dissertation project for someone in the folklore department at UNC.

I remembered some things differently from others in the room. Stories have a way of becoming apocryphal. The search for a headmaster, for one thing, has grown much more extensive, thorough, and discriminating with each telling. At the time it seemed like the best of several risky options. We do need to write this down, now, before access to the original accounts is lost.

Most importantly, though, I was struck by the response of those who were relatively new to Trinity. They were deeply appreciative of the chance to hear the story, to understand the history. Terry Ervin's question was everyone's: What were you all thinking when you started this school? It's not just that we are curious; we who were not charter members of the Trinity community but who are clearly members now want to know how our part in the story of Trinity fits into the larger picture.

That larger picture is not just the tale of Trinity. That would hardly be a story worth emphasizing. The excitement about Trinity's story comes when people realize that the *shape* of the Trinity story is the shape of the Gospel story. It's about foolish and selfish people and a faithful God, who has a plan to bless us beyond our wildest dreams, but hardly in accord with our selfish plans. What's more, the Gospel magnifies the *size* of our story. We started with 39 students and we've grown to 304, but that's a drop in the bucket of K–8 students who are being educated in Durham and Chapel Hill. We're quite a small enterprise, but the size of what we are doing cannot be measured by a head count. We're part of God's bigger story, and only he knows how big the Trinity story will grow as the Gospel goes to the ends of the earth.

So we welcome the newcomers among us. Enter in. Take your part. Ask a veteran to remember a tale or two. And become part of the Trinity story.

1 – Vision

The one who has a Why to live by can put up with most any How.
FRIEDRICH NIETZSCHE, "*MAXIMS AND ARROWS*"

In my time at Trinity, I have found that digging deep into First Things is an inexhaustible source of inspiration and guidance for a school. Schools necessarily spend enormous energy on *how* questions: How many half days for professional development? How should the students dress? How should we teach foreign languages? These and many other such practicalities are necessary, but man does not live by *how* alone. We were made for a purpose, and education is one place where teachers, parents, and students can engage with ideas that motivate us.

Many of these articles have a September date, and there are reasons for this. Summers have always been a good time for me to recharge and reorient myself, through reading and reflection. And coming off of such reveries into the wonderful optimism of the new school year, the first issues of our *Parent News* often seemed the opportune time to wax thoughtful about our purpose.

A Village Called Trinity

September 6, 1996

I remember where I was when I wrote this, the inaugural Parent News *cover. It was a Friday afternoon early in my first year as headmaster (the school's second year). The office had cleared, and I sat down in front of the desktop computer that Christian Smith and his wife had lent us (thank you, Smiths!). It was presidential election season, and Hillary Clinton's* It Takes a Village *was all the rage (literally). The notion of a school as a village was heuristic, and I've heard other heads say that schools are like small towns. From the beginning, we wanted ours to be Christian and classical.*

Trinity School has gotten off to its second year of schooling amidst a political contest in which an African proverb has become a sort of shibboleth to show one's political colors: Does it take a village? Or does it take a family?

In my first week of watching over a school, perhaps I would be prudent to stay as far away from this controversial subject as possible. But then, again, perhaps I would be a coward not to enter a conversation (if that is what it is) so important to any school. Without being partisan, can we be political? For to be political is to concern ourselves with the shape and order of our common life together. And that is what we have, you parents and we teachers: a life together in a community called a school. You will surely be interested to know what sort of answers we give to such important questions, and while this newsletter is hardly the forum for sustained argumentation, I can at least give you some idea of the direction of our school.

At Trinity we believe that it takes a family to raise a child. A school is not a family—cannot be. The family has a unique status in God's economy: When God made the world, he made the family (Gen. 2), in which the mandate to create and sustain what we call "culture" was to be passed from generation to generation. Fathers and mothers were to teach daughters and sons about the One who had made the heavens and about how to subdue the earth.

At Trinity we also believe that it takes a village to raise a child. The work of passing God's interpretation of reality from one generation to another, especially in a complex culture, is a huge task. From the earliest recorded history we see the family enlisting help in educating children. The school is one of the best helps a family can have, but always the school serves *in loco parentis* (in the place of the parent), which is to say that its authority and mandate are delegated and not inherent. Or, to put it differently, a school, unlike a family, is important but not essential to the raising of children. Still, since in our culture schools seem to be unavoidable, we ought to ask ourselves just what kind of school we seek to be.

This brings us to the heart of the matter, for the real question is not whether it takes a village or a family to raise a child. No, the real question is this: What kind of village do we want to be? What kind of village will Trinity School be?

The answer to that question is not my answer, but that of the stream of the classical, Christian tradition, into which we have already launched the ship called Trinity. It is a good answer, time-tested. Easy to describe, impossible to achieve but for the grace of God, this is the classical and Christian conception of the virtuous society. What does such a village, such a *polis* (Greek for "city"), such a republic, look like? It looks like a school where the cardinal virtues of prudence, self-control, justice, and courage are respected, encouraged, and modeled. And under these (as their foundation) and over these (as their crown) are the distinctively Christian virtues of faith, hope, and love. All of these virtues are defined and modeled and fulfilled in Christ: "He is before all things, and in him all things hold together" (Col. 1:17).

And so the crucial question for us is not whether it takes a village or a family to raise a child, but rather whether we parents of Trinity can shape such a village that will help us to do well what God has called us to do. Let us not be presumptuous about this task. Virtue is gained only at great cost. No political party, no school, private or public, has a natural affinity for virtue or an immunity from vice. But with God as our help, let us do what we can and pray for what we cannot.

Why Go to School?

September 20, 1996

This piece was written with an audience larger than our relatively small parent body in mind—I remember recycling these ideas at our early open houses for prospective parents. Two larger concerns inform this piece, directions I still want to push at Trinity twenty years later: the rich and layered texture of education with its several purposes; and the public and universal appeal of a good education, which is deepened and consummated by our Christian mission. We have always aspired for Trinity to be a deeply Christian school that has relevance to our larger culture and community.

Why do we send our kids to Trinity? No one answer to that question seems sufficient. In fact, when we become too fixated on any particular answer, our education can easily lose its balance and falter. At Trinity we believe in a constellation of purposes, at least three of which are worth mentioning here.

First, education is *vocational training*. Vocational training has gotten a bad name in some circles as a subpar education. ("He went to a vocational school, not a real college!") But none of us thinks that getting a job is unimportant business or that training children to be gainfully employed is a sideline. We see our work at Trinity as preparing students to enter into and persevere well in their life's work. Much of what we do between 8:30 and 2:00 is justified by this purpose: learning to read, to subtract, to spell, to memorize, to organize, to socialize. And soon, we hope, to use computers for a variety of tasks.

Some of what we study at Trinity—actually a good deal of it—may not be so easily justified according to this first purpose. For most of us, Latin, Greek mythology, and the history of the pharaohs won't be translated into a paycheck. But these are important things to study because an education is also a *civic training*, an introduction into the vitally important job of being a citizen. By the time students have graduated from Trinity, we hope they will be able to enter into the most important debates that touch upon our life together in this nation and world: about the nature of justice, about the balance between individual freedom and communal responsibility, about the implications of living in a country that subscribes to the notion of *e pluribus unum*. Civic education may sometimes seem impractical, but here we must resist good old American pragmatism to be Americans.

Even less practical is the third purpose for our education. Education is *private cultivation*. Here we attend to those things which, simply, interest us. Here we encourage individuality: this student loves gazing at stars, that one takes to music. Here we promote the enjoyment of what is true, good, and beautiful for its own sake and not because it is useful to make a living or get along with others in a democracy. Much of what we do at Trinity is concerned with such cultivation: the reading of good literature; music and art classes; field trips to museums and planetariums.

One thing more. We are a Christian school, and being Christian affects every one of these purposes. We don't paste a "Christian" wallpaper over a secular structure; instead, we believe that these good purposes for an education are, like all of life, transformed deeply and radically by the Gospel. There is not space here to do justice to this transformation, but a nod of recognition is warranted.

Education for a job becomes for us education toward vocation— that is, answering God's call to use the unique gifts God has given us as providential opportunities arise. In fact, it is the theistic conception of vocation which transforms "having a job" into "answering a call," so that our life's work is much more than a job or a task and becomes a way to serve the Lord Christ in our daily lives.

Education for citizenship becomes education on how to work for the common good, transforming culture with the values of God's kingdom and with the power of that kingdom as manifested by the Spirit of Jesus. We as Christians have as good a reason as anyone for being concerned with "the common good." Far from taking us out of the world, the Gospel leaves us in it as salt and light.

Education for private culture becomes education that awakens and nurtures a sense of awe and wonder at God's good creation, as well as a hopeful and faithful expectation of his better recreation in Christ. And so it was that we began our year, at our opening assembly, singing "Let all things now living a song of thanksgiving to God the Creator triumphantly sing." Teaching kids to wonder and to worship is part of our mission.

As always, we want to be open to discussing these things. Please feel free to let us know your opinions on such matters. We hope that we have some definite ideas about education, hard enough to guide us, but soft enough to be reshaped in helpful ways in the context of this community where we are all learners and listeners.

Experimenting on Our Children

September 5, 1997

> *Janice McAdams, our first Development Director and longtime stakeholder, always cringed when I referenced "experimenting on our children." I listened to her, most of the time, and was reticent to speak this way in public. I suppose I must have written this before she convinced me that Trinity's experiment did not have quite the branded stability that the American experiment had. Lewis and Sayers were strong early influences on us, and they are given their due here. How would we measure the results today?*

Trinity is an experiment in education. The corollary of such a statement is that your children are being experimented upon, an unsettling truth which may become even more disturbing when one considers the venerable and bizarre history of educational experimentation in the Western world.

Plato, in his *Republic*, recommends something like boarding school at a tender age. Rousseau's Emile, being given a truly romantic education, does not learn to read until twelve or thirteen. Louisa May Alcott's transcendentalist father founded the Temple School, where he did not "teach" but "conversed" with the children from ages seven to twelve, while a scribe recorded the comments, both prosaic and precocious. Fortunately for humanity, some of these outlandish experiments were never actually attempted (Plato's Republic is a utopia, which means, literally, "no place") or were short-lived (the Temple School survived only a few years).

Not all social experiments are created equal. Some are impracticable. Some are faddish. But some are of enduring significance and value, like the one we all participate in, the American Experiment. In this grand experiment, for example, our democratic polity is set out to

1 – VISION

test the hypothesis that the natural and inescapable human drive toward meaning and belonging should not be dictated by the state but, in the words of George Mason, the principal author of the Virginia Declaration of Rights, should be "directed only by reason and conviction, not by force or violence."[1] I have heard people who think this experiment to have been a great success and others who are sure it can now be declared a failure; I have not heard anyone argue that it ought not to have been attempted.

May it always be so of Trinity: that it is judged to be an experiment worth trying. Let me briefly remind you of the principal hypotheses that Trinity is out to confirm. These would be two propositions, one educational, the other religious.

The educational hypothesis is stated most succinctly by Dorothy Sayers in her seminal essay "The Lost Tools of Learning": "The sole end of education is simply this," says she, "to teach men how to learn for themselves."[2] This is not faddish. This is not allegiance to anything like technique or loyalty to a particular party or movement. This is, in our view, good common sense, proven by centuries of experience. It is better to teach people to fish than to give them a fish. We might add that it is important, also, for them to want the fish and to enjoy the fishing. The medieval Trivium, which Sayers recommends, is most interesting as a model of education because it takes a child fishing, step-by-step, until she or he is able to fish the stream of any subject encountered. First the children learn how to speak (Grammar); then they learn how to think (Logic); finally they learn how to speak well and cogently (Rhetoric).

---

1. The Virginia Declaration of Rights, sec. 16. http://www.archives.gov/exhibits/charters/virginia_declaration_of_rights.html.

2. Dorothy L. Sayers, "The Lost Tools of Learning." Paper delivered at a Vacation Course in Education, Oxford, 1947. Later published in the *Hibbert Journal: A Quarterly Review of Religion, Theology, and Philosophy* 46 (Oct. 1947–July 1948). http://www.triviumeducation.com/texts/The_Lost_Tools_of_Learning.pdf.

EXPERIMENTING ON OUR CHILDREN

The religious hypothesis could be stated any number of ways. C. S. Lewis (as usual) put it well. In an introduction to an edition of Athanasius's *The Incarnation of the Word of God*, Lewis makes this claim: "Measured against the ages, 'mere Christianity' turns out to be no insipid interdenominational transparency, but something positive, self-consistent, and inexhaustible."[3] By being a Christian school, independent of any particular church or tradition, yet committed to that "something" which is the heart of Christianity, Trinity is putting to the test Lewis's claim. Some may think we need to choose between the Puritan Bunyan or the Anglican Hooker or the Thomist Dante, and, of course, as individuals and families we will. But is there really something, indeed *Something*, that is unvarying and capable of sustaining us and our children in their learning and their living? Something true, good, beautiful? Trinity is founded on the proposition that there is such a something, who is a Someone, whose name is Jesus Christ.

Thank you to all of you who have entrusted your children to Trinity this year. We do not take your trust lightly, and we pledge to work hard to give them a good education. We would rather not experiment on our children, so precious are they to us. What is more, we get only one shot at this thing called "educating our children." Still, truth be told, every school is an experiment and every education is a risk. The trick is to be thoughtful about our fundamental ideas, consistent in our applications, and full of faith as we step out and put our ideas to the test. May God give us grace to pass the test.

---

3. C. S. Lewis, Introduction to *On the Incarnation*, by Athanasius (Crestwood, NY: St. Vladimir's Seminary Press), 6.

Positively Countercultural

MARCH 13, 1998

I am more convinced now than I was in 1998 that being young is hard on a school. I have watched many other new schools go through the same growing pains we did. The opportunities are enormous, but so are the demands. I'm glad I was forty and not sixty back in 1998—I don't think I'd have the energy now for all this. One person who did have energy beyond her years was founding board member Nancy Brooks, and she was wont to speak favorably of being a countercultural school. Such a notion is tricky for any enterprise trying to market itself, but we tried to lay out our vision of a school whose oddness was attractive. It would be an interesting exercise for today's staff to measure our twenty-year-old school by these aspirations.

Trinity's youth is a curse and blessing, both the bane of our days of late and the hope of our hearts for years to come.

Being young is hard. Ask our first graders, who are meeting diphthongs for the first time. Ask our second graders, who are learning cursive this semester, or our sixth graders, who are dealing with new hormones, new emotions. Ask any Trinity board member or staff or teacher, all of whom are meeting new questions six times a day.

If the difficulty of youth is immaturity in the face of big challenges, the advantage of youth is its energy and possibilities. I will freely admit that sometimes I am exhausted by the number of issues that have to be decided, and quickly, in a short space of time around this school: Will we have a seventh grade? What will our site plan look like? What will our mascot be? But I will just as freely insist that being young and (yes, I'll say it) immature, we have our future before us. There are still a few tricks this young dog can learn.

Trinity is still malleable, soft in the hands of those who are shaping it, soft in the hands of God, I hope. It is not too late to dream dreams for our school.

One dream that keeps me going in the harder times is the dream of being a countercultural school: not an anticultural school, not a school dedicated to the bizarre or the rare or the non-Western, but a school that embodies a thoughtful application of this biblical injunction from 1 John 2:15: "Do not love the world or anything in the world." The "world" that we are warned against here is not God's good creation or his providential blessings; it is a biblical term of art which refers to all that stands against God's righteous rule and his peaceable kingdom. John names three particulars of this "world" that we ought to be on guard against: "the cravings of sinful man, the lust of his eyes, and the boasting of what he has and does."

It will be all too easy to let our school become a petri dish for the mold of worldliness. All we have to do is...nothing. Such is the human heart after the fall that without God's grace and our own watchful, prayerful efforts we will easily become a school where the seven sins reign.

But I believe that God has better things in store for Trinity. I believe that Trinity is becoming and can go on to be a school where the counterculture of the Gospel is dominant.

In a world where parents and their children are increasingly segregated and estranged, I want Trinity to be a school where children talk to their parents, where even eighth graders at a sleepover sit around the kitchen table discussing ideas and issues with their parents.

In a world where promiscuity reigns, I want Trinity to be a place where purity is esteemed.

In a world where older students so easily despise and bully younger students, I want Trinity to be a place where the older students guard and protect the younger and become kind, strong leaders of the school.

1 – VISION

In a world where TV and the Internet are teaching us to surf through life disengaged and lazy, I want Trinity to be a place where students attend long and hard to one another and to their teachers, to a book, or to a debate.

In a world where "How much will I make?" is the principal vocational question, I want Trinity to be a place that teaches kids to ask other questions as well: "Where am I called? How can I serve? What are my gifts?"

These are some of the dreams that fuel the fires of my enthusiasm for Trinity. Lord willing, most of our future lies before us, and the possibilities for what we might become are many and bright. May God help us as we fashion this school into a special place, a place worthy to bear the name of the One who is the measure of all we do and are.

The End of Education

September 24, 1999

I have always appreciated Neil Postman's work, as this title acknowledges. His book by the same title is a fine example of thinking about education from the perspective of first things. "Why?" is such an important question for a school to keep in front of itself—I still begin every prospective parent open house with this question. I think that one of the reasons for Trinity's success early on was that we were able to keep this question front and center. People need a big Why. I believe that schools that focus on ends will find advocates and partners, because we were created to live for purpose.

Neil Postman has written a trenchant and eminently readable book called *The End of Education*. I mention it here not because I intend to say anything that he has said there so effectively, but because I want to abscond with his title and I ought to give him credit.

It is a marvelously ambiguous title, so that one does not know at the outset whether the book is about the termination (end) of education as we know it or about the purpose (end) of education. Both ideas are well worth exploring, and both are integrally connected. For the more we ask ourselves, What is the purpose of education? the less likely we are to carry on automatically the traditions of our mothers and fathers. For instance, many of us have grown up in schools where the implicit assumption was that the more subjects one could study, the better. Then along comes Dorothy Sayers, who writes a penetrating essay called "The Lost Tools of Learning" and concludes that "the sole true end of education is simply this: to teach men how to learn for themselves."[1] That being the case, the acquisition of certain intellectual tools is far more important than the mastery of myriad subjects. Thus it happens

---

1. Sayers, "The Lost Tools of Learning," 13.

1 – VISION

that a discussion of the end of education leads us to a practice that ends the education we have inherited.

It is not, however, only the old that is corrected by this fundamental question. The healthy habit of asking why will guard us against stodgy and unfounded traditions; it will also protect us from frantic attempts to keep up with the Joneses in our own educational neighborhood. This is probably the greater temptation. Just as we Americans have a knack for bucking tradition, we have a weakness for following the latest fad, for choosing the pragmatic over the prudent, for chasing after more and more and more without asking why. Asking about the purpose of education has led Trinity to adopt some unique approaches: in the selection of our math curriculum; in the development of our technology program; and in our emerging thinking about the way we go about raising money to build the school.

We are often asked why we call ourselves a classical Christian school. One good answer to that question is that both the classical and the Christian traditions are fundamentally committed to asking this question about ends or purposes. The Greek word for "end" is *telos*, and it is from the Greeks that we have learned to ask why. The unexamined education is not worth learning. Before you begin school, you must ask, "What is the *telos* (or ideal end) of this thing called a human being?" Trinity's motto is taken from a succinct classical answer to this question: Human beings have the unique capacity to grow and be perfected in their apprehension of truth, in their practice of goodness, and in their appreciation for and reflection of beauty. No other organism under the sun has these capacities, and education (in Greek, *paideia*) must be crafted in such a way as to help human beings perfect them.

You have to love the Greeks—when they got it wrong, they got it wrong in such a wonderful way. We Christians have learned (principally through the medium of Greek culture) that this ideal human being is simply not a possibility in the world as we know it. Plato's best hope for an enlightened philosopher king, Dion of Syracuse, let his master down in the end. And the Bible's number one draft pick went to bed with Bathsheba. But the Greek ideal, the *telos* of humanity, is more than a pipe dream: There was once a man and a woman whose humanness was more perfect and more moving than the Venus de Milo, and when they fell from grace God sent the Second Man who "learned obedience from what he suffered and, once made perfect, he became the source of eternal salvation for all who obey him" (Heb. 5:8-9).

Schools are built on dreams, and great schools are built on dreams that have inspired humanity for centuries and millennia, such as the Greek ideal of the wise and virtuous person. And a great Christian school is built on a dream-come-true, the Incarnation. The end of all our learning is that we would bear the likeness of the One who became for us a life-giving Spirit.

Why Trinity?

April 2000

This piece was a brochure before it was a Parent News *cover. It was born out of our first strategic planning process, which Board Chair Bill Cobey led us into. Back in the late '90s, Bill knew that we needed a road map for the growth of the school, and we embarked on a thorough planning process that engaged every constituency of the school. We listened especially to Trinity parents, and out of this was born a four-part answer to the fundamental question. I am gratified that with one change ("educationally excellent" rather than "competent") I could still offer this as a case for our school.*

Many of us share an exciting vision and dream for Trinity School. The dream is already coming true, even as the kindergartners learn letter sounds, as the students chant their Latin, as the fourth graders sift through fossils, as the fifth graders learn Greek myths and the sixth and seventh graders run in Trinity's first track meet. The dream becomes much more real as we prepare to break ground on our new facility in the summer of 2000. As the Trinity board has begun planning the construction of our new school, we have been wrestling with fundamental issues that all come back to one question: Why Trinity? What are the reasons we had for starting this school five years ago? What are we passionate about as a school? What unique gifts do we, as a school, possess? What opportunities are there before us to serve this community? Through this planning process, we have been able to identify four points that define our calling as a school.

A School That Honors Christ

Our culture is secular. The world that we see is touted as "the whole show." The idea of something or someone supernatural, beyond the natural world is, at best, irrelevant to most of what the world does and thinks.

Our aspiration is for Trinity to be a place where children learn that God is at the heart of all that we are and do. God is the *cause* of our existence (i.e., God is real); God is the *reason* for our understanding (i.e., God is truth); God is the *purpose* of our lives (i.e., God is the greatest good). A vision of education rooted in these beliefs promises to be, in C. S. Lewis's words, "no insipid interdenominational transparency, but something positive, self-consistent, and inexhaustible."[1] Our goal is to set our children out upon a journey of exploring such a God and the world he has made. Such an education will not be superficially religious, but will be infused, at every turn, with a sense of wonder and reverence, both for the glory of God and for the glory of the most ordinary things in God's creation.

A School That Is Well Paced

Our culture is hurried and greedy, wanting as much as possible as soon as possible. We find that our world is discontented with a quiet life of minding our own business (1 Thess. 4:11), that it accelerates children and families into a faster and more pressured pace of life, and that it often ignores the wisdom of Ecclesiastes 4:6, "Better one handful with tranquility than two handfuls with toil and chasing after the wind."

Trinity is to be a place where children are free to be children, to learn as children, to play and read in ways that fit their natural bent at each age. A truly rich and intellectual education need not be accelerated: There is so much to master, so much to enjoy at each age. It is important to us at Trinity that we balance the demands of school and of family, leaving time for children to grow in academics, in the arts, in sports and recreation, and in the other opportunities their families

---

1. C. S. Lewis, Introduction to *On the Incarnation*, by Athanasius (Crestwood, NY: St. Vladimir's Seminary Press), 6.

choose to pursue. And it is vitally important that they have leisure to pursue their own interests and to play.

A School That Is Educationally Competent

Our culture is educationally confused. Ask most of us what a good education is and we will mumble and stutter. Ask us why we are doing what we are doing in school and our answer will probably owe more to the latest trend than to the great conversations about education that have been carried on for centuries.

We want Trinity to be a school that is thoughtful about education. We want to relate what we are doing in school to the larger purposes of our lives and to articulate a vision of education that makes sense for human beings across the boundaries of time, place, and culture. And we want to choose the best means for accomplishing those goals. The Trivium is just such a choice, and we are excited to have the chance to put it to the test.

A School That Is Safe for Families

Our culture is not friendly to the family. This is true for people of all political stripes. Industrialization, upward mobility, the specialization of the workforce—these and other social trends have made it increasingly difficult for families to raise their children well.

The dream of Trinity is to be a place that is safe for children and families. Not safe like a zoo, but—as Steve Larson, former Director of Lower School once said—safe like a wildlife preserve, where children have the proper boundaries and protection to grow in their trust and their dominion within God's creation. Trinity is to be a school that partners with parents, that recognizes the parents' primary role in raising the child, that supports rather than divides or erodes the family, and that reinforces the educational and spiritual goals of the family.

Thus we find ourselves at the intersection of these different needs in our culture, stewards of gifts that are uniquely suited to meet those needs, moved by aspirations to build a school that answers to those needs. I hope that you are excited, as I am, to be a part of this vocation.

One Nation Under God?
December 1, 2000

The election of 2000 was hard on Trinity, as it was on our nation, and this column was an attempt to chart a course for the school. This is a theme and a challenge that we have returned to over and over, perhaps most helpfully in 2008, when Trinity parents, close friends, and political opposites Peter Feaver and Ian Baucom (both Duke professors) held a conversation about faith and politics in front of the parent body and some students. That event represented a high-water mark for living out the civil but robust political life that I try to picture here. Trinity continues to be a place more conservative than liberal (in the political sense), but I hope it is a place that is safe for political liberals, especially for Christian liberals, who want to be part of the conversation I am describing here. That kind of culture requires the cultivation of hospitality and the sort of humility and moderation that Hamilton talks about in the passage I have quoted. I should add that since the initial publication of this document, the board has made clear in a stated policy that the school is a nonpartisan institution.

Dear Trinity Parents and Friends:

The remarkable political events of the last three weeks have dominated our national attention, and we at Trinity have felt the amazement, anxiety, and confusion of the rest of the nation. Whatever comes of this election, we know now that at present there are significant fault lines in the American political terrain which call into question just what we envision by a "more perfect union." We are a nation divided, roughly, right down the middle.

How does this impact us at Trinity School? And how should we respond to these events? Are we similarly divided? It is to these sorts of questions that I turn in this open letter. I write not so much to hold forth on politics—a task for which I am ill prepared—as to enter into a conversation about which I care deeply.

Let me start by stating plainly that Trinity School is, by definition, a nonpartisan school. Those who founded this school anchored the school's mission in religious and educational convictions, but they did not intend to connect the school with any particular political party any more than they did with any particular denomination.

To say this is not to say that politics is unimportant. Nor is it to say that people in the school should shy away from public and vigorous political affiliation and discourse. Rather, it is a simple acknowledgement that, like all things, politics is relativized by the Gospel and the lordship of Christ.

Relativized, but not annulled. In fact, the lordship of Christ actually affirms political involvement. To say, "Jesus is Lord" is to say, "Jesus is Lord *over all*." As the Dutch theologian and statesman Abraham Kuyper said, there is not a hand's-breadth of all of creation over which the Lord Christ does not pronounce the word "mine."[1] All of the myriad issues that politics addresses should be of concern to us who follow Christ. It is only right that we urge ourselves and one another to "think Christianly" about this issue or that. It is a fair question for anyone to ask how our Christian faith informs our positions on campaign finance reform, on taxation, on abortion, on gun control. It is part of our mission as a school to help our students do just this, to give them tools of learning that will enable them to arrive at and hold firm to informed positions on important issues. Many of us grew up in communities where religion and politics were taboo subjects in polite company; we mean for Trinity to be a place where this taboo is overcome, where civil but vigorous discussion helps us all to take every thought captive to Christ. Further, I hope that we will always value and honor those whose calling leads them to visible public service or political activism.

---

1. Abraham Kuyper, "Sphere Sovereignty." In *Abraham Kuyper, A Centennial Reader*, ed. James D. Bratt (Grand Rapids, MI: Eerdmans, 1998), 488.

1 – VISION

At the same time, the lordship of Christ has another dimension to it, especially in a world turned inside-out and fallen like ours. To say, "Jesus is Lord" is also to say, "Jesus is Lord *over against all*." None of us is exempt from the dangers of holding the truth hostage, and we need constant reminders that the opinions we hold about a candidate or public policy may turn out to be either misconstrued or guided by impure motives. We would all do well to heed Alexander Hamilton's warning in the first number of *The Federalist*, a series of masterful essays which could hardly escape the charge of being vigorously partisan:

> So numerous indeed and so powerful are the causes which serve to give a false bias to the judgment, that we, upon many occasions, see wise and good men on the wrong as well as on the right side of questions of the first magnitude to society. This circumstance, if duly attended to, would furnish a lesson of moderation to those who are ever so much persuaded of their being in the right in any controversy. And a further reason for caution, in this respect, might be drawn from the reflection that we are not always sure that those who advocate the truth are influenced by purer principles than their antagonists. Ambition, avarice, personal animosity, party opposition, and many other motives not more laudable than these are apt to operate as well upon those who support as those who oppose the right side of a question.[2]

This warning should in no way be construed as an excuse for political agnosticism, as Hamilton's lively political debates with New York's Governor Clinton and later with Thomas Jefferson make plain. It is, however, a clear call for humility and moderation, one that should be affixed to every radio talk show like a surgeon general's warning.

---

2. Alexander Hamilton, *The Federalist*, no. 1. In *Great Books of the Western World*, edited by Mortimer J. Adler (Chicago: Encyclopaedia Britannica, 1952), 29–30.

The people of God have long been called "a peculiar people," and it should come as no surprise that our political involvement, like all other activities, is peculiar. We are vigorously and wholeheartedly involved in causes that we deem just, and at the same time humble about our own capacity to get it right and realistic about the value of such projects in view of the kingdom of God.

The apostle Paul speaks of this peculiar way of living in 1 Corinthians 7:29-31.

> From now on, those who have wives should live as if they do not; those who mourn, as if they did not; those who are happy, as if they were not; those who buy something, as if it were not theirs to keep; those who use the things of the world, as if not engrossed in them.

We might add: "Those who are involved in politics, as if not engrossed in them."

Let's be forthright. In the current political climate, Trinity School's political hegemony is likely to be Republican. I offer this opinion not as an advocate but as a cultural observer. One poll taken the week after the election reported that Republicans garnered huge majorities among middle class families and among those who say they attend church. Is it surprising, then, that a Christian school funded by after-tax income would attract many Republicans? But it is no more to be wondered at that we find among us conscientious Democrats and Independents, who are also trying to translate their faith into political involvement. The challenge for all sides is to respect persons in our community whose political views differ from our own, to refrain from demeaning one another, and to have the courage to discuss openly and charitably our differences.

Listening to the news lately, one could easily lose heart. But even in this intensely partisan postelection climate I will not abandon my personal dream that we at Trinity School could struggle well to live out this peculiar political ethic. Is it not possible, with God's good help, that people of different political persuasions would find here a place where they can live, if not in agreement, then still at peace—not a superficial pretended peace, but a real peace that comes from knowing that our common sin and our shared redemption far outweigh our political differences? Thus may we be a school not for ourselves, but for our community and for our nation, one nation, under God.

Self Education

February 7, 2004

I can never give enough credit to C. S. Lewis's influence on me. I've read so much of his work so many times that I sometimes channel him without knowing it. This piece is strongly influenced by his essay, "Two Ways with the Self." Lewis's essay is deeply and distinctively Christian, but the fundamental distinction between the two ways can be prosecuted in a more secular setting as well. I attempted this recently when I returned to my alma mater, the Webb School, to speak about education more generally. Whether in a Christian setting or a more secular one, I still believe "that education is never easy." Fun sometimes, simple, and engaging—but always arduous and challenging to the self.

There are two ways with the self.

One is the way of the self. The traveler on this road bends, subdues, and manipulates everything in service of the self. The great challenge on this way is how to control reality to suit the self. Saul traveled down this road when he disobeyed the Lord's clear command to destroy the Amalekites but then answered Samuel's rebuke with an incredulous protestation: "But I *did* obey the Lord" (see 1 Sam. 15). Saul had reshaped the large, round peg of reality to fit into that puny, square hole that was his self. Is this not the same road taken by alcoholics in denial? By chronic liars whose belief that they have told the truth is as earnest as it is mistaken? By dabblers in the dark arts who, like Uncle Andrew in Lewis's *The Magician's Nephew*, attempt to manipulate occult forces for their own gain? By technophiles who claim that genetic manipulation holds the key to our true happiness? And lest we think that this is the way less traveled, the road only for addicts, warlocks, and geeks, let us recall that we all live in a world whose billboards declare "You deserve a break today,"[1] where even one of the most altruistic vocations still extant recruits with a siren song to the self: "Be all that you can be."[2] Like it or not, we all bow down, at least now and then, at the high places that our culture has built, everywhere, to the cult of self-worship.

This way of the self is a wide road, wide enough for all of us if we choose to go that way. Parents, teachers, and students walk down that route when we redefine mastery as what the student can already do, apart from study and practice. We parents head right into the traffic jam, too, when we instinctively turn the teacher's correction of our child into an indictment of the teacher. The quest for the easy, royal road to learning is an age-old temptation, but today, surrounded by technological marvels, we are particularly susceptible: we greet each new digital advance with the hope that here, at last, is the secret to making education easy. The truth is, of course, that education is never easy, and we delude ourselves like Saul of old when we think we can change that with some technological legerdemain.

The other way is the way of wisdom, an old road, well traveled if not crowded. It runs exactly counter to the way of the self. The challenge for the pilgrims on that wise way is how to conform the self to reality, and over the years men and women have learned a thing or two and passed them on from mother to daughter and father to son. The Proverbs are replete with simple, profound indicatives—affirmations of reality. The spiritual realities discovered there are as real as the wonders discovered by an explorer in the natural world. No one ever climbed Everest by making the mountain as small as the self; no one becomes wise by pretending that the spiritual mountains are little sand dunes to be shaped to suit the tiny self.

---

1. McDonald's Corporation advertising slogan. Created by Kevin Gavin and Sid Woloshin, 1971.

2. US Army advertising slogan. Created by Nelson VanSant and N. W. Ayer & Son, 1980.

SELF EDUCATION

In the history of Western education, knowledge, self-discipline, and virtue have long been the ways of bringing the self into line with something other, something real. Truth, goodness, and beauty are not only great objective realities against which the self measures itself; they are also transcendent wonders which have the capacity, by God's grace—common and special—to transform that self. C. S. Lewis wrote a poem about that divine alchemy which turns the self into something greater:

> When soul and body feed, one sees
> Their differing physiologies.
> Firmness of apple, fluted shape
> Of celery, or tight-skinned grape
> I grind and mangle when I eat,
> Then in dark, salt, internal heat,
> Annihilate their natures by
> The very act that makes them I.
> But when the soul partakes of good
> Or truth, which are her savoury food,
> By some far subtler chemistry
> It is not they that change, but she,
> Who feels them enter with the state
> Of conquerors her opened gate,
> Or, mirror-like, digests their ray
> By turning luminous as they.[3]

The way of wisdom seems old, as old as Solomon; and the way of the self seems new, faddish, in vogue. But in truth both of these ways are old ways, and we are hardly the first generation to have struggled to find the right road. Long ago Jesus spoke of these two as a wide way and a narrow way. And he pointed out the paradox of the spiritual journey. The map of the soul is counterintuitive, and it's oh-so-easy

---

3. C. S. Lewis, "On a Theme from Nicholas of Cusa (*De Docta Ignorantia*, III.ix)." In *Poems*, edited by Walter Hooper (New York: Harcourt Brace Jovanovich, 1977), 70.

1 – VISION

to get turned around. "For whoever wants to save their life will lose it, but whoever loses their life for me and for the Gospel will save it" (Mark 8:35).

Trinity School is unabashedly dedicated to the way of wisdom, the old road, the way that brings the self into submission to reality. Only by constant renewal and rededication will we keep our way, for the on-ramps to the way of the self are everywhere. But perhaps it will be a little easier to resist the insidious temptations to take the wrong way if we travel together, all of us, in the hope that we may find our true selves hidden with Christ in God.

What Good Is an Education?

September 2004

This Parent News *piece has a lineage. In the summer of 1996, when I had been appointed as headmaster but had not officially started, I sat down to write a personal manifesto by this same title. I had been reading a lot of Augustine in the previous year, and I had also been pondering Luke's narrative of Mary and Martha. What, I was asking, is the point of education in the context of eternity? C. S. Lewis's "Learning in Wartime" was also in the background. I have come back to these texts over and over in the course of Trinity's life, and I still find them to generate important fundamental notions about education in a Christian context.*

My father loves to pass on the joke that Mr. Neely would tell about his son Jack. Jack was a high school classmate of mine who went off to Millsaps College to major in history. Somewhere close to the end of his undergraduate career, Jack's father is supposed to have asked Jack, in a slightly sarcastic tone, "What will you do when you graduate—work for one of those history companies?"

The joke has been passed around by two very different groups of people. To Jack's father, to many fathers, perhaps to all fathers who have footed the bill for college education, the joke is on Jack and his ilk, who think that anything good can come from something as impractical as a history degree.[1] To Jack's defenders the joke exposes the philistine prejudices of people who have never imagined that an education might be good for something other than its earning power. For all of us, Mr. Neely's joke prompts a profound question: What good is an education?

---

1. Jack has vindicated himself admirably over the years, writing numerous books such as *Knoxville's Secret History*.

1 – VISION

A school ought to have an answer to such a question. It is incumbent on those who are running a school that they be able to explain not only what they are doing but also why. The unexamined school is not worth operating. In truth, this is the kind of question that takes a lifetime to answer, but at the beginning of another school year it is good for us to tackle it again, as simply as we can, and to say why we are doing what we are doing. Let us set forth three related propositions:

Education is a great good, in fact one of the greatest goods under the sun.

Measured by the hours invested in founding and running this school, or by the tuition dollars dearly paid, or by the zeal of students and teachers, it is clear that people at Trinity believe in the value of a good education. Furthermore, though we are certainly mindful of the usefulness of an education (to help our children get jobs, for example), we have also been moved by the vision of an education that is a joy in and of itself. We speak of the love of learning around here because we know that the experience of reading a book for the sheer pleasure of it is one of the most "human" activities we can engage in.

Measured against eternity, however, education is far from the greatest good.

As important as we think education is, most of us would assent to this qualification. We know that knowledge can be used or misused, and that knowledge puffs up while love builds up. We all know people whose education is first-class but whose lives are hardly to be envied or imitated. And we know, maybe, a few salt-of-the-earth people, whose ignorance or naiveté is so far overshadowed by their huge hearts that it may give us pause to be getting and spending so much on our education.

WHAT GOOD IS AN EDUCATION?

Measured against eternity, against the immortality of our own souls, and, most importantly, against the God whom to see is either sheer hell or perfect blessedness, education can hardly be considered as the *summum bonum*, the greatest good of our lives. As a Christian school, we regard the goal of our lives this way: to give glory to God by enjoying him forever. And this we believe to be made possible and real to us through Jesus Christ and by the work of the Holy Spirit.

Long ago Augustine used an analogy to teach us this same point. Suppose, he says, that we were wanderers, far from our native country, who could not live in blessedness except at our home. We would need vehicles for land and sea, which could be used to help us reach our homeland, where we would find our true joy. But suppose that the amenities of the journey, the beauty of the scenery, and the marvelous vehicles themselves so delighted us that we should forget about our country and become "entangled in a perverse sweetness."[2] By misusing a good vehicle, by treating a means as an end, we might miss our destination. Now our destination is not a place, but a person, waiting like the prodigal's father to embrace us. In truth, three persons, the Father, the Son, and the Holy Spirit, one God forever blessed. The greatest good that Trinity students can ever hope for is to find their way to this, their home.

The greatest good that an education can be is as a help toward that greatest good.

As Christians, we do not believe, as Plato seems to have thought, that education can "save" us. It may save us from ignorance, but it cannot save us from selfishness and sin. In this sense, to continue with Augustine's analogy, Christ is the vehicle on which we sail home to the Father. But the things of this world, education included, can be like the sails, the rudder, or even the scenery—they play a part in our journey. I can think of several important ways that schooling can help us along the way. Some of these ways are simple, some are profound:

---

2. Augustine, *De doctrina christiana* 1.4.4.

- Through a good liberal arts education, we learn to speak and listen, to read and write—the basic skills of communication, apart from which we cannot enter into relationship.

- At a school like Trinity, we will be teaching students to read the Bible and to listen to God attentively.

- Through an education students acquire the tools of learning that will enable them to tackle any subject that they encounter in life—in this way they are being equipped to fulfill their vocations in God's world, where they are called to live.

- Teachers at Trinity will model the faith, hope, and love that we want to cultivate in our children.

- Finally, in a good school children will enjoy learning in a way that trains them, prepares them for the enjoyment of heaven. To be sure, delight in E. B. White's prose is a far cry from eternal blessedness, but one has to start somewhere, and to the one who has (such joy) more will be given.

I'm hoping that we and our children have a great voyage this year, that we take much joy in the journey, and that we never forget where we are going.

What I Saw When I Looked Up

April 1, 2011

At the 2011 National Association of Independent Schools Conference, I had the chance to sit in on a presentation by Secretary of Education Arne Duncan, and this experience made a strong impression on me. Back at Trinity we followed up on some of Duncan's ideas, going to visit the Durham superintendent of schools and offering to help with the DPS robotics programs, which were part of the DPS Strategic Plan. And our service-learning program, under the able leadership of Lori Easterlin, has pushed us into important areas of community involvement. Still, I sense that Trinity's best days lie ahead when it comes to realizing our public purpose. It's a great question for any institution to ask: If our institution disappeared overnight, who would care?

For the last sixteen years, I've had my head down. It takes a lot of one's attention to get a school going and keep it running. Or maybe the better analogy is driving in heavy traffic—you really need to keep your eyes on the road in front, on the cars around, and on the dashboard now and then. There's not a lot of time to take in the scenery.

But all the while, something has been bothering me. That's why I decided to go to Washington last month. I wasn't going to go to the annual conference of the National Association of Independent Schools (NAIS). It's expensive and time-consuming and—well, I've had my head down. But when I saw that the theme was "The Public Purpose of Independent Schools," I couldn't resist.

We've managed to build a pretty good school in sixteen years. Conferences like NAIS help our schools move from pretty good to pretty great. There was plenty of that at this conference, but I've been there and done that before, and I'll do it again. What was new was an intense focus on the role of independent schools for the public good.

1 – VISION

What's been bothering me, niggling at my conscience, is the realization that for all our good work, the larger story of which we are a part is not a good one. We are managing to do something very worthwhile for 447 students this year. But there are 32,500 students in public schools in Durham County Schools. How are they doing?

And what about the national picture? According to the Programme for International Student Assessment (PISA), the United States ranks 17th in the world, for the most part right smack in the middle of average.[1] The closing keynote speaker at NAIS was Geoffrey Canada, CEO of the Harlem Children's Zone, now famous (and infamous) for his frank-talking, no-nonsense, prophetic voice in the film *Waiting for Superman*. Said Canada, "If our nation allows children to fail, we will not remain a great nation. I don't think people realize the enormity of the problem."[2]

While in DC, I also had the chance to hear from Arne Duncan, Secretary of Education, and two educational policy experts, both smart, well informed, and well spoken: Sir Michael Baker, of McKinsey, and Andreas Schleicher, who oversees PISA, the test of cognitive skills administered to fifteen-year-olds across the globe. Secretary Duncan spoke passionately about the crisis we are in. He cited a 25 percent national drop-out rate, in a time when skilled knowledge workers are essential to our economic competitiveness in a global market.

I don't need to pile on the statistics. They are myriad and depressing. But I may need to pile on the reasons we at Trinity and other independent schools need to be paying attention. We all keep our heads down a lot, but we need to look up and see what is going on.

There is the economic argument. How far behind are we falling? What countries are outstripping us? What can we learn from those

---

1. National Center for Education Statistics, *Highlights from PISA 2009* (US Department of Education, 2010), 17.

2. Geoffrey Canada, "Creating Success for All Children." Keynote speech, Annual Conference of the National Association of Independent Schools (Washington, DC, February 25, 2011).

countries that have improved on measures like the PISA over the last decade? What kinds of policies do we need to reverse the trend of decline in US education? Can our economy recover and stay strong if we continue to stay in the "average" category for the quality of education? What if countries like Chile, Korea, Poland, and Portugal continue to improve and we continue to decline?

But there is another and, to my mind, greater reason that we all need to pay attention to this challenge: it is our civic duty. And enlightened self-interest might kick us in the pants too, since the survival of our democracy is, to understate the case, of interest to us all. Elizabeth Coleman, president of Bennington College and one of the most eloquent speakers at NAIS, lamented that there is really no serious dialogue about the importance of education for the health of our democracy. We tend to start with economics and jobs and our competitiveness on a global scale. But the primary value of an educated citizenry is that it helps us to maintain and regulate our freedom in the best and the worst of times.

We will have to roll up our sleeves and actually do something. Think globally and act locally, as they say. Or, to return to where I started, after you've looked around at the horizon and the landscape and studied the maps, look back down at the road and drive on, with a renewed commitment to doing something worthwhile along the way.

I haven't been called to set educational policy in DC or to guide independent schools across the country. But I have this one little school, and we can make whatever difference we can make, not just for our students, but for our community. It would seem to me that Christian schools ought to be out front in this way. Love your neighbor.

So my takeaways from the conference? Go meet some of the public school principals nearby. Ask them how we can help. (Our Augustine Literacy Project service-learning class is already doing this in a powerful way.) Read the DPS Strategic Plan and do what Dr. Becoats asked of us all at its unveiling: Find one thing you can do and put your oar

1 – VISION

in. Surely there is something our school can do to help Durham and Chapel Hill schools improve.

Trinity can be a school for our community. It would be wonderful if the entire community looked at us and said, "I'm so glad that school is here!"

Truth, Goodness, and Beauty

October 5, 2012

> *Our motto, as this essay shows, plugs our relatively upstart school into a tradition that is as old as education in the West. It is a venerable tradition to be reckoned with, and these big ideas have guided and inspired us. The classical motto has not been without some detractors, as it is less distinctively Christian than some we might have chosen. "Why not faith, hope, and love?" I have been asked. I have always appreciated the wide appeal of this classical motto; it has such cross-cultural versatility and supports our commitment to the notion that all truth is God's truth. And, as I tried to show in this essay, it is fully congruent with the audacious Christian claim that "in Christ all things hold together" (Col. 1:17).*

Trinity's motto is *Veritas, Bonitas, Pulchritudo*. Around Trinity, even those with no Latin have learned how to translate this: Truth, Goodness, and Beauty.

Each of these three bears sustained attention. What do we mean by truth? Can you teach goodness? Where is beauty in our curriculum? But my purpose here is to look at them together. They form a triad that spans not the whole of human experience but a large enough swath of it to remind us that we are complex creatures capable of a rich array of relationships. A good education ought to honor the *whole person* as created in the image of God. We are intellectual beings (truth); we are moral beings (goodness); and we are aesthetic beings (beauty). Ignore any one of these, and Trinity would offer a lopsided education. So one of the values of our motto is that it reminds us, as Charlotte Mason liked to say, that education is the science of relations and that we human beings have the capacity to form relationships with all manner of people and things (art and nature, for instance). We celebrate a rich education.

These three (truth, goodness, and beauty) have quite a history. They go back to the Greeks, and Christians like Augustine brought them into the theological tradition of the early church. Thomas Aquinas extended this thinking in his *Summa Theologica*, and there is a deep and rich tradition of Catholic thinking about these three. Works like Etienne Gilson's *The Arts of the Beautiful* are profound explorations into the nature of these three.

I keep calling them "these three" because we lack a really suitable name for them, considered together. Fine names have been suggested (see below), but none has caught on like, say, "Trinity" has for the Three-Personed One God of Christian theology. Still, the names that have been suggested, while not particularly helpful for marketing purposes, are excellent windows into the nature and value of these three and remind us why we continue to honor them by placarding them all over our stationery and across the frosted glass outside my office.

The Permanent Things

This expression, I am told, comes from T. S. Eliot, who passed it on to his friend Russell Kirk. Kirk believed that truth, goodness, and beauty were part of an *order of reality*:

> There is an order which holds all things in their places: ...it is made for us, and we are made for it. The thinking conservative, far from denying the existence of this eternal order, endeavors to ascertain its nature and to conform to that order, which is the source of the Permanent Things.[1]

This calls to mind C. S. Lewis's claim that there are two ways with the self: we can try to shape reality to conform to the self (a modern

---

1. Russell Kirk, *Prospects for Conservatives*, rev. ed. (Washington, DC: Regnery Gateway, 1989), 36–37. This statement appears in a slightly different form in earlier

or postmodern project); or we can try to conform the self to reality (the classical and Christian project).² All of these thinkers regarded truth, goodness, and beauty as realities against which the wise person would measure and adjust herself. Cultures change, ideas go in and out of fashion, but some things are *permanent* and are thus worthy of our greatest attention. Such a notion would explain, for instance, why geometry is still (since the Greeks) an essential part of most school curricula. It may be useful for building bridges, but there is another, deeper reason for studying the proofs: they are demonstrations of something amazingly *permanent*.

The Eternal Verities

On September 13, 1922, a young man stood before the trustees, faculty, and students of a new Christian school, called the Stony Brook School. That man was Frank Gaebelein, who went on to serve as Stony Brook's headmaster for 41 years. Dr. Gaebelein set forth a vision for a school,

> an enterprise built upon the foundational truths of Christianity. These are the great and abiding things—the eternal verities. Our contemporary philosophy, a large part of our religious thought, is colored by the idea of relativism, the endless ebb and flow of things. Yet the great truths remain. They are immutable, abiding—as much more firmly fixed than the mountains as the infinite transcends the finite. They cannot be shaken; they constitute "the everlasting yea."³

I had not heard this expression before I read Dr. Gaebelein's address, but I found it, later, in a Puritan prayer republished in *The Valley*

---

editions of the book; see, e.g., the second edition (Chicago: Henry Regnery, 1962), 50.
  2. C. S. Lewis, *The Abolition of Man* (New York: Simon & Schuster, 1996), 83.
  3. Frank E. Gaebelein, "Plan and Scope of Stony Brook School for Boys: Address at the Inauguration of the Stony Brook School, September 13, 1922." *The Presbyterian*, December 14, 1922.

of Vision.⁴ Wherever it came from, it is an apt phrase to capture the essence of our motto. Truth, goodness, and beauty "remain" and "abide." Our investment in them is our best investment, sure to last, never to fade.

The Great Transcendents

This is my favorite tag for our motto, but it is surely the least marketable. I have been told never to use a word like "transcendent" in a public setting. I refuse to concede the point, but I will admit that it is readily misunderstood. To transcend is to pass across some important and seemingly impassable divide. Christians will be familiar with the expression, from Paul, of the "peace that transcends all understanding." Paul's meaning is that all the understanding in the world will not get you across the great divide from anxiety and fear to peace. That requires faith and prayer.

So it is with truth, goodness, and beauty. They allow us, in an imperfect but real way, to cross over a great divide between this ephemeral and contingent world into the reality that is the heart of all that is. Truth, goodness, and beauty give us glimpses of this reality. Or, we might say they give us traces. N. T. Wright calls them clues.⁵ They whisper into our ears that there is another reality beyond the one we live in all day long. They suggest to our souls, "This is not all there is."

Think for a moment of the beauty of music. Physicist and theologian John Polkinghorne speaks of the mystery of music as a "window into reality." He asks a profound question: "From a scientific point of view, [music] is nothing but vibrations in the air, impinging on the eardrums and stimulating neural currents in the brain. How does it come about that this banal sequence of temporal activity has the power to

---

4. Arthur G. Bennett, ed., *The Valley of Vision* (Carlisle, PA: Banner of Truth Trust, 1975).

5. N. T. Wright, *For All God's Worth: True Worship and the Calling of the Church* (Grand Rapids, MI: Wm. B. Eerdmans, 1997), 9.

speak to our hearts of an eternal beauty?"[6] The connections we make to this eternal realm are brief and passing, but they are powerful, and as C. S. Lewis attested in his autobiography, *Surprised by Joy*, one will spend a lifetime searching for that connection to the permanent, eternal transcendent.[7]

Our goal at Trinity is to set children and young adults up for the making of these connections. We cannot orchestrate them, but we can set the table, so to speak. Our job is to make sure that the spread is rich, full of truth, goodness, and beauty. And surely it is one of the best jobs in the world to watch as the neurons fire and the Spirit moves.

---

6. John C. Polkinghorne, *Belief in God in an Age of Science* (New Haven, CT: Yale University Press, 1988), 18–19.

7. C. S. Lewis, *Surprised by Joy: The Shape of My Early Life* (New York: Harcourt, Brace, 1956).

2 – Christian

There is not a hand's breadth in the whole domain of our human existence over which Christ, who is Sovereign over all, does not cry, 'Mine!'

ABRAHAM KUYPER, "SPHERE SOVEREIGNTY"

The Christian mission of Trinity has always been central to the school. The first group that gathered in our family room to talk about a school (the group that would comprise the first board) were all Christians. But, by design, they were Christians from different traditions, different churches. We were all evangelicals—committed to the scriptures and to God's personal work in our lives through the truth of the Gospel and the power of the Holy Spirit. And we all shared what C. S. Lewis called "mere Christianity," the fundamental commitment to truth that transcends denominations, traditions, times, and cultures. Since that time, the Trinity board has again and again affirmed the centrality of this Christian commitment. I have tried to choose essays in this section that give some sense of both the breadth and the depth of our thinking about these matters, as well as some examples of how our Christian faith influences the way we go about essential educational decisions.

A School That Changes Lives

SEPTEMBER 1, 2006

*My infallible computer tells me I wrote this in April 2006, but it wasn't published until the next fall. I can't for the life of me recall why I waited to publish this—*Parent News *deadlines were always looming, and anything half-good was often enough. I've often reflected on Augustine's notion of his two conversions, and I think they provide a clear goal for Trinity School. We can expect the first of every student, a conversion to wisdom. We can hope for the second and more important spiritual change. Both of these are, to some large extent, beyond our control, but one can hope. And pray. This piece provides a nice segue from our more general thoughts about vision to our particular and distinctive Christian mission. Trinity has always tried to walk that fine line: being thoroughly Christian, but being open to the community.*

We expect a lot from our schools. Indoctrination or even training is not enough: We want transformation. School brochures are replete with metaphors for such deep change, from the inside out: We ignite the fires of learning, or at least kindle them. We awaken a love of learning.

Private schools are perhaps the boldest to make these claims—parents who are paying thousands of dollars expect schools to open the eyes of the blind and wake the dead.

Such lofty goals have a venerable history. Plato may have started things out with his allegory of the cave, a vision of education-as-enlightenment. But even here, at the beginning, doubts arise about the realism and viability of such an ideal education: Plato's Republic has been called a utopia, a word which means, literally, "nowhere." Is that where we will find the school that changes lives? Nowhere?

What can we expect from our schools? In particular, what can we expect from a school like Trinity, with its classical Christian mission?

2 – CHRISTIAN

I will tell you a true story about the transformation of a young man. His name was Augustine, and he lived from AD 354–430. His mother was a Christian, but he wandered far from the faith in his youth, first in North Africa, then in Italy. Eventually he came back to the faith of his mother and became one of the most important writers and thinkers in church history. What interests me here is how he traveled back to his faith. How, in other words, his life was changed. And what role education played in this transformation. We have the skinny on this because he left us one of the most amazing accounts ever written, his autobiography, *Confessions*.

It turns out that Augustine went through two conversions, as he tells it. The first was a conversion to wisdom, to the love of knowledge; the second was a conversion to Christ. The first change (Book III) came when he was 19; the second (Book VIII) when he was 31. The first was a natural conversion; the second was supernatural.

The first came by reading Cicero; the second by reading St. Paul. The first moved him from the mockery and foolish mischief of youth to the serious study of a lawyer; the second moved him from scholarship to piety. The first taught him to study and learn; the second taught him to praise and pray. The first made him a philosopher; the second made him a Christian.

There is no question that both of these conversions changed him. About the first, he reflected, "All my empty dreams suddenly lost their charm and my heart began to throb with a bewildering passion for the wisdom of eternal truth."[1] And of the second: "In an instant, as I came to the end of the sentence, it was as though the light of confidence flooded into my heart and all the darkness of doubt was dispelled."[2]

There is also no question—at least in Augustine's mind and in mine—that the second conversion was infinitely more important than the first. He would have traded a hundred books by Cicero for one word

---

1. Augustine, *Confessions* 3.4.7.
2. Augustine, *Confessions* 8.12.29.

from God himself. Christ was his sun; Cicero his moon. If it comes down to it, we would be wise to trade all our education for redemption, which alone can make us ready to enter the kingdom of God.

But it does not always come down to it. Sometimes, the Spirit moves in patterns. Sometimes the soil of knowledge and virtue, well tilled, is fertile ground for the fruits of faith, hope, and love. Sometimes, but not always. There will be those who scorn both conversions and go on, like the youthful Augustine, stealing pears and living like a lout for the rest of their lives. And—worse—there will be those who follow Augustine through his first conversion but never make it to the second: They are the learned fools who have found everything except the pearl of great price.

What I want for my children is both transformations, both conversions. I want them to come alive to learning, and I want them to love the Lord Christ first. I want both of these. We are not masters of these changes, but only servants. Like the Baptist, we prepare the way. We baptize with water and look for the One who baptizes with the Holy Spirit. Whether in first grade, or in high school, or nineteen years later, we wait: Come, Lord Jesus, and teach our children.

Where Is the Christian in Christian Education?

NOVEMBER 7, 2003

It is heartening to read this piece, now a decade old, and realize that we are still talking this way to parents at our open houses, to teachers at their orientation, and to our entire faculty in a recent session on being Christian role models. There is, of course, the danger of staleness, of driving one's own idea so many times that it becomes its own cliché. But there is also the danger of drift, which is the story of every institution, and so it encourages me to see this kind of consistency at Trinity. These elements of Christian education make a cord of three strands, not easily broken.

How does your Christianity impact the education you offer at Trinity?

This is a fair question, frequently asked. The school asks it, on the application form, of prospective teachers and staff. Prospective parents invariably ask it. People from nonreligious schools want to know what might be different here.

A Christian education is an education offered by Christian teachers. Every legitimate vocation in the yellow pages can be adorned and honored by a sincere Christian who takes it up with reverence, humility, diligence, honesty, and love. Of education, however, we can say more. Because its currency is ideas and truth, and because its materiel is the human person, the opportunities for doing serious good and serious harm are magnified. Wherever we find honest Christian teachers plying their trade—whether in public schools, independent schools, or religious schools—we should give thanks and pray for their benevolent influence in the lives of their students. At Trinity School we work hard to hire and nurture teachers who are Christians.

A Christian education is an education from a Christian perspective. Frank Gaebelein, first headmaster of the Stony Brook School, defined this as "integration" of our faith with learning in every aspect. Some Christian schools today like to talk about worldview.[1] At Trinity we have chosen these words in our mission: "to educate...*within the framework of Christian faith and conviction.*" Following Christ our *Magister*, we stride into the world with a double posture: enlightened by Christian truth, we meet the world with interest, sympathy, curiosity, and compassion. All truth is God's truth. All that has been well said belongs to us Christians. On the other hand, we know that creation waits in travail and we live in a fallen world, a dangerous place where truth is still held hostage by unrighteousness. Therefore we seek to bring every thought captive to Christ's truth, to scrutinize what we hear according to God's truth, and to sift the true from the false. Both of these postures are essential to Christian education.

If education *by Christians* is possible in almost any school, education *from a Christian perspective* is not possible in many of our schools. A school like Trinity offers Christian education in both of these senses, but also in a third, which is unique: **Christian education can also be defined as education in a community of Christian teachers and students**. This fellowship is vital because education is a communal experience. We learn from one another. The fastest student in the class has a chance to explain indirect objects to her struggling deskmate. And then the deskmate, in turn, asks the best question later in the day. What is true of education is all the more true of Christian education. We are the body of Christ and we belong to one another. Students in Christian schools learn how to value rightly their own gifts and those of their classmates. Moreover, Christianity is caught as much as it is taught, and many of us Christian parents put our children in schools like Trinity because we want the Gospel to be formed in them, in every part of them: from imagination, to intellect, to will. Since our students

---

1. Frank E. Gaebelein, *The Pattern of God's Truth: Problems of Integration in Christian Education* (Winona Lake, IN: BMH Books, 2009).

spend six or seven hours daily in a school setting, it makes sense to ask what sort of community is shaping them.

A school like Trinity offers a Christian education in all three of these senses: Our teachers are believers who give students a framework of Christian faith and conviction in a community that is attempting to live out the Gospel and kingdom values. Any one of these can be a potent force in a young person's life, but the combination of the three can be, by God's grace, life-changing.

The Dilemma of Faith and Learning
February 29, 2008

When the board first hired me as headmaster in 1996, the school was too young and small to provide many of the resources a head would expect. One of the great compensations they made, for which I have always been grateful, is to have written into my contract an annual four-week study leave. It took me many years actually to take this leave, and I still struggle to find the right time and to get away (especially in the age of email), but the times I have taken have been most invigorating for me and (I hope) helpful for the school. I recall writing this piece at the end of one of those leaves, when I set myself down to plough through some of Aquinas's Summa Theologica. *There is so much profundity there, and the sentence I have quoted at the beginning of this piece is dense enough to fuel an entire seminar session. I include this article not because I think I have mastered the great Doctor on this point, but because I am sure that the dilemma I identify is a real one and that Aquinas has something important to say about it. Of all the things that keep me awake at night, this one is at the top.*

> *The love of God is better than the knowledge of God; but, on the contrary, the knowledge of corporeal things is better than the love of them.*
>
> – Aquinas, *Summa Theologica*

For a Christian school, there is always a dilemma: Which is more important, faith or learning?

Faith has a lot going for it. What Christian would elevate learning above religion, one's own intellectual improvement over spiritual development? And we have it on good authority that if we have all knowledge but do not have love, we are noisy gongs and clanging symbols.

2 – CHRISTIAN

Love is better than knowledge, and this conviction leads us sometimes through hard choices: Shall we hire the deeply pious teacher who is passable but not excellent in the classroom? Or shall we hire the master teacher whose faith is, at best, fuzzy and weak? Of course, we would always like to escape the horns of such a dilemma and dream of the spiritually mature master; but reality has a way of forcing such choices on us from time to time. Schools that choose the brilliant non-Christian forfeit, eventually, their birthright as *Christian* schools; heads who hire the faithful mediocre lie awake at night wondering if they have not also sold out for another pot of soup.

For there is something to be said on behalf of knowledge. This is, after all, what schools are for. If not for the cultivation of the intellect, then why have we founded these institutions? There are churches for the spirit, art institutes for our aesthetic side, sports teams for the body and heart (double entendre intended), clubs for our social development, and volunteer societies (like Bible studies) for the training of the will through disciplined habits. But where else, in all of human culture, is there a place devoted to the cultivation and celebration of the intellect? To balance a chemical equation, to discover the properties of the Fibonacci numbers, to trace the intellectual pedigree of a concept like freedom—these are the glories of understanding, to which every member of the human race has an inalienable right. Not to celebrate the dignity of the human mind is a shame, and a Christian school which neglects this for the sake of piety pays no honor to the Creator.

I have long thought that such paradoxes—e.g., that faith and learning are both most important—are resolved somehow in the mind of our Maker. Problem is, I am not privy to such insights. But I am grateful that God has sent us a few Wise, who see more clearly than I, even if not quite up to the divine perspective. One such is Aquinas. I will not spend much time now singing his praises, nor will I pretend that I understand half of what he says. But there are passages in his *Summa*

Theologica that are like bolts of lightning into my darkness, and the one cited above shows me a way out of this perplexing dilemma.

Aquinas is sure that "the intellect is nobler than the will."[1] Why? Because the object of the intellect is more simple and more absolute than the object of the will. The intellect grasps directly "the good as desirable." The will is secondary—one must have some sort of understanding before one can choose something. Faith comes by hearing. But things get a little more complicated, as they always do for Aquinas. "When...the thing in which there is good is nobler than the soul itself, in which is the idea understood, by comparison with such a thing the will is higher than the intellect."[2] This sets up a fascinating tension: When it comes to earthly things, the sorts of things we often study in schools, the soul is superior, and therefore the intellect is the most important thing. But when it comes to spiritual things, where the soul encounters something better than itself (like God's self), the will trumps the intellect. The knowledge of Roman history is better than the love of Roman history; but the love of God is better than the knowledge of God.

We began by speaking of the inherent difficulties of Christian education. Faith or learning? Secular schools have a simpler task and can avoid this distraction. But they do so at their peril. For if Aquinas is right, then an inherent tension between the intellect and the will is always present in our lives and in our schools. If we attempt a school that is simply intellectual, one where learning is supreme, we will betray our souls. If we ignore the plain truth that there are realities before which even our glorious intellect must bow, we miss the most important thing. The love of God is not a sweet platitude added onto education; it is the most important thing. On the other hand, we who are Christians must honor the *imago Dei* which is stamped upon every student. The mind of each one is a glorious dignity which we cannot manipulate, but to which we must pay homage through good, disciplined, brilliant

---

1. Aquinas, *Summa theologica* 1.82.3.
2. Aquinas, *Summa theologica* 1.82.3.

teaching and learning. This is not intellectual elitism; it is the only way to do education well.

And so I accept the challenge of Christian education because I am convinced that it is the best education. Not because faith is better than learning, or the converse, but because only a Christian education can honor the soul as it is, a thinking-willing soul, created in the image of God, ready to think God's thoughts after him, designed to love him forever.

Science and Religion at Trinity School
April 9, 2010

I have included this article for several reasons. The issue continues to be on the top of any FAQ list. Over Trinity's twenty years I have seen many issues come and go, but this one has staying power, and I am glad we thought through our posture and approach early on. Two Trinity spouses were instrumental in helping craft this policy: Don Tyndall, husband of founding board member Kathy Tyndall and professor at the UNC Dental School; and Fred Brooks, husband of founding board member Nancy Brooks and founding chair of the Department of Computer Science at UNC. This article demonstrates what we mean by being a Christian school that is evangelical, orthodox, and ecumenical—three commitments that together create a certain tension but also a possibility for a unique cultural space. I hope that in this short essay on science and religion one can see the school's commitment to the Gospel of grace in Christ alone, to non-negotiable truths, and to a certain charity among believers who differ on the way all this gets worked out.

One of the first policies ever written at Trinity School was on creation and origins. We knew that this issue was challenging, controversial, and defining. It still is, and I am thankful for the wise and careful work of the group that Don Tyndall chaired back in the day. The policy needs a good update (e.g., it was written before Intelligent Design became all the rage), but it is still wise and substantial.

Teaching about origins is challenging because we are committed to two things, neither of which is easy by itself: doing good science and doing good theology. As our forebears would have said, we want to read *both* books of God's revelation: his general revelation in the book of nature, of which science is the primary hermeneutic; and his special revelation in the book we call the Bible, for which faithful understanding is the primary means to knowledge. There is a simple splendor to each of these books, but the unfolding of their stories is far from simple. Just think of the complex and storied history of science, the progressive understanding of physics from the ancients to Newton to Einstein. Likewise, the church's understanding of the life and death and resurrection of Jesus unfolded progressively through the Gospels to Paul and on through the ecumenical councils of the church, until the classic orthodox formulations about Jesus were established. Either one of these books would be challenging enough by itself, but the issue of origins forces us to read them *together*, to integrate them and see them side by side. At the intersection of these two readings is the vexed question of evolution and how we read the book of Genesis.

The matter of origins is not only challenging; it is controversial. The options for relating science and religion are several, and they are by and large mutually exclusive. Physicist (and Duke grad!) Ian Barbour has proposed a helpful fourfold typology[1] for the way that people, Christians included, have related science and religion: *Conflict*—the two are incompatible and one must give ground; it is a zero-sum game; if science is right, religion is wrong, and conversely (e.g., young-earth creationism and atheistic evolutionism). *Dialogue*—recognizing that the two ways of knowing are quite different, this position actively and hopefully looks for connections and for presuppositional similarities (e.g., in their shared assumptions that the universe is intelligible and open; the work of John Polkinghorne comes especially to mind). *Integration*—this is perhaps the most challenging posture of all, for it expects to achieve some kind of synoptic, complementary, and cohesive view of the two disciplines (e.g., natural theologies and classic apologetics from both Design and more recent Intelligent Design theories). *Independence*—science and religion are each legitimate ways of knowing and understanding, but they exist in parallel conceptual uni-

---

1. Ian G. Barbour, "Ways of Relating Science and Religion." In *Religion and Science: Historical and Contemporary Issues* (San Francisco: Harper SanFrancisco, 1997), 77–105.

verses, and it would be futile to try to connect them (many seriously religious academic scientists in institutions where faith commitments are scorned have learned to compartmentalize these two). Christians have taken each of these positions, and some of these positions are fighting positions. No wonder there is controversy.

This is also a defining issue. It is the rare open house for prospective parents where we don't get this question, in some form. Parents realize that the way a school deals with this question will define its core values and shape its culture. How can we be a school that welcomes the knowledge and understanding the world has to offer (think: science) without accepting all the commitments and idolatries the world demands (think: materialistic atheism)? Will we be a school that gives students the answers to these vexing challenges, or one that teaches them to ask the sort of questions which those who follow Christ ought to be asking? I've long thought that one of the best entrees into this question, for older students, is to give them an introductory chapter on evolution from a standard science book and also the first three chapters of Genesis, and ask them to read both and come to class the next day with a list of questions. This is education, Trinity style.

Given the cultural and religious landscape, Trinity will attract families who sort these questions out in different ways. Evangelical Christians tend to end up in one of three positions: Young-Earth Creationism, which claims that God created the heavens and the earth in six literal days and Adam and Eve without the aid of evolutionary mechanisms; Intelligent Design, which allows for a much older earth and micro-evolutionary development, but denies that evolution can account for the complexity of organisms and posits moments of special creation; or some form of Theistic Evolution, which proposes creation *ex nihilo* in the beginning and allows that God ordained evolution as the mechanism through which species originated, including human beings. The book to read is Francis Collins's *The Language of God*.

2 – CHRISTIAN

In this context it will require a strong dose of charity for us all to live and learn together. But we mustn't lose sight of the substantial agreements that these three views have, beliefs which separate us from a purely secular and atheistic evolutionary stance: the amazing creativity of God, the wonder of creation out of nothing, the intelligent design behind the universe in general and the animal kingdom in particular, the unique status of human beings created in the image of God, the ways in which we are fearfully and wonderfully made, and the "language" of creation, the glory of God as the end of all creation, and the summing up of all creation in Jesus Christ.

It was great to be with the students this week as Dan the Animal Man came to show them some amazing creatures (a porcupine, an alligator, and an owl) in the Lower School Assembly. Dan talked to the students about God's wise design, drawing from his deep knowledge of these animals, which he clearly loves. He left many questions unanswered, many controversies untouched. That was appropriate for our Lower School students. The main message was loud and clear: the heavens declare the glory of God, and the creatures are his handiwork. Amen.

All Truth Is God's Truth

September 5, 2011

Each year at Trinity, since maybe our third or fourth, we have chosen a passage of scripture as a theme. There is a gallery of these hanging in the Blue Gym, and each year the entire school memorizes the passage and reflects on the verse. In 2011, we chose Psalm 24:1 and focused on Christ's lordship over all creation. In particular, we thought about creation stewardship, and we read Richard Louv's Last Child in the Woods *and a biography of John Muir for our summer Trinity Reads program. All of this gave us a natural jumping-off point for exploring a constellation of ideas that had been part of the school's DNA from the beginning. The title of this article has been almost an unofficial motto of Trinity, and at the beginning of the year I was able to reflect on some of its meaning and lineage. The concept goes back at least to Augustine, who in his treatise* On Christian Doctrine *(18.28) declared that "a person who is a good and true Christian should realize that truth belongs to his Lord, wherever it is found." It is a venerable idea whose implications still hold currency in our complicated modern world.*

> *The earth is the Lord's*
> *and everything in it,*
> *the world and all who live in it.*
> *– Psalm 24:1*

If you asked ten people off the street whether they thought Christian education was enlarging or constricting, I'm afraid I know how things would come out. Most people think of Christianity as something that holds us back and somehow makes us less than what we'd like to be. To many, Christian education means education by subtraction, education that is defined mainly by what it doesn't do: books we won't read, subjects we won't cover, questions we won't ask.

2 – CHRISTIAN

The truth of the matter is that Christian education ought to be the widest, most expansive, most open-hearted and hospitable education on the planet, for our God is the Lord of all, as our verse for this year assures us. All truth is God's truth, so we are not afraid to go where the truth leads, for it leads us to God. As Justin Martyr, the second century Christian philosopher and apologist said, "All that has been well said belongs to us Christians."[1]

The idea of common grace means that God showers his undeserved blessings on all people, religious and irreligious, Christian and non-Christian. We Christians are glad to acknowledge that God's gifts of humor, of scientific insight, of musical genius, of innovation, of mathematical acumen, of powerful storytelling are not given to Christians alone. Sometimes I think they are seldom given to Christians, though of course there are notable exceptions. God seems to do a pretty good job of reminding us that these are grace gifts, undeserved. There is nothing in us that deserves to be wise or articulate or musical or brilliant or talented—nothing in us Christians, and nothing in our unbelieving friends and colleagues. But wherever we find such gifts, we celebrate them and acknowledge that all of this comes from God, and we love him more for the truth that we see, wherever we see it.

So it is that our education is wide and expansive. It is often wider and more expansive than the education our secular friends give their children in secular schools. For there it is verboten to cross the religious line of separation. Take the issue of origins. Our graduates are able to explain the idea of evolution as fully and accurately as any graduate of a school where the teachers might all be committed materialists teaching evolution as one of their core values. But Trinity students will also have to articulate other viewpoints: young- and old-earth creationism, intelligent design, theistic evolution. And not only will they have wrestled with the best science that has been done thus far in human history; they will also have wrestled with the best theol-

---

1. Justin Martyr, *Second Apology* 13.4.

ogy. And, most importantly, they will have read and interpreted the biblical text, which we hold to be God's revelation of his purposes for this world.

Much of our teaching at Trinity will look like good teaching at any school, but there is a difference. The teachers and many of the students are glad to acknowledge that God is the Lord of all they study. Abraham Kuyper, the Dutch theologian-statesman, famously said, "There is not a square inch in the whole domain of our human existence over which Christ, who is Sovereign over all, does not cry: 'Mine!'"[2]

Which leads us to another cultural objection. "Mine" can sound petty and selfish, like a toddler who hasn't learned to share toys. That, of course, is not God's way with the world he owns. The whole notion of creation means that God chose from the beginning of our world to share its truth, goodness, and beauty with us all. He could have kept it to God's Triune self and been gloriously happy forever without us. But he didn't. He gave, he risked sharing, he loved us enough to reveal himself through his works. And then, more gloriously still, God's redemption of the world in Christ is the most gracious and generous act in all of history. The scriptures teach us that Christ's "Mine" is the claim of a husband for a bride he loves deeply, one he has sacrificed himself for unto death. And, most glorious of all, we are promised (1 Cor. 15) that one day Christ will hand this redeemed and perfected creation back to the Father and say to him, "Yours!"

We belong to God, and we are glad of it. Whatever he has to teach us, we will learn. This has been the posture of learning and teaching here at Trinity from the beginning of the school. Welcome to this big tent of learning we call Trinity School.

---

2. Abraham Kuyper, "Sphere Sovereignty." In *Abraham Kuyper, A Centennial Reader*, ed. James D. Bratt (Grand Rapids, MI: Eerdmans, 1998), 488.

3 – Classical Learning

We may give the Greek, Jewish, and Christian idea of man: man as an animal endowed with reason, whose supreme dignity is in the intellect; and man as a free individual inpersonal relation to God, whose supreme righteousness consists in voluntarily obeying the law of God; and man as a sinful and wounded creature called to divine life and to the freedom of grace, whose supreme perfection consists of love.

JACQUES MARITAIN, EDUCATION AT THE CROSSROADS

I have always paused inside whenever someone has asked me about Trinity's distinctive pedagogy. "Are you a classical school?" "Is Trinity a Charlotte Mason School?" "Are you child-centered? Project-based?" The streams that have flowed into the river that is Trinity School are several, and their confluence has created something that is not easy to describe. I envy my colleagues, say, at the local Montessori school, who can nail their pedagogy with one word and leave it there. Further, as the school has grown (adding grades) and matured (adding years and wise leaders), our understanding of what it means to be Trinity has come into sharper focus. Over twenty years, we have had different dialogue partners in the larger culture (from E.D. Hirsch to Thomas Friedman to Daniel Pink). Over twenty years my own thinking has changed some, and I have tried to mark a few of those important changes in the footnotes of this section. But at the heart of Trinity remain four funda-

3 – CLASSICAL LEARNING

mental commitments: Christian, classical, rich, and unhurried education.

The following sections attempt to unpack each of those last three in some depth, to show how far back they go, and to chart the development of my thinking on this to some extent. The best guide for these continues to be Trinity's Expanded Mission Statement, available on our website. This document has been thoroughly vetted by our educational leaders and approved by the board, so it supersedes anything I have said in these reflections.

Classical can mean many things in education. Tell-tale signs of classical influence include the teaching of Latin (and sometimes Greek), an emphasis on the Trivium as a way of ordering curriculum and pedagogy, a focus on the ancients and the Great Books, a focus on the liberal arts, and an interest in Socratic ways of teaching and learning. In Christian schools, there has been a resurgence of classical emphases over the last twenty to thirty years, and we all owe much to the work of organizations like the Classical Christian School (CCS) movement led by Doug Wilson and the professional organization, the Society of Classical Learning (SCL). Trinity's classical emphasis has always been broad and generous, seeking to mine the best from the long tradition of education in the liberal arts and to temper certain strains of classical emphasis with complementary models—most notably, the creative tension between Charlotte Mason's more child-centered model and the classical ideal. We continue to think that the classical model, interpreted in this broad and hospitable way, has several abiding values for Trinity: It connects deeply to our Christian faith (e.g., the rich tradition of what has been called Christian humanism), and it remains (despite its dusty reputation) a surprisingly fresh and adaptable way of thinking about education for the future. I hope that the articles in this section will support these claims and inspire many future Trinity leaders to continue to pursue the classical vision.

A Liberal Education

November 6, 1998

This essay, written in the third year of the school, my second as headmaster, is an attempt to explain what a liberal education is, in its essence, and why the Trivium was so interesting to us as a metacognitive pattern of learning. The most important ideas here are the notion of intellectual freedom (i.e., the glory of learning for learning's sake), the centrality of language, and the inseparability of thinking and speaking. I also fully admit to having two ulterior motives in this piece: to stake out some ancient territory for a classical education that was wider than the classical Christian school movement in the 1990s, and to rehabilitate the word liberal in a political climate that saw it as a shibboleth. The friend I refer to, by the way, was Robert Phay, my wife's former boss at the Principals' Executive Program (PEP), and a great fan of Mortimer Adler, whose book he gave me. I should give credit here to PEP, along with my wife's training and connections there—they were a source of wise counsel and aspirational direction in our early years.

Even the staunchest conservatives will send their children to a liberal arts college, a fact which makes us all do an intellectual double-take and wonder what in the world it means to call an education "liberal." Nowadays it is hard to hear "liberal education" as something other than a political description, but it has not always been so.

In the classical tradition, of which Trinity is a grateful though not uncritical beneficiary, a liberal education is, in essence, the sort of education that is fitting for free persons (from the Latin *liberalis*, meaning free). Although too often in the past those who were "free" to receive this kind of education were a certain privileged elite, the essential distinction is not between person and person but between person and animal. The notion of a liberal education is born of the conviction that humanity, being possessed of a rational soul, is free in ways that other living beings are not. In particular, we humans are free to speak and to think rationally. This is what a friend of mine had in mind when he gave me a book on whose flyleaf he had inscribed the salutation "Here's to a liberal education for every child!" Indeed.

Traditionally, a liberal education begins with the liberal arts. In the finely ordered and articulated medieval system, these are seven in number. The seven liberal arts are divided into two groups: the first three, called the Trivium; and four others called the Quadrivium. Together they comprise an educational system that was designed to cultivate those unique capacities that we humans are free to exercise: thinking and speaking.

The Trivium is, essentially, an educational program that teaches students how to use language well and to think clearly. Thinking and speaking cannot be separated, and the Trivium involves both. It comprises grammar, logic, and rhetoric, three distinct but inseparable "arts." When a student has mastered these three, he or she can confidently and competently listen and speak, read and write.

A student who is skilled in the use of these arts will have a freedom that only discipline can yield. Only the trained horseman is free to explore the trails. Only the liberally educated is free to learn any subject. All others will be chained to the few subjects they have been given, without the knowledge of how they are to be gotten or sustained. The Quadrivium, which followed the Trivium in the classical curriculum, was in fact a regimen of four standard subjects (geometry, arithmetic, astronomy, and music) and provided the student with a standard curriculum to be explored with these tools of learning. In our own world of the wide web of information and the expansion of knowledge, these four cannot continue to reign alone or hold pride of place for every student. Nevertheless, the educational pattern remains standard: One learns first *how* to learn (through the arts) and then one proceeds to pursue learning various subjects, going as deep into a field as one's calling and interests allow.

Our goal at Trinity is to equip our modern students with these very same tools of learning. Grammar, logic, and rhetoric are not outmoded parts of a medieval syllabus, but the very arts that anyone must master who will be free to speak and think and go on learning as only human beings can. Mastery of these arts is much more important than the collection of various "subjects" in our students' heads. Subjects enough they will get along the way of their lives, but our goal is to give them the tools that are adaptable to any task they will face in this changing world. To this end we work, and we thank you for your partnership.

Paideia

September 8, 2000

I remember writing this piece after returning from a summer conference in Texas sponsored by Bruce Lockerbie's Paideia group. The conference with other Christian school leaders gave me a chance to reflect on what it meant to offer a classical education. I remember also working on a proposal to the board that counted the cost of launching our Upper School with our vanguard class, which that summer was rising from seventh to eighth grade. We had committed to telling those parents a year in advance whether Trinity would have an Upper School for their students. Our answer: Not yet. It would be six more years before we deemed ourselves ready for that great launch.

The notion of "enculturation" is key to this essay. Human beings are, by all mammalian standards, slow to grow up. One reason is that it takes a long time to teach the complex and richly textured interpretation of reality we call culture. This essay pays proper homage to the Greeks, but it also reminds us that a good education, wherever it is found, involves a complete orientation into culture, which includes the religious. The classical and the Christian fit nicely together.

Trinity opened its doors this past Tuesday to 154 students and nearly 30 faculty and staff for the start of our sixth year. The rainy weather couldn't dampen the excitement of teachers and students alike, and one parent captured the mood of many as she pulled through the long carpool line: "We've really grown, haven't we?"

Indeed we have. From 39 students to nearly 160. From one campus to two. From our original combination K–1 class to two sections of first grade this year. Like the students who have returned after a summer of growing, we're bigger than we used to be. And like those students, we have grown in ways that can't be measured with a yardstick or a calculator. I trust that as the years pass, we will grow in wisdom and in our understanding of what it means to be a classical Christian school.

We keep going forward by going backwards, trying to understand the rich legacy that has been left us by many who have gone before. Some of our best teachers are the Greeks, who can be regarded as the founders of liberal education, and to these Greeks we turn again now at the start of this year to be reminded of a truth well worth remembering.

It is ironic that the Greeks had no distinctive word for education. The word they did have—*paideia*—can be translated as either "education" or "culture." The fact that the Greeks could not even distinguish between education and culture is a clear indication of how tightly these two ideas were bound together for them. Education was a way of passing on their particular and fascinating culture to the next generation. Education was "in-culturation."

Most civilized communities have followed the Greeks in this tradition. C. S. Lewis put it like this: "Education in most civilized communities...has taught civil behaviour by direct and indirect discipline, has awakened the logical faculty by mathematics or dialectic, and has endeavoured to produce right sentiments...by steeping the pupil in the literature both sacred and profane on which the culture of the community is based."[1]

When we start talking about culture, people get nervous. "Whose culture?" is usually the first question asked these days. Hermann Goring, head of Hitler's *Luftwaffe*, is alleged to have said, "When I hear anyone talk of culture, I reach for my revolver." Others of a less violent and impulsive bent may wonder whether "culture" is anything definite enough really to mean anything. Check out a dictionary and you may wonder if there is anything under the sun that can't be called "culture."

In an important and insightful essay entitled "Notes Towards the Definition of Culture," T. S. Eliot wrote that culture can be described

---

1. C. S. Lewis, "Our English Syllabus." In *Rehabilitations and Other Essays* (London: Oxford University Press, 1939), 81.

3 – CLASSICAL LEARNING

"simply as that which makes life worth living. And it is what justifies other peoples and other generations in saying, when they contemplate the remains and the influence of an extinct civilisation, that it was worthwhile for that civilisation to have existed."[2]

Eliot goes on to argue that no culture "can appear or develop except in relation to a religion."[3] Lest we think that this is simply the self-serving conclusion of an Anglican of high cultural sensibilities, let us remember that he has a lot of support.

To wit, the Greeks again. Greek education began and continued with the reading and extensive memorization of Homer. Homer was a best-selling potboiler of a book, but this fact alone hardly accounts for his immense popularity. In *The Iliad* and *The Odyssey* were contained a perfect knowledge of accepted practice and proper feeling. The Greeks read their Homer with the same devotion that our forebears read their Bibles. Alexander the Great slept with a copy of Homer under his pillow. Generations of Greeks (and Romans after them) were formed by Homeric stories in the same way that Louisa May Alcott's little women were shaped by their reading and re-reading of *Pilgrim's Progress*.

In short, *paideia*—whether as education or culture—is impossible without a unifying story that can help us understand how to treat our parents and raise our children and act toward our enemies.

At Trinity School we have just such a story. The scriptures are our Homer. Our youngest children learn it by heart and become familiar with its stories. Our older children wrestle with its deeper meanings. And all of us, together, are learning to live as disciples of the One it points to and tells us about. As we go about our lives and work at our vocations, we sleep with it under our pillows.

I doubt whether Alexander had much leisure for reading his Homer as he stormed through the Persian Empire. Likewise, our days are filled

---

2. T. S. Eliot, "Notes toward the Definition of Culture." In *Christianity and Culture* (Orlando, FL: Harcourt, Brace & Co., 1976), 26.
3. Eliot, *Notes*, 77.

with many things, and I wouldn't want to leave anyone with the impression that we sit around school doing nothing but reading the Bible. Five minutes in most any class will dispel such a misunderstanding. The point is this: that without the unifying narrative and values of such a story, all the skills and techniques and competencies in the world cannot add up to what could be called an education.

The Education of Abraham Lincoln
February 12, 1999

This essay, written on the occasion of Lincoln's birthday (which is also my mother's), was an attempt to show how an unusual way of educating an extraordinary man honored the fundamental and ordinary arts of learning (the Trivium) we had adopted from early on at Trinity. In 1999, after pausing at sixth grade for two years, we had launched forth with a seventh grade. The modular unit on the new Pickett property had not yet passed all its inspections, and our teachers packed students into Hope Creek Church like sardines while we drove the school furniture around in a Ryder truck, awaiting the green light from the city to move in. Maybe I took some subconscious assurance in recalling that even Lincoln's education had been, shall we say, a little bumpy, too?

Abraham Lincoln was educated, as he said in his inimitable fashion, "by littles."[1] All his formal schooling—a week here, a month there—did not amount to one year, and mostly he educated himself by borrowing books and newspapers. He loved *Robinson Crusoe* and the tales of *The Arabian Nights*, a biography of Washington, and the poetry of Shakespeare and Burns. Someone recalled, "I never saw Abe after he was twelve that he didn't have a book in his hand or in his pocket. It didn't seem natural to see a feller read like that." Fond of talking and storytelling, he found a book called *Lessons in Elocution* and began practicing his public speaking from a tree stump.

Many of us would be afraid to let our own children's education follow Lincoln's course, and perhaps with good reason; but can there be any doubt that Lincoln acquired the tools of learning that would serve him (and his country) well throughout his life? In fact, it is most

---

1. National Park Service, "Learning by Littles." Lincoln Boyhood National Memorial (Indiana) website, http://www.nps.gov/libo/historyculture/leaning-by-littles.htm.

instructive to reflect on Lincoln's learning not as an aberration but as an exemplar of a good education. All the elements of a classical education are there: *grammar*, the learning of language and the acquisition of knowledge; *logic*, learning to think critically; and *rhetoric*, learning to express oneself elegantly and persuasively. These three can (and should be) distinguished, and there is an order to them: Lincoln began with a copybook, moved on to his borrowed books, and then imitated traveling preachers and politicians. But the mature Lincoln, the man who had mastered the arts of learning, was able to ply all three of these tools as one in order to debate Senator Douglas and to deliver the Gettysburg Address.

The Gettysburg Address might be exhibit A in the case for a classical education. On a cold November day in 1863, in the middle of a war that was going badly, on the very site where fifty thousand soldiers had died only months before, Lincoln delivered a speech that could have been written only by one who had mastered the tools of learning.

That Lincoln could not have written his famous speech without the rudiments of grammar is almost too obvious to need telling. On the other hand, what might seem paltry praise will rise in our estimation if we simply set Lincoln's first sentence before a sixth grader and ask her a few questions: What is a score? Multiply it times four and add seven. Without looking it up (Lincoln wasn't likely to have had an encyclopedia with him on the train to Gettysburg), compute how long it had been since the nation was "conceived." And, by the way, spell *conceived*. Explain the difference between a continent and a nation. Let me dictate this first sentence and you copy it perfectly, punctuating it correctly. Finally, name the famous document to which Lincoln alludes in this first sentence and recite its first two sentences. These are the sorts of things one ought to be learning at the grammar stage.

While all of these questions may teach us a thing or two about our children's education (or our own), they hardly bring us to a true understanding of Lincoln's classic speech. For that we need to appreci-

3 – CLASSICAL LEARNING

ate Lincoln's mastery of the second liberal art, logic. The address is essentially an argument, brief and succinct, but complete. It begins by reciting a proposition that it assumes to be true, "that all men are created equal" and a consequence, that all people ought to live in liberty. It goes on to ask a question about whether a nation founded on such a proposition can endure. And it argues that the horrible war that was being fought was the great test of whether the bold experiment of American democracy ("government of the people, by the people, for the people") was viable in the long run. It is not Lincoln's purpose, in a two-minute speech, to debate or prove either the truth of his propositions or the validity of his argument; but it is important to realize that even in such a short speech the skeleton of a clear line of reasoning is present.

Perhaps it is Lincoln the orator, the master of rhetoric, who shines most brightly in this address. It has been said that the three goals of rhetoric are to teach, to please, and to persuade. Lincoln does all three. By his reinterpretation of the carnage of Gettysburg as a test of fundamental democratic principles, he instructs his audience. By his brevity (which was highly controversial on the occasion of his delivery), by his skill as a wordsmith ("the last full measure of devotion"), and by his use of rhetorical tropes ("we cannot dedicate—we cannot consecrate—we cannot hallow..."), he wins our attention and makes us open to his argument. By his appeal to the great sacrifice of the brave men who fought, he persuades us to "increased devotion" to their cause.

I have tried to analyze this speech because I want us to see the fine work of a well-educated man and to aspire to the same kind of education for ourselves and for our children. Nevertheless, I would not want to leave this marvelous speech, as it were, on the dissecting table. Its form and its subject are too great for that. I have taken it apart, but I hope that on this occasion of Lincoln's birthday we might all put it back together by reading it again ourselves and honoring the man who practiced what he preached and did himself give "the last full measure of devotion" to our nation.

Math Matters

November 19, 1999

It is a shame, in a way, that I had to write such a piece, but I did. Trinity, like many schools, was founded by experts in the humanities. How different the history of the school would have been if its founding headmaster had been an engineer or a physics major! Probably then everyone would have known in their bones that math and science belonged right in the center of the curriculum. But we needed to make sure this was clear from the start. It is easier now: we have a growing cadre of excellent math and science faculty, strong Christians who are faithful in their vocations to teach students to love the patterns of math and the wonders of science. Our robotics program is thriving, giving students the chance to bring their creative gifts to the challenge of programming, design, and problem solving. But in 1999 it was important to put a stake in the ground. Today I would add just this: that math is an art, the art of finding and playing with patterns, and that the love of math is a beautiful thing, not to be desiccated by overzealous rigor in solving problems. Here again, a rich and unhurried education looks a little different.

> *Arithmetic is a kind of knowledge in which the best natures should be trained, and which must not be given up.*
>
> – Plato, *The Republic*

There is a silly idea abroad that a classical Christian school would not much care about math and would make arithmetic a sort of ugly stepsister to the favored humanities. I will not even attempt to trace the paternity of such foolishness, but I will say, briefly and frankly, why I think it wrong-headed. Both the classical and the Christian heritage speak against it and tell us that math is an essential, beautiful, and elegant part of a child's education.

3 – CLASSICAL LEARNING

We have to be philosophers and not simply shopkeepers to appreciate fully the value of math. It is important enough to be able to make change, and we all know how much our children will need to be able to balance a checkbook and to be able to calculate eight percent compounded over fifteen years. And for some of our children, facility with statistics or with calculus will help them earn their salaries. But can such knowledge, no matter how complex, really compare to the sublime examples of heroism and virtue that history and literature afford? Yes, and by all means!—if we will only think about it philosophically.

Plato thought that the study of pure mathematics—involving not visible or tangible objects but abstract numbers—helped the soul to lay hold of true being. While many other subjects (like poetry and history) were about *becoming*, math was about *being*.[1] Similarly, in his *Amalgest*, Ptolemy argued that mathematics provides the best argument for divinity because of its consistency and incorruptibility.[2] Even the dullest among us can follow the philosophers here, for we all must bow before the awesome truth that a certain equation will always and everywhere yield the same incontrovertible answer. Math problems are as demanding and unforgiving as Mt. Everest: there may be more than one way up, but if you get it wrong there is no argument and no mercy. The sheer cliffs of an equation or a geometrical proof are as awesome and terrifying as the law of God. It is by the analogy of the simplest mathematical equation that we come to respect the God whose Hebrew name means "I AM WHO I AM."

The idea of the Trinity, that one God exists in three persons, is the foundation for mathematics as we know it. There is unity and there is plurality; both are true ways of understanding reality. *One* is a true number, reflective of reality, but so is *two*. We are not Hindus who believe that at the most basic level of reality all is simply *one*—for the God who has revealed himself as the bedrock of all reality is

---

1. Plato, *Republic* 7.525.
2. Ptolemy, *Amalgest* 1.1.

three persons, Father, Son, and Holy Spirit. At the same time, we do not despair that the "many" parts of reality have no unity. With the Israelites we confess that "the LORD our God, the LORD is one."

Another noble and ennobling reason for studying math is that it teaches us about God's creative genius. Scientists and mathematicians have often marveled at the simple but profound fact that a few mathematical equations actually predict and explain reality as we know it. For instance, the famous Fibonacci number sequence (1,1,2,3,5,8,13, etc.) models the complementary spirals in a pinecone or a sunflower. And are we not amazed that by mathematical equations scientists can actually predict which nights give us the clearest view of the Leonid meteor shower? Isaac Newton wrote in his *Principia Mathematica*, "This most beautiful system of the sun, planets, and comets, could only proceed from the counsel and dominion of an intelligent and powerful Being...This Being governs all things, not as the soul of the world, but as Lord over all."[3]

Math, I am sure, is a part of the curriculum of every school across America. It has a language, a grammar if you will, of its own. What, you may ask, is distinctive about the way a classical Christian school teaches math? One answer—and there are others—is that we should be seeking to make our students not simply shopkeepers, but also philosophers, when it comes to math. We should be teaching them the language, the vocabulary, the thought patterns of math. But all of this is to be related to the eternal and the sublime. Galileo describes our mandate this way: "The great book of nature lies ever open before our eyes—but we cannot read it unless we have first learned the language and the characters in which it is written. It is written in mathematical language, and the characters are mathematical symbols."[4] So long as Trinity keeps this book open before our children and leads them to pages they can read for themselves with the math they are learning,

---

3. Isaac Newton, "General Scholium," *Principia Mathematica* 3.42.
4. Galileo, *The Assayer*, 4.

we will have not only a competent math program but even an excellent one, rich in the classical Christian tradition.

The Genius of a Classical Education
November 2, 2000

This piece is overly simplistic, but it is at least clear in its distinctions. I hope that the historical perspective is helpful, and I hope that it is clear that Trinity's goal was to find a third space in the creative tension between these two educational postures. I would want to add here that two of our earliest influences, Dorothy Sayers and Charlotte Mason, were both creating just such a space: Sayers in a theoretical way in her essay, "The Lost Tools of Learning," and Mason in a real learning environment in her Teacher's College and her schools. Another way to say this is that Sayers was quite child-centered in her classicism and that Mason was quite classical in her child-centered approach, which resembled that of certain Romantics. I came to Trinity with a strong classical bias, and it took me several years to warm up to Mason, to whom Jane Adams and Kathy Tyndall introduced me. I have grown and changed my mind about Mason, whom I first mistook as a hopeless Romantic; I have also changed my mind about Sayers in a few important particulars, as the footnotes show.

There are two ways to do education: a subject-centered way and a child-centered way. This is the first simplification I give you, and the second is like it: in the history of Western civilization, the subject-centered way came first and the child-centered way succeeded it.

A subject-centered education is an attempt to address one principal question: What should the child master in order to be educated? Greeks answered "Homer" and Puritans said "The Bible," and both agreed that there was a great story and a body of cultural knowledge that each new generation must learn to live by. In a more general way, the medieval syllabus of grammar, logic, and rhetoric provided a sort of "meta-curriculum" that lasted for centuries and defined a set of skills without which no one could really claim to be educated. In America, most academies of the eighteenth and nineteenth centuries offered two standard courses of study: a "Latin Course," consisting of a classical curriculum founded on Latin and Greek, with mathematics, science, and history; and an "English Course," which de-emphasized some of the classical requirements and added subjects useful for business. But in both cases, the curriculum was definite and consistent.

Somewhere along the way this all began to change, probably around the beginning of the Romantic Movement, about the time Rousseau wrote a book called *Emile* (1762). Emile is a young boy whose education consists, mainly, of doing what he wants to do when he wants to do it. He is removed from society and is put under the care of a tutor who declines to "teach" him and simply tries to put him in situations where he can learn for himself. For Rousseau, the principal educational question is not about cultural mastery but about the child: Who is the child and how does he or she learn? Like all sea changes, this one was gradual but overwhelming. Rousseau's speculative masterpiece was followed by Pestalozzi's actual school and Froebel's "kindergarten." Mix in a little of Piaget's developmental psychology, a measure of Dewey's democratic zeal for encouraging the child's capacities, and a strong dose of unadulterated American individualism and you get what we have today: the unquestioned dogma of a child-centered approach to education.

It has to be admitted that neither the subject-centered nor the child-centered approach to education is sufficient in and of itself. The deficiencies of the former are fairly obvious to us, since this approach is no longer in vogue. A strictly enforced core curriculum is a fine thing, unless, of course, students fail to master it. As Neil Postman has observed, "Teaching and learning are now understood as transactional, which is to say, we understand that there is no sense in saying you have taught something if it has not been learned."[1] Images of Professor Dry-

---

1. Neil Postman, "Education." In *Building a Bridge to the 18th Century: How the Past Can Improve Our Future* (New York: Alfred A. Knopf, 1999), 157.

as-Dust droning on about some important but terribly boring subject haunt us all.

On the other side, harder for us to see because of our culturally tinted glasses, are the deficiencies of a purely child-centered education. What could possibly be objectionable about suiting the subjects, scope, and sequence to the child's natural development? This: that some learning, despite Rousseau's pipe dream, is simply "unnatural." Or perhaps we should say, "supernatural." Learning to read is one of the truly amazing things that happens to a human being. Spelling, phonics, grammar, and times tables are not things that Emile would probably ever have had the impulse to take up on his own. It would do us all good to read E. D. Hirsch's critique of a Romantic view of education in his 1996 book *The Schools We Need*.[2] The genius of the classical approach to education is that it attends to both of these questions and addresses the weaknesses of both. In her essay "The Lost Tools of Learning," Dorothy Sayers observed that the classical Trivium of grammar, logic, and rhetoric fits the natural development of the child. She proposed a three-stage development: from the "poll-parrot" stage, in which learning is easy and pleasurable and reasoning difficult, in which memorization and recitation are natural; to the "pert" stage, which yields the child who contradicts, answers back, catches people out, and propounds conundrums; to the "poetic" stage of full adolescence, when the child is self-centered, restless for independence, expressive, creative, and eager to do some one thing in preference to all others. Miss Sayers was no child psychologist nor even a parent, but all the parents I have ever asked have found her description right on target. Most profound of all, however, is her observation that "the layout of the Trivium adapts itself with a singular appropriateness to these three ages: grammar to the Poll-parrot, dialectic [or logic] to the Pert, and rhetoric to the Poetic age."[3]

---

2. E. D. Hirsch, *The Schools We Need and Why We Don't Have Them* (New York: Doubleday, 1996).

3. Sayers, "The Lost Tools of Learning," 7. I have come to believe that such distinctions and compartmentalizations are not actually true in the experience of the young persons who learn in our schools. Today I would say that the three liberal arts

3 – CLASSICAL LEARNING

This classical approach honors and respects the child. One doesn't attempt to teach critical thinking to an eight-year-old or demand that fifth graders spend a lot of time on creative writing.[4] These will come, soon enough, and there are much more valuable lessons for the young student in the grammar stage. At the same time, as a course of study the Trivium is as firm and demanding as any course, and the skills that are acquired will suit the student well for a lifetime of learning. The one who runs the course to the end knows how to listen attentively, how to think clearly, and how to speak well. Ask your favorite college professor if she would be glad to have such students in her freshman class.

---

of grammar, logic, and rhetoric are present in every stage of learning, at every grade. Thus, an eight-year old is quite capable of critical thinking, though not perhaps ready for syllogisms. And creative thinking and writing (or pre-writing) are inherent in learning at every stage. Developmental differences surely still pertain, but the arts of learning are more subtle than I give them credit for here. I owe this change in my thinking largely to Warren Gould, our Director of Upper School, who pushed me to examine these things more carefully.

4. I would now say, "A good teacher will differentiate the way she teaches critical thinking to an eight-year-old or designs a lesson that engages fifth graders in creative thinking."

Teaching Students to Think for Themselves

MARCH 9, 2001

> *This essay explains the nature of academic freedom, that core value of the modern educational institution. Alan Wolfe's exploration of Wheaton provided a cultural moment to dig into this question. I would say that as Trinity matures and grows, the challenge of this question becomes only greater and greater. Stott's kite analogy is a good one, but the kite is not animate, not free to cut its tether and fly on if it wants to. As I reread this essay it occurred to me that a discussion of these very matters would be valuable for our own Upper School students, say, in their senior Theology class. We have learned that education is a glorious but risky business.*

Dorothy Sayers's 1947 essay, "The Lost Tools of Learning," has served as a sort of manifesto not only for Trinity School but also for a resurgence of classical Christian education around the country. Miss Sayers's concluding words might even deserve to be etched somewhere in the blocks and brick of our new building: "For the sole true end of education is simply this: to teach [students] how to learn for themselves."[1] What Miss Sayers is promoting, particularly, is the training of the mind for both a negative and a positive purpose: She aims to equip young minds with the analytical tools to resist the dangers of specious propaganda; and she hopes to fit these same minds for a vigorous and self-sustained pursuit of knowledge for a lifetime. This sort of education has long been called "liberal," from the Latin root meaning "free," and most of us would be glad to think that our children are receiving what could be called a solid "liberal arts" education. Not coincidentally, the first three of the traditional liberal arts are grammar, logic, and

---

1. Sayers, "The Lost Tools of Learning," 13.

rhetoric—and you can't be around Trinity long without hearing those ancient names. Independent thinking as cultivated by the liberal arts, then, is heralded as an essential outcome of a good education.

Now turn with me, if you will, to a more recent tribute to independent thinking, this time in a specifically Christian context. Last October in *The Atlantic Monthly*, Alan Wolfe documented the revitalization of evangelical higher education in an essay entitled "The Opening of the Evangelical Mind."[2] Wolfe visited Wheaton college and researched several other evangelical institutions, and his conclusions seem to have surprised him. Instead of an intellectual backwater, he found vibrant seminars, bright students, and interesting faculty. Wolfe was impressed by the "liberalism" inherent in the classes he attended, by which he meant a willingness to discuss difficult questions dispassionately and to consider answers that might not benefit one personally. But Wolfe's tribute to "vigorous, intelligent, and informed" education at these Christian schools is qualified by a huge reservation: "The requirement that students and faculty members sign a statement of faith is bound to make a modern liberal uncomfortable. It is rightly considered hostile to academic freedom."

Ah, there's the rub. There is the mother of all questions for any school that wants to be serious about both Christianity and the life of the mind. The relevance of this question for Trinity School should be plain to us all. We too have a doctrinal statement to which all our faculty and staff subscribe (not our students and parents, by the way, in contrast to some of the Christian colleges Wolfe interviewed). And we too are seeking to cultivate a community of learning that is committed to unfettered inquiry into all of the important questions about people and the world we inhabit. Wolfe's charge essentially calls into question whether an educational experiment such as Trinity is really viable.

---

2. Alan Wolfe, "The Opening of the Evangelical Mind," *The Atlantic Monthly*, October 1, 2000, http://www.theatlantic.com/past/docs/issues/2000/10/wolfe4.htm.

A truly liberal way of approaching this question would listen to all sides. The modern liberal (there's something of him in all of us who live in 2001, whether we like it or not) would sit down at the seminar table with the traditionalist. G. K. Chesterton called this "an extension of the franchise...giving votes to that most obscure of all classes, our ancestors."[3] One such ancestral vote in favor of the compatibility of doctrinal commitment and a real quest for truth is cast by Augustine, the Bishop of Hippo at the beginning of the fifth century AD. In his *City of God* the brilliant bishop (I tip my hand, I know) says that God communicates truth directly to the mind, "the highest of man's constituent elements, the element to which only God himself is superior."[4] Here we have a glorious yet humble assessment of the human mind. Our minds are such marvelous things that nothing in all creation ought to hold sway over them: not the opinions of others, not the tyranny of power, not scholars, not angels, not devils. But there is one thing—not *in* creation but *beyond* it—which is superior to our minds, and that is God himself. I confess that it is hard for me to understand how one can be a Christian and not assent to this proposition.

And so, in the end, I think Wolfe is mistaken in his criticism of Christian education. For, to borrow an analogy from John Stott, our doctrinal commitments are not like the bars of a cage that keep the bird from soaring; they are like the string of a kite that keeps it flying. We all know what will happen to the kite if the string is cut. Likewise, we who are created "in the image of God" are on a journey towards the truth along the way of faith. This is not a journey we can make on our own, like some wild bird soaring unfettered. Rather, it is the journey which the Son of God, who himself is the Truth, has made for us and bids us follow.

What does all of this mean for a school that wants to teach children to think for themselves? It means that we help our students understand

---

3. G. K. Chesterton, "The Ethics of Elfland." In *Orthodoxy* (San Francisco: Ignatius Press, 1995), 53.

4. Augustine, *City of God* 2.9.2.

3 – CLASSICAL LEARNING

what it means to be created in God's image. It means that we respect and even revere their minds, recognizing that parents and teachers cannot hold sway over that to which only God is superior. And it means that we work and pray toward the end that they will grow up to honor Christ with all that they have and all that they are. May God help us so to teach.

The Classical Ideal

FEBRUARY 22, 2002

> *The classical element in Trinity's education has always been the hardest to get our minds and words around. We have tried to find our own path and not simply franchise the popular Classical Christian School movement that was all the rage when Trinity was born in the mid-nineties. Our approach has been more eclectic, mixing elements from other fine Christian educational traditions. So the question "What is classical?" is complicated for us. We keep searching, as we should, for the simplicity beyond the complexity, and I do think this article identifies one of those simple and fundamental questions: What does it mean to be human? This question, by the way, has been reiterated in our Expanded Mission Statement, citing the profound and provocative answer of the Thomist Jacques Maritain.*

It's that time of year when we get a lot of visitors to Trinity School. Prospective parents visit our open houses and tour the classrooms. Teachers drop by to check us out and wonder, "Would I ever want to teach here?" Old friends stop by, and every now and then someone starting a new classical Christian school will call or drop in to learn what they can from our successes and mistakes.

Many of these people often ask, as they should, "What is the essence of a classical education?" They want to get at the marrow of it. They have a sense—and I think they are right—that many of the most noticeable features of a classical school may not be the heart of the matter. What makes a school classical? Learning Latin? Memorizing states and capitals? Teaching logic? Reading the "classics"? Writing essays? Emphasizing grammar, logic, and rhetoric? Learning the history of our Western cultural heritage? All of these have a place in a

3 – CLASSICAL LEARNING

classical curriculum, but none of them is the bull's-eye of a classical education.

At the heart of a classical education is an Idea: an idea of humanity, an ideal of humanity. This ideal is bigger and better than any one of us, and it assumes that there is something we could call "human nature." Contrary to modern ideas, this human nature is a constant across time and cultures. It is against this standard, and not simply against ourselves or the person in the seat next to us, that we should measure ourselves, for the closer we come to this standard the more fully "human" we will be. This is why, incidentally, the studies that make up an important part of a classical curriculum are often called humanities or humane letters. They lead us to this human ideal.

The classical tradition has always kept this ideal in mind. Cicero's text on rhetoric is entitled *De Oratore*, that is to say, *On the Ideal Orator* or *On the Orator as Such*. Says Crassus, one of the key interlocutors in this dialogue and one of the most esteemed orators of his day, holding up this ideal and measuring himself as well as others: "You must remember that I have not been talking about my own ability, but about the ability of the true orator." One of the reasons that classical education advocates reading the classics is that in them are found exemplars of this ideal. Achilles, Odysseus, Roland, and Henry V all show us something of this. Dead white males, all, and we should be looking hard for women like Dorothy Day and Africans like Nelson Mandela to add to our lists. But let us not, ever, lower the bar of greatness that has been set for us by the tradition before us. Perhaps James Boswell sums up this standard as well as any at the end of his justly famous biography of a great man of the eighteenth century:

> Such was Samuel Johnson, a man whose talents, acquirements, and virtues, were so extraordinary, that the more his character is considered, the more he will be regarded by the present age, and by the posterity, with admiration and reverence.[1]

---

1. James Boswell, *The Life of Samuel Johnson*, vol. 4, Oxford English Classics

A classical education is founded on the conviction that it will do both you and me (whoever we are) good to take careful stock of a man like Samuel Johnson, to measure ourselves by his greatness, and thus to attain to two goals: to have a sane estimate of our own abilities; and to improve ourselves as best we can toward the ideal. In order to do this, several prerequisites apply: one needs habits of attentiveness and patience (Boswell's biography is no easy read) and a respect for authority; one must be able to read, to think, to converse intelligently with others who can do the same; one must also have some sense of history in general and a fairly decent understanding of the intellectual and cultural scene in eighteenth century England. Thus it becomes clear why reading, narration, history, grammar, logic, and rhetoric are such an important part of a classical education.

My son is learning to play the violin by the Suzuki method, and we've been working on three Bach minuets at the end of the first volume for some time now. We've made some progress in mastering the left hand, in bowing, and in tone. All this comes about through practice, but there is one other part of the Suzuki method that is considered essential: one is supposed to listen to the piece on CD twice a day. Why? The recorded performance is an ideal that is inspiring, humbling, and instructive. To learn to play really well, my son must measure himself by an ideal greater than the self. This is a model of classical learning.

In violin and in life, however, no one plays perfectly. Boswell's Johnson was a man whose faults were as enormous as his physical frame and as striking as his virtues, leading the famous biographer to conclude that "man is, in general, made up of contradictory qualities."[2] The more we study greatness in humanity, the closer we come to understanding the tragic side as well. Oedipus and MacBeth are great men too.

(London: Talboys and Wheeler, and William Pickering, 1826), 393.

2. Boswell, *Life of Samuel Johnson*, 389.

This impossible ideal would be the reef that wrecks the classical ship if not for one man. That one man is, according to the scriptures, the First Man (i.e., the archetype), the Last Man (i.e., the finished product), the "radiance of God's glory and the exact representation of his being" (i.e., the perfect model).[3] And, as if this is not enough, this one man promised to send his Spirit to live inside those who trust him and to give power to live the ideal. Christian classicism thus transcends the boundaries of the old ideal in two ways: the Ideal was made flesh and lived for a while *among* us; and the Ideal offers to live forever *inside* us. Not only is the Great Master playing Bach's minuet *before* us; he offers to play it *for* us, *within* us. This is the obedience that comes from faith, and this is what we offer our children when we say we are a classical Christian school.

---

3. Heb. 1:3.

Fishing for Answers or Fishing for Men?

APRIL 2, 2004

> *The impetus for this essay was dual: my own teaching, which had often devolved into precisely the sort of fishing I decry here, and my reading Merton's* Seven Storey Mountain *and hearing him speak so admiringly about his teacher, Mark Van Doren. I still use this passage from Merton in orienting new teachers to their work at Trinity. I know that not every pedagogical moment can be like this, but I long for more of them and hope that Trinity is full of them. It is a risky and scary thing to teach like this—going on an adventure that may end up in a place you hadn't planned on. But this is where the best learning happens.*

Good teaching is hard to come by; but bad teaching is like falling off a log. There are more ways to get it wrong in the classroom than I can name, and those of us who have had the inestimable privilege to sit under a good teacher would do well to stop right now and give thanks. We might do better still to take out a note card and let that teacher know of our abiding gratitude. But I digress, for I mean to talk, first, of bad teaching. And of a particular kind of bad teaching that is to good teaching what playing the kazoo is to mastering the flute. I see it often (though, thankfully, not at Trinity), and I have practiced it more than I care to confess, particularly when I am ill prepared to face the class.

I am talking about fishing for answers. We've all been the victim of this kind of educational quackery. The teacher asks, "Who knows what the main difference between a communist and a socialist is?" What she means, in fact, is this: "Who will make my next point for me, which is to tell you what I understand to be the main difference between a communist and a socialist, but it would be much better if one of you would make it for me and I could leave the class thinking that someone has really learned something." A fail-proof sign of this sort of fishing expedition is the look of disappointment and even frustration on the teacher's face when someone gives an "incorrect" answer. Then follows a somewhat awkward transition, "What do some of the rest of you think?" (A good teacher knows that incorrect answers are the threshold to the house of understanding, and she will not pass by that door so quickly.) Sometimes a mountebank teacher in this predicament has to run through half the class before landing on the right answer. And sometimes things grow truly desperate and the teacher shrugs her shoulders and says, "Let me just tell you what the difference is." At this point the teacher has spent ten minutes of the class's precious time doing what she might have done in thirty seconds, and no one is the wiser for it.

I suppose it could be argued that the students in the class have been taught something, in a way. But they have not been *educated*. Good teachers do not go fishing. They go exploring. They walk into the class with a great respect for the material (usually something everyone has read or is about to read) and for the students who have read it. They come with expectations, and they come with questions, but not the artless questions which simply give back what that teacher (or some predecessor) has stuck there, like a post-it note on their cerebral cortex. The English word *education* is derived from two Latin words which mean, literally, "to lead out," and a good class is really a lot like a spelunking adventure, with the teacher as the wise guide who knows the cave but does not know what, this time, the students will bring forth into the light. By her own vital interest in the subject at hand, the good teacher brings forth, or educes, ideas and thoughts from her students which neither she nor they knew were there.

Mark Van Doren (of the Great Books fame) was such a teacher. He taught Thomas Merton, who immortalized his teacher in his autobiography, *The Seven Storey Mountain*. Van Doren knew the Socratic secret that the good teacher does not "put sight into blind eyes" but awakens in each student an inherent power to learn:

FISHING FOR ANSWERS OR FISHING FOR MEN?

> Mark would come into the room and, without any fuss, would start talking about whatever was to be talked about. Most of the time he asked questions. His questions were very good, and if you tried to answer them intelligently, you found yourself saying excellent things that you did not know you knew, and that you had not, in fact, known before.[1]

In this Van Doren, who was no stranger to the order of grace, was shadowing the Great Teacher, whose parables were really questions put to his disciples. If the teacher must go fishing, he will be casting for men and not for answers. I seem to recall that he told a parable about a net and some fish. And in that same text he left us this picture of the teacher: "Every teacher of the law who has become a disciple in the kingdom of heaven is like the owner of a house who brings out of his storeroom new treasures as well as old" (Matt. 13:52). This haul we call education.

Teachers who can teach like this are excellent indeed. And schools that have such teachers are not ordinary places of learning. If you find such a school, stay there. If you find such a teacher, take every course he teaches. If I could leave a legacy to Trinity, it would be that masters like this walk our halls. Already they do; may their tribe increase.

---

1. Thomas Merton, *The Seven Storey Mountain* (Orlando, FL: Harcourt Brace, 1998), 154.

4 – Rich Learning

> *Education is a life. That life is sustained on ideas. Ideas are of spiritual origin, and God has made us so that we get them chiefly as we convey them to one another, whether by word of mouth, written page, scripture word, musical symphony; but we must sustain a child's inner life with ideas as we sustain his body with food.*
>
> Charlotte Mason, *A Philosophy of Education*

By rich we mean, of course, a deeply textured and abundant learning experience for students. Not an education for the rich, not an education that is necessarily expensive. The love of learning is at the heart of this value, and this is certainly one of the softer qualities of education that are much harder to measure. Still, I would claim that students and parents know when an education is a rich one. We are wont these days to speak of engagement, and there is a strong correlation between rich curriculum and student engagement.

This would be the place to give full credit to Charlotte Mason, whose philosophy of education was as rich as any we know. Some have suggested that Trinity include Mason in its mission statement, but I have always balked at that idea, just as I would balk at putting Dorothy Sayers or Augustine or Lewis there. It is important to make our debts clear and to give credit where credit is due, but an educational philosophy is larger than any one person, and Trinity's richness is formed by the intersection of several different threads of educational thought.

4 – RICH LEARNING

Still, Mason has much to say when it comes to richness, and she receives her due in some of the essays in this section. As with classical, I am continually gratified and surprised (honestly) to learn how these old ideas are reborn in contemporary notions about what is good practice in education. If we can get past her Victorian trappings, we might see in Mason a richness that any proponent of twenty-first century education would be glad of.

Why Trinity Reads

June 2005

> *The Trinity Reads program has a long history, and this moment was an important one. The National Endowment for the Arts study of reading habits mentioned below corroborated our fears and steeled our intention to keep swimming against the current. I am glad to say that teachers in the Lower School still read to students at lunch, that we still launch a Trinity Reads book each summer, and that the first question on the Trinity teacher application has not changed.*

Fifty years from now, will anyone be reading? I wonder. Seriously, I wonder. I wonder because I see what power video games and iPods have on young boys in particular. I know how little time our busy schedules leave for leisure reading. The time we used to spend reading P. D. James we now spend checking email and surfing the web. I wonder because I see that movies, not books, are already the lingua franca of youth culture.

Of course *someone* will be reading, fifty years from now. But who? Will we have reading clubs, like knitting clubs, designed to revive a lost art? Will readers be the eccentrics among us? Will we pass someone reading a book and look back in curiosity, as though she were churning ice cream by hand or pecking at a manual typewriter?

Until recently, I could regard my musings as the dark specters of a pessimistic old English major. But now I know that I am not crazy—and would that I were! A recent study by the National Endowment for the Arts (NEA) shows that Americans' reading habits have declined ten percent in the last decade.[1]

---

1. National Endowment for the Arts, *Reading at Risk: A Survey of Literary Reading in America*, Research Division Report #46 (NEA, 2004), 30.

4 – RICH LEARNING

This is no crackpot report, nor is it an impressionistic buffet of anecdotes. Based on US Census Bureau polling, this report summarizes the responses of 17,000 Americans—a huge sample. For the first time in modern history, less than half of the adult population reads literature (fiction, drama, and poetry), and other sorts of reading are also on the decline. Further, the rate of decline in reading is accelerating, and this decline cuts across gender lines (though the decline in male reading is steeper), racial lines, and age groups. The steepest decline—and this is most worrisome for schools—is among the youngest Americans.[2]

One result of this survey is vindication of the classical notion that reading is not a natural act, not a given, or something that will happen if we just leave human beings alone and let them do what they want to do. It is more like juggling than like eating. One needs to learn a trick or two to master the act, and people can live, procreate, and die without it. We have lived in a literate country for so long that we tend to take this strange act for granted. We can do so no longer. Twenty years ago the landmark study *A Nation at Risk* warned of a growing mediocrity in our schools. This more recent study, aptly titled *Reading at Risk*, warns that it is not simply our schools that are in trouble: our culture is at risk.

We ought to care deeply about this problem at Trinity School. I don't know, for the life of me, how our civilization will continue as a just society and an effective democracy without good readers, lots of them. I don't know how police officers and judges and doctors and teachers will be able to carry out their essential vocations without what Russell Kirk called the moral imagination, a capacity for vision, prudence, and judgment that is acquired, primarily, by reading works of enduring literary value. I just returned from our seventh grade field trip to Washington, DC, and I was struck by the enduring power of *words* in that town. The monuments to Jefferson, Lincoln, and Roosevelt, as well as the new WWII Memorial, are etched with words that have shaped our nation. Moreover, as a Christian school, we ought to

---

2. Paige P. Parvin, "The Vanishing Bookworm," *Emory Magazine* (Spring 2005). http://www.emory.edu/emory_magazine/spring_2005/reading_at_risk.htm.

care about this dire trend. Christianity has always been a most bookish religion. Reading is no virtue, but it prods one to virtue. Reading is no grace, but reading scripture is a spiritual discipline through which the Holy Spirit does indeed impart grace to us who believe.

What can we do about this disturbing trend? Emory University's Mark Bauerlein, who has publicized the NEA report, says, "This is a problem of cultural and personal behavior, and it has to be addressed in a million different ways by hundreds of programs."[3] We at Trinity will do our small part. We will rebuild our section of the wall and guard it as well as we can, God helping us. Our summer reading program this year, Trinity Reads, is aimed at encouraging families to read together, out loud, in order to model good reading habits to all. Children who see adults reading, who read with adults, learn to value reading. Further, by having us all read the same books (*Misty of Chincoteague* and *The Yearling*), we will be encouraging both adults and students to talk about books. A community that carries on conversations about books is a community that builds readers. We will also continue reading at lunchtime to the children. This is one of my favorite traditions at Trinity School, and I am going to renew my own efforts to get into the classrooms to enjoy some books with the children.

Finally, I pledge that we teachers will continue to strengthen our own habits of reading. This starts, by the way, when we hire teachers. I was fascinated to see that the question that the NEA study asked Americans is the very first question that has been on the Trinity teacher application for a decade now: What books have you read in the past twelve months? An applicant's answers to that question tell me more than her résumé ever will. But good reading habits don't stop at the hiring—I'm looking for teachers who love to read so much that not even the demands of teaching will keep them away from books. And in keeping with that love, our teachers always read together a book each

---

3. Mark Bauerlein, cited in Paige P. Parvin, "The Vanishing Bookworm," *Emory Magazine* (Spring 2005). http://www.emory.edu/emory_magazine/spring_2005/reading_at_risk.htm.

summer and come together in August to discuss it. This summer we will be reading Richard Adams's *Watership Down*, an adventure story about community, just and wise governance, leadership, and the importance of stories in the life of a culture. We can't do a million things or carry out a hundred programs. But this much we can do.

So I bid you farewell for the summer and I hope that wherever you go, you will find a good book. Enjoy it, as you do your small part to make our nation again a people of the book.

Beyond Educational Tourism

MAY 23, 2003

My friend (and onetime Trinity teacher) Don Rose organized the wonderful seventh grade field trip to Washington, DC, in the spring of 2003, when both of our daughters were in that class. This trip was a tradition in the days when the Middle School was Trinity's top division. These reflections were in no way meant to gainsay Don's fine planning and the inestimable value of such trips for class bonding. But the trip did afford me a chance to reflect on the difference between learning that is meaningful and what I have called here educational tourism. Today we would use the word engagement. It is still a goal, and still a challenge.

I spent three days last week in Washington, DC, touring museums and monuments with our seventh graders. Ostensibly, I was there for crowd control and transportation, but I really had a secret mission, unknown even to the CIA and the Department of Homeland Security: I was on a quest to learn what captures the interest of a seventh grader. I am writing now to report my findings.

The first thing that seventh graders are interested in is other seventh graders. This we already knew and did not need to go to DC to verify, though the students themselves are exceedingly glad that we did go because eight hours in a car and three days without classes give them unprecedented time to giggle, gibe, gossip, grin, and gawk their way into one another's lives in ways that are fortunately not possible during a normal school week. It was good for me to be reminded of the adolescent way of being in the world, but my mission lay elsewhere.

As we walked to the Jefferson and Lincoln Memorials on our first afternoon, I was watching the students, sizing up their curiosity, weighing whether there was any significant connection between them and the ideas and people that were enshrined there. The way I figured it, the social force is so strong among this group of students that any trace of real intellectual engagement is way up there on the Richter scale.

A couple of lengthy paragraphs from the Second Inaugural Address and the Gettysburg Address are etched in the marble of Lincoln's monument, and it was instructive to watch the students' reactions. Some of them were decidedly uninterested and would have been just as happy to be visiting Southpoint Mall, so long as they got to stay in a motel at night. Others—and these were the vast majority—were interested in what I'd call Lincoln trivia. They were angling for a good photo of themselves with Abe in the background. They were looking for the North Carolina inscription on the entablature above the columns. This kind of interest is not without a certain passion, and several students greeted me with an enthusiastic challenge: "There's a misspelled word in that quote. Can you find it?"

I had kind of hoped that one of them might come bounding up to me to throw down a more serious gauntlet: "There's a truth in that quote. Can you find it?" I suppose that I expect too much of seventh graders, but I'm not the only one who's had a dream on the steps of the Lincoln Memorial, and I refuse to give it up.

I got a glimpse of that dream come true as we were leaving. I spotted a National Park Service docent in a serious conversation with a parent chaperone and a couple of our students. I sidled up close enough to hear the end of the discussion, which was all about Lincoln's carved hands. The left is clenched and the right is open, and the docent was helping the students interpret those gestures, referring to the determined theme of the Gettysburg Address and the open-handed charity of the Second Inaugural, respectively. For a few brief minutes there, I saw a couple of students (and adults) meaningfully engaged in a conversation that could never be called trivial. It was moments like those that made the trip worthwhile for me.

The best learning—indeed, the only true education—moves beyond educational tourism and a guided tour of the famous sites of history and culture. The best learning happens when students stop and think, stop and ask questions, engage. Another high point for me was a late afternoon pause on the Mall when several students asked, with real concern about some of the modern sculpture we were viewing, "Mr. Ranck,[1] I could make something like that. Why is that art?"

Three things have to happen in order for us to move beyond tourism into education. First, we need a big idea. Lincoln the implacable but merciful is a big idea; the typo on the wall is not. There is nothing wrong or unhealthy about filling the often wide interstices between profundities with trivial pursuits. But factoid snacks alone, however enjoyable, will not support a healthy life of the mind. We need the protein and vitamins of seminal ideas and large questions.

Of course, one wonders, if this be the case, why students visiting the Lincoln Memorial do not sit at their teachers' feet with uplifted faces and open palms, ready to be sated upon the feast of wisdom. For the solving of that mystery I can only point to its nutritional analogue: Why will students skip a good breakfast but beg incessantly for a stop at the food court for one more round of nachos? Part of the answer, at both the biological and intellectual level, is that our desires are all out of touch with reality. In order to put things back the way they are supposed to be, we need good habits. Good eating habits, good learning habits. Students must practice learning to get good at learning. And the more you practice, the better you get, the more you enjoy what you do. If there was ever a place where Jesus's proverb rang true, surely it is in the realm of learning: "To him who has, more will be given." Students whose parents have taken them to art museums are a lot less likely to hurry through the galleries to get to the museum shop. Good habits of learning are the second essential.

The third is a relationship with the big idea. Real learning is knowledge, and knowledge is not possible apart from relationship. It is no accident of language that the biblical term for that most intimate sort

---

1. Chris Ranck, Trinity's eighth-grade teacher.

of relationship is also a term of knowledge: "Now Adam knew Eve his wife, and she conceived..." (Gen. 4:1 [ESV]). Such relationship starts with simple familiarity. Students who have memorized the Gettysburg Address will have a more natural interest in the Lincoln Memorial than those who have not. But the sort of relationship that is wed to true knowledge is constituted by a vital and personal interest. Martin Luther King, Jr., when he stood upon those steps, knew that the life of Lincoln was vital to his own dream. Students today who ponder the tragedy of 9/11 have an opportunity to become intimate with Lincoln's own struggles with the atrocities of war and the judgments of the Lord. In this way we hope that students will discover not simply history, but *tradition*, what Chesterton called history from the inside, the story which is part of their own story, the story which is essential for their own story to make sense. Thus we hope to be graduating learners, not tourists.

The Developmental Approach to Learning

OCTOBER 2003

Trinity and the Gesell assessment go way back. Our first admission director, Cheryl Wolfe, is now a world-renowned Gesell trainer, and she still does many of our assessments. I sat through this training in 2003 at Trinity because I wanted to understand the approach from the inside out, and I was glad I did. Trinity has always put a premium on paying close attention to the developmental patterns of children, and this essay attempts to give some philosophical and perhaps even theological justification for that practice. Our admission measures and procedures are more complex now (we are also admitting ninth graders, not just kindergartners), but the questions are still the same: Where is the child on the road of human development, and how would she thrive and succeed in this class at Trinity? I've included this article in this section because I think that the sort of deep and personal engagement that a rich education affords is best realized when students are taught according to their nature and the pace of their own growth.

People are more like flowers than rocks. This we know for sure, and it makes all the difference here at school. Rock School would be vastly easier to build and maintain: it would consist of large classes of identical rocks. If a rock did not fit into our curriculum, we would chisel it down to size and make it fit, and so far as we can tell the rock would be none the worse for such procrustean measures. Flowers, on the other hand, require a different kind of handling. One must ask a lot of questions at Flower School: When do they bloom? Are they annuals or perennials? How much light do they need? How much water?

4 – RICH LEARNING

The medievalists would have said that the flower has a soul and the rock does not. Some of us may balk at the notion of a flower-soul, reserving that honor for humanity. But let us suspend our post-Enlightenment skepticism and humor the medievalists for a moment. Gregory the Great, for example, posited three kinds of souls: vegetable, sensitive, and rational. A woman has a rational soul, a cow has a sensitive soul, and an oak tree has a vegetable soul. There is a hierarchy here, with the vegetable soul at the bottom. Each of the ascending souls encompasses more, but never less, than the lower forms. Thus a cow has the powers of the vegetable soul along with its sensitive soul; and the woman has the powers of the sensitive soul, in addition to her rational soul. What distinguishes these three souls is a fascinating study in itself, but today I am interested in what they have in common. All souls have three basic powers: nutrition, growth, and propagation. Flowers need water and sunlight; they change over time from seed to plant to flowering plant; and they give birth to new flowers that can do the same. Rocks do none of these.

Because children are organisms with these powers of soul, school is a more challenging thing to pull off than a rock collection. Like flowers, these little people are always needing to eat (literally and figuratively); they are always changing; and they are always moving toward adulthood, when they may produce other little people just like they once were. This view of children impacts the way we teach them at Trinity School.

Last week Trinity hosted a workshop led by the Gesell Institute for Child Development.[1] Developmental approaches to learning, like Gesell, regard the child, fundamentally, as an organism. An organism, according to this approach, has several essential qualities:

- An organism is a living being—distinct from inanimate objects.

---

1. http://www.gesellinstitute.org/.

THE DEVELOPMENTAL APPROACH TO LEARNING

- An organism is a living being with interrelated systems of life—in the human organism, this includes intellectual, emotional, social, and physical systems.

- An organism, by definition, comes into existence at some point (birth) and then ceases to exist (death).

- An organism changes or grows through stages that are predictable and patterned.

- An organism, in other words, is distinguished by the essential qualities of soul.

We administer the Gesell Assessment to every child applying for transitional kindergarten, kindergarten, and first grade. Why? Because children grow and develop over time, in patterned ways. We believe that we will do the best job of educating these children if we learn as much as we can about where they are along this path of development, and the Gesell Institute has decades of experience in plotting out the patterns of growth.

At the same time, we believe that developmental assessments are a necessary but never sufficient tool for making student placements and other important educational decisions in the lives of young children. For one thing, as the Gesell Institute itself advocates, parental input and teacher input are two other invaluable sources of information leading to an accurate read on the child's developmental age. Moreover, developmental age is but one of three key components in the child's growth. The other two are biology and environment. One must also take into consideration the uniqueness of each child. Anyone who has tried to find the exact picture of a mystery leaf in a botanical guide will appreciate the fallacy of thinking that one can plot the exact pattern and shape of any organism's development.

Our approach is to utilize the developmental assessment with confidence but also humility. We are confident that children are more than flowers, but never less. Humanity is a "little world," encompassing all of existence. The patterned growth of flowers is not beneath us—we also grow in stages and phases, along predictable lines. Environment modulates and inflects our growth, but it never determines it. A flower never blooms before it sprouts, and even Jesus grew in wisdom and stature. At the same time, humility is called for. Human beings are so much more than flowers. God has made us a little lower than the angels, and we have, in addition to our vegetable soul, a soul with traces of the angelic. We have the powers of the rational soul, understanding and reason, and we are open to the influence of God's Spirit. All of this is somehow united to a body, making us what Bruce Cockburn calls the "angel-beast."[2] The little people who come through the doors of Trinity School every morning are not like anything else in all of creation. Woe to any of us who would say that biology + environment + developmental age = the child.

Children are like flowers, but so much more than flowers. Like flowers they bloom. And blooming, like all intransitive activities, is a glory. But the blooming that we look forward to among our students is a glory that makes the flowers fade. I speak of the blossoming of understanding, in service of Christ's lordship, for the good of the kingdom. When we make their grade placements, we're hoping to put them in a well-watered spot in the sun.

---

2 Bruce Cockburn, "Burden of the Angel/Beast," *Dart to the Heart*, Columbia Records, 1994., #B000002954, compact disc. Produced by T. Bone Burnett.

On the Sacredness of Personhood

May 11, 2007

Charlotte Mason was there when Trinity was born. When we were designing the curriculum for our first students (in grades K–4), Kathy Tyndall and Jane Adams introduced us all to Mason. Jack Beckman, then at the Intown Community School in Atlanta, visited Trinity and helped us wrestle with Mason's pedagogy. Over the years, my understanding of her ideas and my respect for her wisdom have grown. Her influence is still strong in our Lower School, less direct in our upper grades. Keeping Mason strong at Trinity will be one of our ongoing challenges. I hope this essay helps her cause by highlighting a few of her profound insights.

> *Our crying need today is less for a better method of education than for an adequate conception of children—children, merely as human beings, whether brilliant or dull, precocious or backward. Our business is to find out how great a mystery is a person* qua *person...[W]e cannot commit a greater offense than to maim or crush or subvert any part of a person.*
>
> – Charlotte Mason, *A Philosophy of Education*

Perhaps the cornerstone of Charlotte Mason's educational philosophy is the notion that *the child is a born person*. The child is endowed at birth with something *sacred,* which is something *given*. Adults do not grant this to the child; God does. Therefore, children are due the utmost respect. The teacher and the parent must look on the child as an equal. It would be a gross misunderstanding of Miss Mason or of any sound education based on her thought to think that this means an undermining of the adult's *authority* in the life of the child; however, that authority is relative and not absolute, and it is the authority of one who knows that the child has much to teach the adult. It is also the authority of one who knows how splendid and how fragile is this little person.

I use the word *fragile* with some reservation, for Mason was not afraid of the skinned knee or the skinned ego. She expected children to be corrected, and her classrooms were the farthest thing from what most of us imagine when we hear the words "child-centered." She was not afraid to tell a child, "No! Not here!" Not anywhere! Never!" But she was afraid of something, and that something is the subject I want to pursue briefly.

She was afraid of maiming the child-person. Not physically, not even so much emotionally, but especially—as far as schools are concerned—volitionally. She knew that children are capable of being moved by a wide array of influences. We do what we want, but we want what we learn to want, and this is where education, at home and at school, is so vital. There are many strings of the instrument we call a child, and a teacher or parent can make each of them resonate. We can pluck the strings of fear, love, and the desires for approbation, emulation, avarice, or power. Some of these (and there are others) are always wrong. Many of these are not wrong in themselves, but Mason knew that the effect would be disastrous if any one dominated in the child's life. We are all amused and even impressed when the parent parades the child before the adult dinner guests and asks her to recite the Lord's Prayer in Latin; but if this is done too much, if the child learns to live for this sort of approbation, something perfidious happens. Certainly the result is not a child who prays well.

But there is more. One desire is, like Tinkerbell, best of all and the most fragile. This is the *desire for knowledge.* Children are born with a natural and healthy desire for knowledge, even as they are born with a natural desire for food and drink. We do not have to manufacture this desire, only to feed it. It can, however, atrophy. I suppose that it can atrophy from starvation, but it is hard to imagine, really, a child being starved of knowledge. The world is much too full of it; there are few droughts or famines in the world of knowledge. But there are two other dangers we must be aware of: First, there is a lot of junk food out there—perhaps more today than ever before. And the greatest danger is the teaching of trivia, what Mason called "twaddle," which cripples the desire for knowledge. This is like feeding them sawdust, giving them something they really can't digest. The second danger comes when we make students work for inferior ends (like showing off for adults). The desire for knowledge is inversely proportional to so many other desires of the child. If they learn to live for those other desires, the good and noble desire for knowledge will be choked out. This is, by the way, the reason Miss Mason was so chary of using external rewards to elicit learning. Any benefits of behavior modification have to be weighed against the atrophy of this precious desire for knowledge. A job well done is its own reward, and an idea understood for its own sake is delectable. It needs no sauce or seasoning, and the child will come back for more, again and again, to this fine feast.

Thus will we teach students the love of learning at Trinity School, with God's good help.

Education from the Inside Out

September 14, 2007

This piece from 2007 is a sort of ten-year retrospective on the idea of a richly textured education. It gives credit where credit is due to the early proponents of Charlotte Mason, whose writings are full of this notion of richness. It also gives a nod toward the Trinity Listens program of the summer of 2007. That program, the brainchild of former Division Director Steve Larson, was a riff on our longstanding practice of reading something together as a school community (the Trinity Reads program). That summer, through the encouragement of the Society of Classical Learning, I had read James Taylor's Poetic Knowledge *and had been deeply influenced by it. We had spent much of the first decade of the school agonizing over how a classical model might be fused with one influenced by Mason; this piece represents one of the most important ways in which the two resonate in harmony. A classical education can be a rich education, and should be.*

There is education from the outside in, and education from the inside out.

When my wife and I homeschooled our eldest in second grade, the year before Trinity started, we spent some time going through *What Your Second Grader Needs to Know*.[1] I remember being more than a little disappointed with my seven-year-old's lack of engagement with that encyclopedia of things he should know. I will lay the fault at the feet of his second-grade teachers and not at E. D. Hirsch and his cohorts at the Core Knowledge Foundation. I was Professor Gradgrind to

---

1. E. D. Hirsch, *What Your Second Grader Needs to Know: Fundamentals of a Good Second-Grade Education* (New York: Dell, 1993).

him that year: "Now, son, what I want is Facts." This was education from the outside in. And not very far in.

One of the serendipities of that unremarkable homeschooling experience is that Desirée said to me midyear, "You know we really should get serious about this idea of starting a school." Several influences—my own mediocre experience with homeschooling, some splendid chapters in my own educational story, reading seminal educational thinkers like Charlotte Mason and Mortimer Adler, and the partnership of some fine educators like Rita Davis, Kathy Tyndall, and Jane Adams[2]—these all guided me toward a better understanding of education. There is a form of knowledge that approaches its subject *from the inside out*. This is knowledge not *about* the subject but *of* the subject. It is an encounter with reality that is not first and foremost analytical, but beautiful, "awe-ful," spontaneous, mysterious. It is founded on a sense of wonder, and it affirms the intuitive understanding of which the youngest children are capable, and which the oldest among us never outgrow.

It is belief in this *poetic knowledge* that led us to sponsor the Trinity Listens program this past summer. Our goal was not some insipid form of cultural exposure; rather, we hoped that our students would learn to love what is beautiful. Take a look at the *Messiah* projects upstairs in the Lower School and you'll get a sense of how these children engaged with that great work. This morning I watched tenth grader Grace Bidgood perform an amazing juggling act to "And the Glory of the Lord." To quote Homer (the Greek bard, not Bart's dad): "This, to my way of thinking, is something very much like perfection."[3]

I owe this term, *poetic knowledge*, to James Taylor (the humanities professor, not the singer), who wrote a marvelously dense and profound

---

2. Rita Davis was one of the first teachers hired at Trinity. She taught in Trinity's Lower School from 1995 to 2013. Kathy Tyndall and Jane Adams, both gifted educators, crafted Trinity's original curriculum, and Kathy also taught in Trinity's fifth and third grades from 1999 to 2013.

3. Homer, *The Odyssey*, 2.4.

book by the same title.[4] I'm not sure I understand half of what he wrote, but this much I get: It is better by far to develop a child's relationships with real books and things, to nurture a sympathy for these and close familiarity with them; and from this sympathetic and intuitive connection will flow all sorts of other knowledge and understandings. "Many scholars forget," wrote Helen Keller while she was at Radcliffe, "that our enjoyment of the great works of literature depends more upon the depth of our sympathy than upon our understanding."[5]

Such learning is not just for children, as though we graduate beyond the poetic when we get a BA or a real job. In the last year or so, I've taken up cycling. I started for my body, but I've kept at it for my soul. I've found a surprising pleasure in being outside, in God's country, with the wind in my face. I've come to know the roads around here more personally and intimately than ever before. Before I started biking, I think I could have told you that Cornwallis intersects with Highway 70 somewhere up north of Trinity. But now I can tell you how many hills there are on Cornwallis, between Kerley and 70. I know which hill is the longest. I know what time of day the magnificent Pleasant Green house catches the afternoon sun at its most splendid light. I know where Coach K lives and (I think) why he lives there. I know where the buffalo grazes and where the pavement is all cracked. And from the fount of this poetic knowledge (from the inside) flows a keener interest in the sort of knowledge that comes from the outside. In my wife's real estate office hangs a huge map of Durham and Orange Counties. I've been caught several times loitering in front of that map. Before I started cycling I did not find the map any more interesting than my son found the list of things a second grader should know.

---

4. James Taylor, *Poetic Knowledge: The Recovery of Education* (Albany, NY: State University of New York Press, 1998).

5. Helen Keller, *The Story of My Life* (New York: Bantam Dell, 2005), 72.

EDUCATION FROM THE INSIDE OUT

If you start from the outside, you're not likely to get very far in. But if you can find a way to the inside first, there's no end to all the places a student's mind will go.

Mind Food

November 8, 2013

> *This is a recent piece, a précis of my remarks at the 2013 Headmaster's Dinner. The Headmaster's Dinner has become an annual opportunity for the community to come together around the mission of the school. Creating that space has allowed the benefit auction to be an auction (without speechifying by the headmaster). I also like the notion that all Trinity parents, and not just major donors, are invited to participate in this event. Mason's dominant model of learning—digestion—shapes this talk, but the ideas are not just Mason's. The numerous quotations and references give a sense of the widespread agreement with her fundamental notion that ideas are food for the mind.*

> *Education is a life. That life is sustained on ideas. Ideas are of spiritual origin, and God has made us so that we get them chiefly as we convey them to one another, whether by word of mouth, written page, scripture word, musical symphony; but we must sustain a child's inner life with ideas as we sustain his body with food.*
>
> – Charlotte Mason, *A Philosophy of Education*

The job of a school is to attend carefully to the minds of its students. Those minds are not disembodied—they are part of the whole person: body, soul, and mind. And like the body, the mind needs sustenance: it is neither self-existing nor self-supporting. Like our bodies and our entire selves, we can speak of the mind flourishing and thriving; we can also speak of its atrophy and weakness. And when we do, we are not speaking primarily about ability or IQ, but about whether a particular individual's life of the mind is healthy and strong.

The antidote for mental anorexia is a strong dose of good ideas. Judith Shapiro, the former president of Barnard College, once said, "You want the inside of your head to be an interesting place to spend the rest of your life."[1] Ideas are what makes that inner life interesting. Barbara Goldsmith's biography of Marie Curie tells the tale of a woman whose life of the mind was keen and sharp: "Like the parched earth, she soaked up education as a life-giving force. In what was to become an enduring pattern, when she studied, the world around her vanished. She seemed to live on air." And ideas. One reviewer of Goldsmith's biography remarked about Curie: "She had radium in her soul."[2]

An idea is different from a fact. Or from a piece of data. Or from an opinion. An idea is a coherent and meaningful pattern, sometimes propositional, but not always. At the recent Headmaster's Dinner, I shared five ideas to launch our evening discussion. Some were in the form of statements (the opening lines of Tolstoy's *Anna Karenina* and Einstein's theory of special relativity), but one was visual (Rembrandt's *Simeon in the Temple*), one was mathematical (a right triangle with one side as the diameter of a circle), and one was musical (John Coltrane's *A Love Supreme*). All of these coherent patterns of thought are inherently interesting, worthy of a student's attention. Not just for what the student can do with them, but more importantly for the fact that they are, simply, interesting. Fascinating, really, if we will take the time to reflect on them. We speak of ideas "seizing" us, "catching hold of" us, "impressing" us, even "possessing" us.[3] This manner of speaking accords with Charlotte Mason's claim that an idea is a "live thing of the mind."[4]

---

1. Andrew Delbanco, *College: What It Was, Is, and Should Be* (Princeton, NJ: Princeton University Press, 2012), 33.
2. Barbara Goldsmith, *Obsessive Genius: The Inner World of Marie Curie* (New York: W. W. Norton & Company, 2005), 51.
3. Delbanco, *College*, 63.
4. Charlotte Mason, *Philosophy of Education*. Vol. 6 in the Original Home Schooling Series (London: J.M. Dent and Sons: 1954), 105. Originally published by Kegan,

4 – RICH LEARNING

With Mason, we can call ideas "spiritual," by which we mean invisible, leaving traces in the world. Like Marie Curie's "radium of the soul," this invisible dawning of an idea is challenging to measure. But even if we cannot see the thing itself, we can see traces of it, and we can know that it is real. Educators have always seen this. Frank Prescott, the iconic aging headmaster in *The Rector of Justin*, says, "The older I get, the more I realize that all a teacher has to go on is the spark in a boy's eye."[5] I don't suppose that our parents would be very happy if our report cards came home with this comment: "I think I've seen a spark in Charlie's eye." We have to do better than this at assessing real learning, but at the end of the day, it is true, as Charlotte Mason says, that "education, like faith, is evidence of things not seen."[6]

The way that ideas pass from mind to mind is a bit of a mystery, but one we must attend to and honor in our teaching. "Mind must come in contact with mind through the medium of ideas," said Charlotte Mason.[7] Likewise, Cornell's Roald Hoffmann, a chemist, observed, "The more I taught beginning classes, the more important it became to me to explain the gleam of truth, or of a connection." This is most likely to strike the mind "not in isolation but in discourse with another person."[8]

John Dewey had a similar way of speaking about the passing transmission of thinking. According to Dewey, whenever we hear about a new idea, one we can't easily assimilate, we have only three possible responses: (1) we can ignore the idea; (2) we can misunderstand the idea, so that we make it resemble some idea we already have; or (3) —and this is really the only option that leads to learning—we can stop and think about it.[9] We can do the hard work of slow thinking. The

---

Paul, Trench, Trubner (London, 1925); citations are from the reprinted edition reissued in 1989 by Charlotte Mason Research & Supply.

5. Lewis Auchincloss, *The Rector of Justin* (Boston: Houghton Mifflin, 1964), 45.
6. Charlotte Mason, *Philosophy of Education*, 39.
7. Charlotte Mason, *Philosophy of Education*, 39.
8. Roald Hoffman, "Research Strategy: Teach," *American Scientist* 84 (1996): 20–22.
9. John Dewey, cited in Donald L. Finkel, *Teaching with Your Mouth Shut* (Ports-

learner must reorganize her previous thinking to make room for the new idea. It is only when the learner does the thinking for herself that real learning happens. This is why Emerson said, "It is not instruction, but provocation, that I can receive from another soul."[10] We may think that someone like a teacher gives us an idea, but at best this is only an indirect gift. Learners construct ideas for themselves. Teachers design learning experiences in which the learners are provoked into this kind of learning.

So what?

For parents, I have this simple suggestion:

Read to and with your children. This is a simple action that pays immense dividends. In 1995 Hart and Risley published a groundbreaking study that showed that children's IQs and language abilities are relative to the amount parents speak to their children.[11] Children's academic successes at ages nine and ten are attributable to the amount of talk they hear from birth to age three.

Hart and Risley use the term "language dancing" to describe the sort of talk that makes a difference in young children's lives. Not the business talk of "Let's get your pajamas on" or "What do you want for snack?" but talk about "What if...?" or "I wonder...?" Language dancing is face to face; it is open-ended; it is creative; it is playful. It chats, thinks out loud, wonders, reflects. Television and screens cannot supply this kind of interaction. It is personal and unscripted. For example, it might entail reading a book together aloud and then talking about the book. It might be playing a game with words.

---

mouth, NH: Heinemann, 1999), 151.

10. Ralph Waldo Emerson, "An Address." In *The Essential Writings of Ralph Waldo Emerson,* edited by Brooks Atkinson (New York: Modern Library, 2000), 66.

11, Betty Hart and Todd R. Risley, *Meaningful Differences in Everyday Experiences of Young American Children* (Baltimore: P.H. Brookes, 1995). See also Clayton M. Christensen, Michael B. Horn, and Curtis W. Johnson, *Disruptive Class: How Disruptive Innovation Will Change the Way the World Learns* (New York: McGraw-Hill, 2008), 150–53.

4 – RICH LEARNING

Secondly, we want to encourage our children to PLAY with ideas. This is, by the way, one of the principal reasons we promote our summer Trinity Reads/Trinity Views program. I hope many of our families had some fun playing around with Benton's *Spring on the Missouri*. And I still hear Trinity families talking about Tolstoy's *Two Old Men* as a story by which they are coming to understand their own lives.

We teachers must attend to the realities that these truths impose upon our teaching and our students' learning. Again, Mason:

> Probably [the student] will reject nine-tenths of the ideas we offer, as he makes use of only a small proportion of his bodily food, rejecting the rest. He is an eclectic; he may choose this or that; our business is to supply him with due abundance and variety and his is to take what he needs. Urgency on our part annoys him. He resists forcible feeding and loathes predigested food.[12]

We teachers are midwives, attending the birth of ideas, but not conceiving them. We must design learning experiences that will bring forth the life of the mind. We must also realize that holding forth in front of the class, espousing ideas, is to the students just opinion, which can never be a real idea to them, unless they do the hard work of thinking for themselves.

And one of the most important jobs of a teacher is to select the materials upon which the learning experiences will be based: books, natural objects, objects of art. These should have three essential components, as set out in our Expanded Mission Statement: they should be thick, adaptable, and public (that is, time-tested and vetted).

Ideas are inherently interesting and nourishing, but as a Christian school we know the Great Secret that nothing but Jesus Christ can ever satisfy these students who come to us at Trinity. We set before them a rich feast of learning, and we hope that they learn to enjoy learning,

---

12. Charlotte Mason, *Philosophy of Education*, 109.

in a way, for its own sake. But in another way, we hope that they "see through" this joy of learning and the engagement with ideas to see the one in whom all good ideas make sense.

The Gospel of John tells us that Jesus Christ is the Logos, which is translated "Word." John is claiming that Jesus Christ is the organizing center of meaning for all of reality. Our challenge at Trinity is to help our students discover and rediscover this truth in every fascinating idea they pursue throughout their lives. There is no true, good, or beautiful idea that coheres in their minds apart from the Logos of God, Jesus Christ.

Such discovery must be genuine, never facile, never contrived. We want them to find deep connections. For the Word of God, Jesus Christ, goes deep down to the beginning. In him we live and move and have our being.

Thus may we all work together at Trinity, for the students' sake and for the glory of Christ, to make Trinity a place where ideas matter. Where the life of the mind is honored and respected. Where the word "rich" is not just a word in our mission statement, but describes a profound and vibrant community of learners.

5 – Unhurried Learning

The woods are lovely, dark and deep,
But I have promises to keep,
And miles to go before I sleep,
And miles to go before I sleep.
Robert Frost, "Stopping by Woods on a Snowy Evening"

This is the strangest word in our mission statement. We chose it because we wanted to stake out some territory that we thought was both universally important and particularly relevant in our current cultural moment. By "unhurried" we mean that good education attends to pace, to rhythm, to patterns of work and rest. These are deeply biblical concerns (see, for instance, the first chapter of Genesis), and we think that attending to them makes for human flourishing. We believe that the right kind of unhurried education will aid and abet an education that is Christian, classical, and rich. The essays in this section explore these themes, and you can see that whenever we set out to talk about one aspect of the mission we end up talking about something else, often the whole mission. For the making of books, this connectedness is a challenge; but for the education of children and young adults, the connections are organic and often quite lovely in their manifestation.

Nancy Brooks must get her due in this section. In the beginning, we all had our particular passions, and this was hers. She had seen the coastline eroding in her violin students from Chapel Hill and Durham,

5 – UNHURRIED LEARNING

and she championed this idea from the beginning. Charlotte Mason was a friend to unhurried, and there were biblical strands (Ecclesiastes 4:6) that guided us. But in the beginning this idea seemed odd, and I confess to being a slow convert to its importance. I now regard it as one of the best ideas we've had, and I hope that future generations of Trinity leaders will find ways to protect, promote, and rehabilitate it.

An Education of Classical Proportions

DECEMBER 3, 1999

The opening paragraph of this essay reminds me of the early Trinity auctions. They were part auction, part community celebration, part Headmaster's Dinner: too much to sustain in one evening over time, but for those of us who were there, important markers of the work that God was doing in our midst. I still remember the late Chip Stam, whose wife Doris was one of our music teachers, as emcee teaching us all about the classical orders with hand motions. Many people worked many hours in selfless devotion to the cause to put on these auctions. We should have a gallery of their portraits in the Advancement Office.

Balance and moderation are important classical notions, and they find biblical resonances too, as I try to show in this piece. Interestingly, this article, which is ostensibly about our classical mission, really lays a strong foundation for an unhurried (balanced, well-paced) education. Thus do the various strands of Trinity intertwine and support one another.

Thanks to Mr. Chip Stam, our illustrious emcee at the recent Trinity Benefit and Silent Auction, many of us in the Trinity community can identify the three orders of classical architecture. Complete with hand motions worthy of our kindergartners, Mr. Stam drilled us repeatedly on the distinguishing marks of these orders of columns: Doric, Ionic, Corinthian. Who can forget?

If you missed this dinner at the Carolina Club and Mr. Stam's mnemonics, not to worry. There are other—dare we say better?—ways of learning about these things. Claude Perrault, a seventeenth century scientist and one of the principal architects of the Louvre, studied the Italian Renaissance adaptations of Roman and Greek orders and produced

5 – UNHURRIED LEARNING

his own copper-plate versions of the five (Mr. Stam didn't tell us the whole story) orders of classical architecture, complete with a modular scale from which the proportions of the various parts could be read, memorized, and repeated.

One of the most striking things about this drawing is the definition of classical proportions. The ratio of the column's height to its width, the relationship between the size of the pedestal and the column itself, the height of the entablature—these had all been standardized and, if you will, canonized, by the time Perrault set to work. Take the Doric column (the second from the left): The pedestal is seven modules, the column twenty-four, and the entablature six. The diameter of the column is three modules, so that the ratio of the column's height to its diameter is 8:1. The beauty and fit of this ratio may escape many of us, but if you have ever helped fifth graders make a model of, say, the Parthenon, your eyes have probably been opened to all sorts of dumpy or spindly alternatives.

It is a mark of the classical that it attends carefully and well—I do not say perfectly—to balance and proportion. The size and spacing of the columns in the Parthenon, the posture of the statue of Aphrodite that we may all view at our North Carolina Museum of Art, Aristotle's definition of virtue as the perfect mean between two excesses, the Greek rules for good taste in their plays—these are all examples of the classical passion for balance. "Moderation in all things" was a Greek ideal, evident around every corner in the streets of a classical Greek city-state.

AN EDUCATION OF CLASSICAL PROPORTIONS

As a Christian, and particularly as a Christian educator, I have long been drawn to this Greek ideal. Not that excess is always misguided: Was our Lord not immoderate in his anger at the moneychangers in the temple? Not that the Greeks were always able to match their deeds with the ideal: witness the disastrous Peloponnesian Wars. Still, the ideal is inspiring and true. Balance and proportion matter to the Lord, who commands us to love him first and our neighbor second, in the same measure as we love ourselves. Luke tells us that Jesus's growth was not extreme or one-sided, but full-orbed, "in wisdom and stature, and in favor with God and man" (Luke 2:52). The prophet Micah taught us that we cannot measure our lives along only one dimension: "What does the Lord require of you? To act justly and to love mercy and to walk humbly with your God" (Micah 6:8). A life of justice without mercy is as ugly as a Doric column of perfect height and skinny as a flagpole.

Many of the practices and policies of our school reflect our strong desire to maintain these critical balances in our lives. Seeking to balance the intellectual, moral, and aesthetic sides of our students' growth (truth, goodness, beauty), we schedule service projects and art classes alongside math and Latin for our older students. Our commitment to a balance between the structured, formal work of learning and the unplanned leisure of play has shaped the length of our school day and the way we run our recess. Similarly, the balance of the school agenda and family priorities means that we attempt to limit the amount and kind of homework that the students are assigned.

The Greeks' passion for moderation and balance led them to build small but beautiful temples. This preference for perfection over magnitude is a biblical value as well: "Better one handful with tranquility than two handfuls with toil and chasing after the wind" (Eccles. 4:6). Trinity is a small school, but the work that is going on in these classrooms is something we can be proud of. Like the small pottery factories of classical Athens, where gifted craftsmen labored over the proportions of an exquisite vase, our classrooms are the places where talented teachers work carefully, sometimes slowly, to shape the minds

5 – UNHURRIED LEARNING

and hearts and bodies of these students, who will be the leaders and citizens of the twenty-first century.

On Dealing with Problomes

October 4, 1996

> Dear doctor Denton We Have Hade Problome. Beacase The Second Grad Have Ben Steleno ur Beads And Wood. If you can do sonthing about it that Wood be Great.
>
> Love,
> DIANe Jenny Will
> Erika
> Lauren
> Isaac Roleig
> Ben

Translated:

Dear Doctor Denton,
We have had a problem because the second grade has been stealing our beads and wood. If you can do something about it, that would be great.

Love,
[students' names]

During my first fall as headmaster, I received this letter on fluorescent pumpkin-colored paper written with a no. 2 pencil and signed by eight six- and seven-year-olds. Dorrie McKoy was our first grade teacher that year. And I am sure that my daughter's part in this was bigger than just her signature. It is a nice window into life at Trinity in those early years, and one can see themes here that endure. I hope that play is as important to us now as it was back then—that is certainly a challenge. I am gratified to know that the first graders are still building forts in the *woods along the Penny property line on the north side of campus. The "problomes" have gotten more challenging, and I hope I've moved beyond expecting a school without one. I've learned over time that though they hit you in the gut, these challenges can be some of the best opportunities for good and for growth.*

This letter has sat on my desk for about a week now, and it has given me no end of pleasure to read over it again and again. I am deeply gratified to know that Trinity is a place where children play. Play is not work, but it is not inactivity either. Play is different from studying lessons, but it is an important part of children's growth and development. These kids are working hard at their learning, and recess is a good break for them. It is not, however, a break from profitable activity. In the words of Charlotte Mason, "Boys and girls must have time to invent episodes, carry on adventures, live heroic lives, lay sieges and carry forts, even if the fortress be an old armchair; and in these affairs the elders must neither meddle nor make."[1] The economy and the architecture of the "Indian village" outside is as good a tribute as any to this imaginative and spontaneous wonder of childhood. We cannot, in our school schedule, devote much time to such play; but such time as we do have is valuable, and we encourage all of our parents to create the schedule and the space for children's play at home after school. It is for just this reason that we de-emphasize homework in the lower grades.

There is a danger that some of you will think we are frittering away your children's precious time here—oughtn't they to be working hard while they are here? Are you paying for them to play? I think that play has its own justifications, and I hope that the glimpse you get in this letter will be persuasive. In any case, you can see from it that something we can only call "work"—a child's work, but work all the

---

1. Charlotte Mason, *School Education.* Vol. 3 in the Original Home Schooling Series (London: J. M. Dent and Sons: 1954), 37. Originally published by Kegan, Paul, Trench, Trubner (London, 1925); citations are from the 1954 edition reprinted in 1989 by Charlotte Mason Research & Supply.

same—is going on here. These are little people with real minds, and you can see them working. Most obviously, they are writing. They are putting words together, working with the basic phonetic building blocks. There is even a certain complexity to their writing: "Hade" (had a) is as logical a contraction as "didn't" (they'll learn the conventions soon enough). And clearly they are beginning to tackle the "problome" of the silent *e*.

The letter also stands as a pleasant reminder to me of the importance of age-appropriate goals for each of our classes. Not that such standards are easy to settle upon, but across a large range some things are clear. I am exceedingly pleased that our first graders are learning to write words and construct sentences. The words misspelled according to the phonetic rules don't bother me; nor do the sentence fragments. It would be an interesting exercise to ask each of the other grades to "correct" this draft. Third graders ought to be able to correct most of the misspellings. Fifth graders might be able to detect that the causal clause of the second sentence is misused.

Reflecting on all of this gives me pleasure, but perhaps the deepest gratification comes when I hear the utterly serious entreaty from these little people. They are dead serious. There is a real "problome" and they don't know what to do. Taking pen in hand to appeal to the school head is a fine example of civility and creative problem-solving. Such lessons are invaluable. Even as I read this first-grade epistle, an Israeli prime minister and a Palestinian leader have been struggling to find a way to keep talking about an adult "problome" of serious proportions. I take this pint-sized appeal seriously: I have written back to them, and their teacher Mrs. McKoy and I are talking to them about their "problome."

This brings me to a more sobering reflection on the letter. As much pleasure as I have taken in this letter, I am still bothered by it. I wish it were not so, but Trinity is a school with problems. Some of these problems we can deal with summarily. The first graders have dubbed their

5 – UNHURRIED LEARNING

garrison "Fort Poison Ivy" for reasons that are evident on the arms and legs of several students; but soon, thanks to Rick Frothingham and some pesticide, Fort Poison Ivy will be conquered and a new flag will fly there. Would that all our "problomes" were so tractable! Our elementary letter is a window not only into the wonders of childhood but also into the darkness that lurks there. The second graders have been stealing beads and wood. Theft and tribalism are here at Trinity (and we didn't even have to establish a committee!). Worse still, upon investigation, Mrs. McKoy has discovered that the second graders are not the whole problem. The first graders seem to be overly competitive among themselves, and we have had to ban beads altogether, at least for a time. All of this reminds me of another letter once written by G. K. Chesterton, in response to a London paper's inquiry into the principal problem with the world. "The problem," wrote the renowned journalist and author, "is me. Sincerely, G. K. Chesterton."

Some of you, perhaps, were hoping to find a school without problems. I was. This little letter has served to disabuse me of that pipe dream and to help me get down to the business of dealing with problems in a mature and responsible way. May God help us to look these "problomes" straight in their ugly faces, not to lose heart as we work toward real (even if only partial) solutions, to exercise charity and forgiveness, and to keep a grateful heart for all that is going well. "Rejoice always; pray continually; give thanks in all circumstances, for this is God's will for you in Christ Jesus" (1 Thess. 5:16-18).

Homework: Friend or Foe?

February 28, 1997

> *I chuckle to read this now. Some things are so different. All the things I said I hadn't heard complaints about—well, I've heard them by now. And the homework conundrum described here is so Lower School. I had no idea back then what would face us once we launched our Middle and Upper Schools. But not everything has changed. Homework continues to be a constant topic at Trinity—and it may help current parents to see that the struggles we are having now with homework have a venerable history. I still believe that Aristotle's mean is a good principle to go by here. And the three purposes still stand.*

Homework is something I hear about. I don't hear about fire drills or assembly speakers or the selection of music being taught in second grade. I don't even hear much anymore about carpool or the school calendar. But homework is another matter.

Homework is something you care about. When a few of us gathered to discuss the subject at last week's Headmaster Lunch, there was some emotion in the things that were shared. From time to time someone will call with a strong opinion.

I ask myself: Why do we care about homework? I hear the passion and the concern in your voices. What are we afraid of? Seems to me that our fears are of two sorts.

Some of us are afraid of homework's *excesses*. We have seen how the misuse of homework can sap our children of the desire to learn and defeat them. Karla Boreiko, whose daughter attends a public high school in our area, voiced this fear in an article that appeared recently in the *Chapel Hill Herald*:

5 – UNHURRIED LEARNING

> I have a problem on my hands. [My daughter] studies for hours and hours but doesn't reap the benefits. She came home once and said, 'That's it. I give up.' The lesson in life is supposed to be if you try really hard, you will succeed. But average kids come out of this system feeling really stupid.[1]

Karla's problem is a complex thing, I'm sure, but homework surely figures into her predicament. Because of the amount of homework her daughter has ("hours and hours"), she can ill-afford to pursue extracurricular interests. If school were everything or if everything were to be learned in school, this would be no problem. But at Trinity we are dedicated to neither of these propositions. As important as we think school is, it is hardly the totality of a student's (especially a child's) life. And we are not so arrogant or misguided to think that it is our job to teach children to play the violin, to save money, or to pirouette. Excess homework can make it difficult for families to teach such things, and we have stated in our handbook that "Trinity teachers will avoid excessive homework."

Imagine that we were sitting around a table discussing these matters. Some of us have just held forth on the dangers of homework, the value of free time for young children, the importance of time to play, to reflect, to be with family. Someone else on the other side of the table is squirming inside. And not so much from disagreement as from another fear, a fear that is either ignored or (possibly) heightened by such attention to homework's excesses. This is the fear of homework's *defects*. If no homework comes home, or if it is namby-pamby work that does not challenge or drill, questions loom: Is learning fun and games, or is it hard work? What is the role of discipline, of learning to overcome our flaws and incompetencies? Is there a royal road to learning that avoids the steep slopes? If the home and the school are teaming up in this work of education, don't I as a parent need to know

---

1. Karla Boreiko, *The Chapel Hill Herald*, (local edition of the *Herald-Sun*, Durham, North Carolina), February 13, 1997.

what skills and knowledge my children are being challenged with? It does not appear that we can answer such questions without some serious homework, and so it is that in the Trinity policy we have asked our teachers to focus on homework that reinforces skills and knowledge requiring practice, that bridges the gap between home and school, and that encourages reading.

There are those who want to pressure us to choose sides. They will tell us that one fear is the true fear, the one that must be combatted at all costs (including ignoring the other fear). Sometimes I am tempted myself to hash this over again in my mind and decide which side I will be on. But the voices of reason, experience, and authority call me back to the middle. One such voice is Aristotle:

> It is in the nature of moral qualities that they are destroyed by deficiency and excess, just as we can see (since we have to use the evidence of visible facts to throw light on those that are invisible) in the case of bodily health and strength. For both excessive and insufficient exercise destroy one's strength, and both eating and drinking too much or too little destroy health, whereas the right quantity produces, increases and preserves it. So it is with temperance, courage and the other virtues.[2]

And so it is with homework. The one who shuns and fears drill and practice will never learn the grammar of any subject; what is more, she will never learn the habits that make a person educated and lead to a lifetime of learning. On the other hand, the one who is so busy memorizing the classification of plants that he never has time for a walk through the botanical gardens is not truly educated. What we want is not forced, coerced habits of learning, but internalized ones.

In an attempt to avoid falling off the horse on either side and (more importantly) staying on for the ride, I would like to say a thing or two

---

2. Aristotle, *Nichomachean Ethics* 2.2.

5 – UNHURRIED LEARNING

about each of the three positive purposes for homework that are stated in our handbook. I write these things to parents and teachers, in an attempt to help us all work together for our children's better education.

Reinforcing skills and knowledge that require practice

We believe in memory work at Trinity. Your children should be learning math facts and poems, Latin nouns, state capitals, and spelling words. These things do not come without effort, and regular and frequent drill is important for two reasons. Only by drill do they acquire the knowledge, and by drill they improve their capacity to learn. Mental discipline is like weight training: the more you lift, the more you are able to lift. If your children are not bringing home some drill work, please talk to their teacher. It may be that the drill work going on in the class is enough for your child at this point. But in areas of your child's weakness, you should feel free to devise, along with the teacher, a plan for practice at home to supplement the work at school.

Sometimes the greatest challenge is communication. Parents are busy (as are teachers) and students are forgetful. Some students are remarkably incommunicative. All this adds up to a problem of parents not knowing what the teacher expects. This is not, however, an intractable problem. Parents would do well to give the teacher a call or stop by just to review what exactly is being assigned. Teachers would do well to devise, as far as they are able, a regular plan that will facilitate parents' being well informed: Spelling tests every Friday, words are copied in the homework journal every Monday. Special projects and assignments need to be communicated in special ways.

Bridging the gap between home and school

Trinity parents have delegated to the teachers at least two responsibilities: first, to solve the problem of ignorance that every child is born with; second, to awaken in them the love of truth. These are big jobs, and we at school can't tell you everything we do to try to fulfill our responsibility, but we can tell you something. Homework is one of the ways to bridge the gap that too easily develops. One parent said to me, "I never get to see him do math." Now there may be logistical and pedagogical reasons why a teacher would choose to focus homework in, say, spelling rather than in math. But parents do need to see children doing math. Irrespective of the issues of drill and practice, parents need to watch their fourth grader trying to do long division with a remainder. They need to see where the snags are and what comes easily.

Encouraging reading

I will go so far as to say that this is the principal homework that a Trinity Lower School student should have. To my way of thinking, a good day of homework in the life of a third grader would look like this: ten minutes of practice on multiplication tables, ten minutes of practice on spelling words, and twenty to thirty minutes of reading a good book. That reading ought to be the students' own, though being read to is a pleasure we ought to grant our children as long as they will bear it.

No Trinity child ever comes home without homework. Even if there's nothing else assigned, there is always reading. Your child's teacher will always back you up.

And here we come back to the matter of habit. Build into them the habit of reading. It's a far better habit than watching TV. At first they may not enjoy it, though even then there are lots of things you can do to make it fun: a cozy couch, a warm afghan, a great story, a good light, a parent beside them to read aloud. Eventually, probably imperceptibly, they will pass over the great divide: from reading because they must, to reading because they may; from being students who read, to being readers. Reading then is not so much something they'll do as a part of who they are. Then we can truly speak of them as being *educated*.

On Being Bored
September 26, 1997

I was a year old as a headmaster when I wrote this. I don't remember which particular bored child inspired (provoked?) this article, but every school has them. It's seldom easy to diagnose the cause accurately and prescribe the proper cure, but there is a difference between what I call boredom (which the school needs to own) and Boredom (which involves a fundamental assumption on the part of the child). I've included this piece because the word unhurried suggests to some a lackadaisical posture toward learning that is bound to bore. Not at all: the education that is unhurried assumes that the world is a fascinating place, and the sort of time it takes to explore that world is often an unhurried time. I first heard the Agassiz story in college, when my InterVarsity staff leader gave us the fish story as a case study for how to do Bible study. I've used it since as part of the orientation for new teachers, and I think it captures a rich and unhurried learning experience perfectly.

It is a truth universally acknowledged that children who are bored need something to do.

They need something to do over the summer. They need something to do in the car on long trips. And sometimes even in school. We don't worry too much about the summer or the car trips, but boredom in school is a different matter altogether, especially at a school that is fairly clear and vocal about aiming to nurture a lifelong love of learning.

There is boredom and there is Boredom. Boredom can sometimes be the mother of imagination, as when children who have no toys are forced to invent games to amuse themselves. This I would call superficial boredom. On the other end of the spectrum is the child who, when presented with a vast array of interesting options can only groan, "That's boring!" Such a child is fundamentally bored.

Children are different, and we will all of us do well to learn the unique ways that our own children and students are put together. For all of them, regardless of their temperaments, we parents and teachers ought to be working to instill a fundamental fascination and interest in the world that God has made. We have good reasons, as Christians, to do so, as the psalmist reminds us:

> How many are your works, O LORD!
> In wisdom you made them all;
> the earth is full of your creatures.
> There is the sea, vast and spacious,
> teeming with creatures beyond number—
> living things both large and small.
> — Psalm 104:24-25

When we or our children experience the world as dull or monotonous, we know that something in us is awry. This is not the way things are supposed to be.

Our children need to see us model the psalmist's fascination, both at home and at school. They need to see us asking questions, reading, wondering, turning over rocks, and learning new crafts and ideas.

I've been inspired by people who model this kind of wonder. One such man was Louis Agassiz, who was born in French Switzerland in 1807 and, after a notable career as a naturalist in Europe, came to the United States in 1846 and became professor of zoology at Harvard. He was brilliant and industrious, and it has been said that in him "American natural history had found its leader."[1] His primary area of study was ichthyology, especially extinct fishes of Europe and the fishes of Brazil; but he also studied glacial effects and a number of other zoological areas.

---

1. Jules Marcou, *Life, Letters, and Works of Louis Agassiz*, vol. 1 (New York: Macmillan & Co., 1896), 283.

5 – UNHURRIED LEARNING

In America it was as a teacher that Agassiz gained his greatest fame. His method was to give students contact with the natural world rather than information. Well known is the story of the student who stared at the dead fish for days until he finally began to "see" things. Said Agassiz, "It's not textbooks we want, but students. The book of nature is always open."[2] This great teacher understood well the danger of boredom and knew that the way to overcome it was through a careful and passionate study of nature. "If you study nature in books, when you go out of doors, you cannot find her," he remarked.[3]

Children who are bored need something to do. We can entertain them or distract them or busy them with this or that. What's much harder is to take them by the hand and lead them out into God's wide world, or lead them down deep, teaching them that reality is dense with layer upon layer of design, all of it, to use Agassiz's words, "associations of ideas in the Divine Mind." But the hard work will be worth it and here, as so often, it will make us better persons, to become better parents.

---

2. Cited in Nora Archibald Smith, "The Book of Nature." In *The Child Welfare Manual: A Handbook of Child Nature and Nurture for Parents and Teachers*, vol. 2 (New York: The University Society, 1915), 101.

3. David Starr Jordan, "Agassiz at Penikese," *Popular Science Monthly* 40 (April 1892): 721.

The Art of Teaching

December 4, 1998

Comenius gets his due in this piece, but I should also acknowledge my debt to Mortimer Adler, who taught me so much about the cooperative arts in general and the art of teaching in particular. Comenius was ahead of his time in so many ways: he was a strong proponent of education for girls; he was an ecumenist in an age of strong sectarian sympathies; and he was a pioneer in what today we would call evidence-based education. He spoke from his own observations about the ways children learn, and his particular calling was to bring his Christian faith to bear on education. His work had a wide influence, even upon the Christians on this continent who formed the first universities, especially Harvard. I think we have not learned all that we could and should from this great predecessor, and I am glad to include this tribute to his prescient understanding of the value of a well-ordered and well-paced education. This was an early attempt to show that what we call unhurried was neither quirky nor faddish, but substantial and important.

> *If we take nature as our guide,*
> *she will never lead us astray.*
>
> – Cicero, *De Officiis*

Teachers, farmers, and doctors all work at humble and marvelous crafts. All three set out to do a good work by *cooperating* with nature. The doctor heals, the farmer grows, and the teacher educates; yet, in a very real sense none of them really does this work. For all his skill, my orthopedic surgeon simply abets the natural processes of healing that are at work within me. For all his skill and wisdom, the farmer does not produce corn in the same way that a computer programer writes code. So also with the teacher. Socrates, the teacher par excellence, spoke of himself as a midwife who simply assists at the birth of knowledge. Such a view of teaching is quite humbling, but it is nonetheless marvelous. Who of us can witness the birth of a child and not marvel? And what parent has not sat by in wonder as a six-year-old begins to sound out those first words?

Cooperative arts like medicine, farming, and teaching all work on (we might say *with*) organic material: bodies, plants, minds. By "organic," I mean the sorts of things to which the Greeks would have ascribed a psyche, things which had the powers of life: birth, growth, and decay. Any craftsperson or artisan must attend to the nature of the material with which he works—a carpenter needs to know which way the grain of the plank runs. But when we are working with a mind or a body or a plant, there is an even greater need to attend closely to the way that this organic thing comes to be, grows, and decays. Good teaching comes about not by genius or creativity (though these will surely augment a good teacher), but through sensible and wise attention to the natural way that the mind grows to maturity.

John Amos Comenius was a seventeenth century Bohemian educator who thought a good deal about what nature can teach us about education. Just as a farmer must fit his work to the soil and the seasons, so the teacher must fit the order and pace of learning to the human person. In a priceless book called *The Great Didactic*, Comenius lays out a number of principles of sound pedagogy that can be gleaned from observing nature. Let me share a couple of them with you.

"Nature observes a suitable time," says Comenius. Just as a bird does not set out to lay its eggs in winter, nor in summer or fall, but always in spring, when the sun brings life and strength, so must the teacher do all in season. The right time for mental exercise must be chosen, and the season of youth, when "life and mind are fresh and gathering strength," is the best time for teaching.[1] Comenius draws three very practical conclusions from this principle:

- The education of men should be commenced in the springtime of life, that is to say, in childhood.
- The morning hours are the most suitable for study, for the morning is like the spring, when children are vigorous and when learning strikes root deeply.
- All the subjects that are to be learned should be arranged so as to suit the age of the students, that nothing which is beyond their comprehension be given to them to learn.

"Nature is not confused in its operations," Comenius tells us, "but advances distinctly from one point to another. For example, if a bird is being produced, its bones, veins, and nerves are formed at separate and distinct periods."[2] (Although Comenius's embryology was primitive and naïve at points, modern science would generally vindicate his observation.) So also with students and schools: confusion arises when we attempt to teach students too many things at once. Or when we attempt to teach them something that ought to wait. "Let us imitate [wise craftsmen] and take care not to confuse scholars who are learning grammar by teaching them dialectic, or by introducing rhetoric into their studies."[3]

Comenius' advice runs generally counter to popular wisdom at the end of the twentieth century. It is increasingly assumed that the earlier we can move students into more advanced learning, the better: If a child can learn to read at four instead of six, all the better. If third graders can learn to reason abstractly like seventh graders, then we are ahead of the game. If we can get our sixth graders into Algebra I then we will be a truly excellent school. Comenius would call this kind

---

1. John Amos Comenius, *The Great Didactic*, trans. M.W. Keatinge (London: Kessinger Publishing, n.d.), 112–14.
2. Comenius, *Didactic*, 118.
3. Comenius, *Didactic*, 119.

of thinking foolish, a "deviation" from nature. Nature's way is not to hurry, but to grow the organism at a steady and ordered pace. Far from being an inferior education, such growth strikes deep roots and builds strong minds that can face the winters of life.

So the next time you hear someone speak about the "unhurried" education we are attempting to offer at Trinity, don't think that this means "slack" or "lazy." It is an education in accordance with nature, one that respects the students for who they are: people created in God's image, with minds and souls whose growth is not ours to determine, but only to guide as best we can.

> Let the main object of this our Didactic, be as follows: To seek and to find a method of instruction, by which teachers may teach less, but learners may learn more; by which schools may be the scene of less noise, aversion, and useless labour, but of more leisure, enjoyment, and solid progress; and through which the Christian community may have less darkness, perplexity, and dissension, but on the other hand more light, orderliness, and rest.[4]

---

4. Comenius, *Didactic*, 156.

The Myth of Multitasking
March 23, 2012

My Secret Encourager (something we do every year among the faculty and staff) gave me Kahnemann's book, and I found it fascinating reading. Thank you, Muri Pugh! I continue to hear multitasking touted as the great goal for this upcoming generation, but the brain research does not support this. Cathy Davidson at Duke has written a book entitled Now You See It *that celebrates a shift in attentiveness, but it is really just a case for attention to things we have been in the habit of ignoring. Teaching and learning in the digital age will have to take into account the realities I outline in this article. I am thankful for our division directors and teachers, who are being thoughtful about this in the design of their lessons and the ordering of students' lives.*

There is multitasking, and there is multitasking. The trick is to keep them straight.

If you are an event planner, we want you to be able to handle multiple phone calls coming in at once, to direct the vendors while talking on the phone, and to be aware that an urgent text is coming in from the chair of the auction. And it's reasonable to expect this, because you have been doing this for a while and most of these tasks are routine for you. They are performed by what Princeton psychologist and Nobel Laureate Daniel Kahneman (*Thinking Fast and Slow*) calls your System 1 mode of thinking. This system operates automatically and quickly, with little or no effort. For most of us, System 1 does things like detects that one object is closer than another, reads words on a large billboard, and orients the source of a sudden sound. Experienced event planners acquire the capacity to perform with minimal effort tasks that require focused attention from the rest of us, such as estimating the square footage needed for a reception tent or determining whether the

5 – UNHURRIED LEARNING

caterer's estimate includes waitstaff. Chess grand masters can find a strong move by just glancing at the chessboard, but for most of us these kinds of tasks need our System 2 mode of thinking.

System 2 thinking requires effortful, demanding mental work. This "slow" thinking involves agency, choice, and concentration. Try multiplying 13 X 23 in your head. Unless you are Rain Man, you will be practicing System 2 slow thinking to do this.

The control of attention is shared by the two systems. But whereas System 1 demands and achieves attention with minimal effort, often involuntarily (like reading the words on this page), System 2 requires effortful and intentional attention. It is possible for System 2 mental work to seem effortless—this is what psychologist Mihaly Csikszentmihaly calls *flow*, the enjoyable state of keen focus and immersion in activities such as art, play, and work.[1] But for most System 2 activities, we must *pay* attention—the expression is apt. Focusing attention on challenging mental work costs us something in effort and intention. As Kahneman says,

> You dispose of a limited budget of attention that you can allocate to activities, and if you try to go beyond your budget, you will fail. It is the mark of effortful activities that they interfere with each other, which is why it is difficult or impossible to conduct several at once. You could not compute the product of 17 X 24 while making a left turn into dense traffic, and you certainly should not try.[2]

This is why molecular biologist John Medina says, "To put it bluntly, research shows that *we can't multitask*. We are biologically incapable of processing attention-rich inputs simultaneously."[3]

---

1. Mihaly Csikszentmihaly, *Flow: The Psychology of Optimal Experience* (New York: Harper & Row, 1990).

2. Daniel Kahneman, *Thinking Fast and Slow* (New York: Farrar, Straus and Giroux, 2011), 23.

3. John Medina, *Brain Rules: Twelve Principles for Surviving and Thriving at*

THE MYTH OF MULTITASKING

What does all this brain research mean for schools? For students, teachers, and parents?

First, teachers should be designing learning experiences that are full of "attention-rich inputs." Medina has some very practical suggestions for ways in which our presentations can capture and hold attention. The artful teacher will explore many ways to engage students, beyond the "sage on a stage" model of teaching.

Homework assignments should aim to engage students in System 2 kinds of mental activities. This means taxing memory retrieval, complex computation, and problems that require some serious thinking. It means investing time in the *construction of good questions*, questions that require sustained reflection and relentless pursuit. Our aim should be to design work for students that cannot be done well without attention and heavy cognitive lifting.

Parents should guide students to plan for interruption-free zones, when they can work on demanding homework assignments without the interruptions of cell phones, texting, instant messaging, and email. Help them master these tools and not be mastered by them—turn off the notification that announces every incoming email while they're trying to write a paper.

Students will need to accept the counterintuitive truth that they cannot multitask effectively on challenging mental activities. It is a myth generally believed by the young that they can function effectively while doing many different things. But the truth is that they are not really multitasking: they are either doing routine System 1 mental work (which probably means a poorly designed assignment) or they are shifing back and forth quickly (and inefficiently!) from one System 2 task to another. This is not a smart way to get work done.

I should know. I decided to write this article on a day when I was away from the office—I've lived long enough to know that the inter-

---

Work, Home, and School (Seattle: Pear Press, 2008), 85.

ruptions of a school day are not conducive to the sort of sustained thinking I need to do in order to write a newsletter column. My wife was undergoing some minor surgery, and I thought the morning in the ambulatory surgical center would be a good time to focus on this work. I was wrong. Interruptions abounded, from doctors and nurses and solicitous friends, from pharmacy runs and the demands of keeping the polar ice machine running. So now the article I started about 8:30 this morning is still in process at 7:00 p.m., when I should have been finished long ago. This is the opposite of flow. Writing is not a multitaskable enterprise. I should have known better.

We live and learn. My goal for our students is that they will learn to order their work well, to know what kind of work is required by different tasks, and to have the self-control and wisdom to arrange their lives so that they can flourish in whatever work they are called to.

Unhurried Generosity

September 6, 2012

Trinity Reads was born early in the life of the school. It used to be very easy to find one book that we could all read, when we were a small group of parents with students all in the Lower School. Hans Christian Andersen stories or a children's version of Pilgrim's Progress *were successes back in the early days. As we have grown into a TK–12 school, it has gotten harder, but the choice in the summer of 2012 to read Tolstoy's story "Two Old Men" was a coup. It captured many imaginations and made a great impact that is still felt around school. This essay explores the connections between the narrative and Trinity's notion of being an unhurried school. And it goes beyond the intellectual and academic concerns (which are usually front and center) to delve into the moral implications of being unhurried.*

By now I hope many of us have read Tolstoy's story, "Two Old Men." I would be glad if this story worked its way into our collective consciousness and shaped us in important ways. It is that good.

It portrays a remarkable but believable picture of generosity, our theme for this year at Trinity School. I am interested in what Elisha and Efim, the two old men of the story, have to teach about this virtue. Elisha, you may recall, is the bald-headed, short, and dark one, who kept bees and lived on good terms with his family and neighbors. Efim, his erect, long-bearded friend, was a village elder who neither smoked nor drank and kept his affairs in good order.

The Trinity faculty took a morning during our August in-service to reflect on this story and some of its deep connections with scripture and our lives. One of the angles we took was to explore how the generosity of Elisha was related to that mysterious thing we call "unhurriedness" at Trinity School. Many of us identify with Efim, with his long list of

5 – UNHURRIED LEARNING

things to do, his many cares, his constraints, his obligations. And many of us looked to Elisha as an example of one who knew how to leave a thing or two undone, who allowed for interruptions, who seemed usually to be joyful, cheerful, and kind. Most of us would like to be like Elisha when we grow up. I know I would.

Elisha took his time. It would not be quite true to say he was a plodder, for he pressed on at a steady pace and the two men would never have embarked on their excellent adventure if not for his initiative. Still, Elisha had trouble keeping up with Efim, and he needed to stop to get a drink. That's when all the trouble that makes the story began. It was unhurried Elisha and not the fast-walking-no-thank-you-I-don't-need-a-drink Efim who encountered the family in dire straits and paused long enough (quite long, really) to help them.

It turns out that Tolstoy's narrative hunch has been corroborated by modern psychology. In 1973 Darley and Batson performed a study establishing that people in a hurry are less likely to help people in need, even if they are running off to speak about the parable of the Good Samaritan.[1] They recruited seminary students and asked them to prepare a talk on the Good Samaritan. Then they sent them off to another building to finish the work and deliver the talk. Some of these students they sent off with the message, "You're late; you need to hurry and get over there." To some they gave more time. On their way from one building to the next, everyone encountered a man slumped in an alleyway, who moaned and coughed twice. Of those not hurried, 63 percent offered some help (of various degrees); of those highly hurried, only 10 percent offered any help.

One of the details of this study is that "many subjects who did not stop did appear aroused and anxious when they arrived at the second site. They were in a conflict between helping the victim and meeting the needs of the experimenter. Conflict rather than callousness can ex-

---

1. J. M. Darley and C. D. Batson, "From Jerusalem to Jericho: A Study of Situational and Dispositional Variables in Helping Behavior," *Journal of Personality and Social Psychology* 27 (1973): 100–108.

plain the failure to stop." I think I see that same conflict in Elisha, who did stop to help the family in need. One of the peculiarities of the story is that Elisha is extremely reticent to share the details of his pilgrimage with his family and even with Efim when he returns. "God's business," is all he will say. I think of Elisha as humble, but I am not sure that he sees himself that way. He asks the Lord's forgiveness for losing his money and lagging behind his companion. When he talks to himself, he says, "You've slipped your cables and lost your reckoning!" These are not the words of a man who is completely at peace with himself and his choices. I believe that Elisha had a classic conflict of codes (to use Chester Barnard's categories in *The Functions of the Executive*).[2] He had a weighty obligation to go with his friend to Jerusalem—it was a vow he took very seriously and he had even persuaded his friend to make the trip on the grounds that they must tend to their own souls first. Once he encounters the family in need, however, he faces another obligation, which he knows in his bones is one he cannot ignore. But the Elisha who chooses this way of living is not an Elisha without inner conflict. "A nice coil you've got yourself into, brother Elisha!" I believe that at least some of Elisha's humility at the end of the story comes from this deep sense that while he did one good thing he also left something important undone.

Likewise, our decisions to live lives of unhurried generosity will put us in conflict—and not just with bad things we ought to forgo (like too much TV), but with good things we ought to do. An unhurried life will help us notice and respond to the good we should do, but in turn it will leave unfulfilled some hope or even some duty. This is especially true when it comes to raising and educating our children. Keeping up with the educational Joneses is a little like keeping up with Efim. We cannot have our educational cake and eat it too—there are hard choices ahead for all of us. Something has to give: club soccer, piano, robotics, Boy Scouts, gymnastics, Recorder Club, the Duke TIP program,

---

2. Chester I. Barnard, *The Functions of the Executive* (1938; repr., Cambridge, MA: Harvard University Press, 1971).

5 – UNHURRIED LEARNING

learning Mandarin, Children's Chorus, the AP Chemistry exam, pottery classes, the after-school job, the spelling bee, applying to twelve colleges. My point is not to critique these choices—they all represent some good we might have an obligation to provide for our children or they for themselves. The point is that unless we are willing to live like Elisha, we might just go through a life of frenzied excellence and never see the wounded man on the side of the road. And that, according to our Lord, would be a great shame.

Perhaps Elisha's greatest strength is his willingness to cast himself completely upon the Lord's mercy. "As for me, I'm afraid I shall never fulfill my vow in this life," he says at a decisive point in the story. "I must be thankful it was made to a merciful Master and to one who pardons sinners." My prayer for Trinity this year and every year is that we, like Elisha, can keep ourselves focused on the good of our souls and the mercy of God, and thus find our lives enriched by generous acts of service. And, imperfect though we be, perhaps we too may live under the Mercy, kindly and cheerful as we go.

Homework 2.0

September 5, 2014

In preparing to publish this book, I asked for feedback from several readers. One of them, Kristen Blair (mentioned in the article below), commented that the pieces on homework were very dated. True enough. We have done a good bit of thinking about homework over all our years, and there are certainly policies and handbooks and memoranda I could point to; but I did not find just the right article to carry Trinity's unhurried stance on homework into this new century when we are graduating students and sending them to college. So this essay is fresh and not tested by time. Still, I hope it will be helpful as a way of interpreting Trinity's mission in a way that is consonant with our past and sensitive to the ever-changing future.

We started Trinity, in part, because we did not want to send our children to schools where they would burn out on excessive workloads that robbed them of sleep and the sort of life in which they could flourish. There were horror stories in the letters to the editor of the Chapel Hill paper, and Trinity founder Nancy Brooks had long noticed the trend toward stress in her violin students. It was the mid-1990s, and parents were busy herding their children from soccer to piano to Boy Scouts to SAT prep. And then there was homework—hours of it.

This is the context for that most unusual word in the Trinity mission statement: "unhurried." I remember debating with others about the best word to capture what we wanted to embody. "Unhurried" is a negative, and some of us wanted a positive affirmation instead. But no alpha adjective emerged, and the privative survived into our current mission statement. I have grown to love it, even if I have struggled to embody it.

5 – UNHURRIED LEARNING

In the early years of the school, when we had no students above eighth grade, these discussions were easier. Cutting back on homework for a sixth grader is a lower octane move than for a high school junior. What is more, the next level beyond Trinity was high school—important enough, but not the holy grail of college. We could afford to be a bit more countercultural and march to our own unhurried beat. This is not to say that there weren't homework battles—early *Parent News* articles are evidence that even back in the day we wrung our hands a bit over workload and rigor.

During the early aughts, when we were still TK–8 but planning for an Upper School launch, we were watching the cultural trends carefully. There were emerging voices that vindicated our decision to aim for unhurriedness: David Brooks' *Atlantic Monthly* article, "The Organization Kid," described the unhappy results of a generation of overscheduled wunderkinds at a place like Princeton; Billy Collins's Choate Rosemary Hall graduation address was published in the *Independent School Magazine* under the wonderful title, "On Slowing Down"; and Duke professor Harris Cooper emerged as a prophetic voice warning of the negative effects of too much homework ("Does Homework Improve Academic Achievement?" in *Duke Today*). And so it was that when we launched our Upper School in the fall of 2006, we renewed our commitment to an unhurried education.

What goes round, comes round. Here at the beginning of our twentieth year, it is our turn now to step up and reclaim this important word for our own. It is not easy; the culture has not shifted in our favor. Trinity parent and education writer Kristen Blair has recently surveyed several studies of homework woe (see "When Homework Becomes Overwork," *Carolina Journal Online*). She cites the recent *Atlantic Monthly* article, "My Daughter's Homework Is Killing Me" and the long-running film *Race to Nowhere* (which Trinity viewed and discussed two years ago). In particular, the culture of high-performing and privileged schools (that would be Trinity) is prone to creating harmful stress, physical maladies, and life imbalances in the lives of students (see "Nonacademic Effects of Homework in Privileged, High-Performing Schools," in the *Journal of Experimental Education*).

Because we recognize these dangers and the challenges of swimming in these waters towards college admission, we have taken a couple of important steps in the last two years. First, we have revised and updated the Unhurried section of the school's Expanded Mission Statement. The previous version was written, understandably, with Lower and Middle Schools in mind. It was important to revise this essential document to take on questions about athletics, extracurriculars, and holiday assignments. Second, this past spring the board's Education Committee approved, and the board endorsed, a Family and Student Time Policy, which attempts to describe the current workload and time that the school is claiming and to draw boundaries at those points: this far and no farther, says the policy.

Some think we should have been more draconian and pushed back the boundaries even further. The horror stories that birthed our school could be, sadly, recounted with passion by current Trinity students and parents. We are not immune from the ills of our age. What is more, every excellent teacher wants more time, and the work multiplies.

I want to call the Trinity community of teachers, students, and parents to live up to our unhurried mission this year. I believe that it is one of the great values we can add to our students' experience, something they are unlikely to get anywhere else (unless they move to Finland). And I believe that a strong adherence to this principle will make Trinity a better place and will help our students flourish in ways that they cannot otherwise.

To this end, I call us to these commitments, which are in line with the policies I have cited above:

1. Let us all agree that school is important for our students. Its purpose, in large part, is to train students to master complex intellectual challenges—school is inherently rigorous. Other things (sports, friends, Facebook) do not matter as much as this. So we should plan

5 – UNHURRIED LEARNING

our time in school and out of school to give pride of place to the work that schooling requires. Some of our problem (not all, by a longshot) is that we try to do too many other things and do not leave margin for that which is at the very center of the calling of these young men and women. (The book to read is Amanda Ripley's *The Smartest Kids in the World*, which follows several American exchange students to Finland, Poland, and Korea. Her take-home? High-performing countries like these have what she calls a "consensus around rigor.")[1]

2. Let us work together to give students the rest they need. In order to achieve the important academic work of schooling, students need rest. Research says they need nine hours a night. Sleep is productive and restorative. Can we students, parents, and teachers collaborate to make sure that we put adequate sleep into our students' schedules first, and then work the other things in?

3. Let us limit Upper School homework to 2.5 hours per night. Research shows that more than this is not productive and can even be harmful. Certainly it works against the previous goal of sufficient sleep. We must admit at the outset that this limitation presents serious limitations for the teachers. Upper School classes meet, generally, for 75 minutes on a rotating schedule. This limitation means that no teacher can assign more than 45 minutes of homework for any given class period—far less, say, than the college class we are preparing them for. With these limitations, teachers will need to be creative and smart about the kinds of homework assignments they give. The job of the teacher is to design learning experiences, and homework is part of that experience and thus an essential part of the design work of a teacher. Homework must be rigorous, but I believe that rigor need not be equated with excessive time on task.

4. Let us talk to each other. Communication is essential. Regulating homework is like regulating the thermostat in our (nonsmart) house.

---

1. Amanda Ripley, *The Smartest Kids in the World: And How They Got That Way* (New York: Simon & Schuster, 2013), 118.

One person is hot, another is cold. The temperature changes through the day, and doors get left open. Seasons change. We have to talk to one another about these kinds of things. Students should become their own advocates in this collaboration, and teacher must be open to feedback and adjustment.

5. Let us differentiate in homework just as we do in our instruction and our assessment. Homework loads vary widely within any given class of students: Some students work quickly, and some are slower. Some assignments require fast thinking, some slow thinking. For this kind of differentiation, experience is invaluable. Teachers learn over time what kinds of assignments will take more time for certain students.

6. Let us allow for a few exceptions. Flow is one. In the book *Flow: The Psychology of Optimal Experience*, psychologist Mihaly Csikszentmihaly has written about this optimal learning/working experience in which the individual is completely absorbed into the work, so that he or she loses track of time and is energized by being immersed in the work. While we cannot expect all (even most) homework assignments to lead students into this optimal experience, we ought not to quibble about the clock when it does happen. I have known students who have experienced this through reading a novel that completely captured their imaginations, through preparing for real-world tutoring in the Augustine project, and through diving into the annual challenge in the robotics pit. These too can become excessive, but let us not rob our students of this wonderful experience that will instill in them a true lifelong love of learning.

I cannot imagine a school where someone is not complaining about homework. But I can imagine a school where the students, teachers, and parents are working together to do homework well. Let us be that school.

6 – Moral Education

We are what we repeatedly do. Virtue, then, is not an act, but a habit.

ARISTOTLE, *NICOMACHEAN ETHICS*

Habit is ten times nature.

ARTHUR WELLESLEY, DUKE OF WELLINGTON

For a Christian school, moral education is both easier and harder than for other schools.

Easier because it is expected. There is a given code and a dominant narrative. There are even secret weapons in our arsenal: the power of the Holy Spirit to motivate and help students to live lives that please the Lord. The school is staffed and parented by people who are Christ-followers, examples for the students. And, at least in theory, we all expect our students to be wounded sinners who will sometimes fail but who also are capable of repentance, reconciliation, restoration, and amazing virtue.

Harder because our moral failures reflect poorly not only on ourselves and our school, but also on the one we call Lord. Temptations to self-righteousness and hypocrisy are legion, and nothing stinks so much as religion gone bad. We expect so much more of one another as Christians, and we sometimes forget that being Christian does not make us any better than someone else, only (we hope) better than we would have been if we weren't following Christ.

The essays in this section reflect a concern to avoid two dangers. One is culturally specific: succumbing to the moral relativism of an age that has lost touch with the "steep good" of virtue. I feel the tug of this temptation whenever I hear, in the context of a student discipline case, "I don't want to make any excuses for him, but...." The other is the timeless temptation of legalism. Anyone who has tried to write a student handbook with conduct codes will know this temptation, and at the start of Trinity we were all too aware that Christian schools were often defined in the larger culture by what they do not allow. I believe with all my heart and mind that the Gospel offers a liberating way through both of these dangers, and I hope the essays here chart such a course.

A Steep Good
October 25, 1996

I can still remember which students were lost on this field trip, and so can Janice McAdams (former board member and director of advancement, and parent of Trinity alumnae) and Rick Adams (former board member and also parent of Trinity alumni). If you read Trinity's Student-Parent Handbook today, you can find traces of this incident in our rules about field trips. Almost twenty years later, having been through some mishaps steeper than this one, it is easy to look back on this and smile. But at the time it was hard and frightening, and the history of Trinity continues to prove the dictum that "the next opportunity for prudence will not look like the last." I have come to regard this virtue, practical wisdom, as one of the most important in a school's arsenal. I am thankful for the cadre of wise leaders at Trinity, who every day exercise this virtue in making numerous decisions about students and families. I like to think that the practice of virtue, like physical strength and endurance, though hard, is made easier by practice. And I am afraid that it is true that, like physical strength, it is much easier to lose one's moral stamina than to regain it or maintain it.

We've been learning some lessons at Trinity and I'd like to reflect on them with you in this *Parent News*. Putting it as simply (though probably not as clearly) as I can, I would say we have been learning about prudence. Prudence is an outdated word; most of us would say wisdom nowadays, and we needn't quibble about the distinctions. Prudence is the first of the cardinal virtues, in a tradition of moral discourse at least as old as Plato's *Symposium*, where prudence appears with the other three cardinal virtues: justice, fortitude, and temperance. You may recall from our first parent newsletter that I had proposed these four, along with the three Christian theological virtues, as the model for the sort of community of learning we want Trinity to be. It was with a

6 – MORAL EDUCATION

certain seriousness about this task of moral education that the teachers and I sat down last week to discuss this "intellectual" virtue. We had done a little reading together—some excerpts from Aquinas, from C. S. Lewis, and from Mark Noll's *The Scandal of the Evangelical Mind*. We had an interesting discussion about the importance of the intellect and the anti-intellectual trends in our culture. Thankful for the collegiality among our faculty, I went away from that discussion thinking that moral education is a comfortable venture, rather like a pleasant stroll in the autumn countryside.

I had not remembered well (which is one of the marks of imprudence) the reality and truth I had met before. I had forgotten my own words from that first newsletter: "Virtue is gained only at great cost." I had not kept in mind Aquinas's notion that prudence, like all the virtues, is not knowledge acquired without great difficulty, but in fact, a *bonum arduum*, a "steep good." A steep and dangerous hike is a better metaphor for moral education than a pleasant stroll, and it took just such a steep hike to teach me, along with others at Trinity, a thing or two about wisdom.

On Friday a week ago, two of our classes were scheduled to go on a rather long field trip in conjunction with a science unit on rocks. The weather on Friday was volatile and threatened rain, and we made a decision to change the venue of the hike to our local Eno River State Park. The trip was, by all accounts I have heard, a fine one until the end. After hiking independently for most of the morning, the two classes merged near the end of the trail, where they both back-tracked along a stretch they had hiked earlier that day. The children were excited to see their Trinity friends, confident along a familiar stretch of trail, and eager to finish (and to finish first) as they came to a point where the trail ascends about thirty feet up a steep set of steps. At the top of that hill two Trinity students came to a place where another trail veered off to the left. Children sometimes climb hills faster than adults, and these two children happened to be out of sight of the adults ahead and behind them when they decided to take the turn to the left. It was only about five minutes before the children were discovered missing, but since they kept hiking it took over an hour to find them. Needless to say, there were some anxious parents and teachers. The two students were safe and unharmed, and surprised to learn that they were such celebrities and the object of so many prayers.

Some will think it the height of imprudence for me to recount this tale. "Be glad that nothing serious happened and let it be forgotten"—this is the common "wisdom." Although I am cognizant of the dangers of telling this story, particularly in a litigious society, I am convinced that it is good to tell it. And the particular good that can be done in the telling is the exercise of prudence. Prudence has at least two faces: one that looks back and one that looks forward. If prudence is "reason perfected in the cognition of truth," then we must be busy about that perfection as we look both ways at the particular realities of our lives. This means telling last week's story and reflecting on it.

Telling this tale helps us to grow in wisdom as we look back. We are told by moral theologians that backward-looking prudence consists of at least three things: memory that is true to reality, a proper open-mindedness to things as they are (and not as we would wish them to be), and a certain objectivity in unexpected situations. In many conversations that I have had since this incident, I have witnessed such backward-looking wisdom: the parent who remembered well but painfully his own carelessness in passing that fork in the trail; the fifth-grade students who faced the fact of a lost classmate and gathered to pray; the teachers, parents, and rangers who recognized the danger and acted swiftly with the eyes of clear-sighted vision to find the children.

Wisdom looks not only to the past but also toward the future, and the perfection of prudence at Trinity means that we have opportunities to act with foresight, which is to say that we should be growing in our capacity to estimate, with a sure instinct, whether a particular action will lead us where we want to go. I trust that already this chapter of the Trinity story is about learning such foresight. Both teachers involved and some parents have suggested improvements to our field trip policy. David Hancock, chief of the Durham Search and Rescue, is coming to Trinity on November 5 to talk to all our students about safety in the woods and elsewhere and about how to respond if lost. All of us have a heightened awareness of the priority of safety both on and off campus. And I for one face the future with a keener sense that this world can be a dangerous place and that actions have consequences. "The prudent give thought to their steps" (Prov. 14:15).

The virtue of prudence, like all the virtues, is not a moral trick or technique that we can memorize. Rather, it is a difficult craft to be mastered. The next opportunity to practice wisdom will not look like the last; it will be a different fork in the trail, up a different steep slope, and it will take us by surprise. Prudent protocol and policy are certainly called for, but our greatest need is people who act with prudence. If Trinity can be the kind of school that trains people for these "steep climbs," then we will be doing something right.

Some Thoughts on Moral Education
September 18, 1998

> *The crisis that precipitated this article, of course, was the Clinton sexual scandal. Everyone was talking about it, so it seemed wise to make something good out of the opportunity. I have long held that every school teaches morality, whether it says so or not. Being ethical is part of the fabric of our humanness, and Christian schools are not unique in their claim to teach students how to be good. I like to think that they are more explicit, and certainly more distinctive, as they hold forth the example of Christ as the measure of all things. And the resource of the Holy Spirit to motivate and sustain the virtues is our great secret power. The shaping of the will and the habits of the heart may be the most lasting impression a school leaves on the student.*

Ethics, increasingly the domain of specialists, has lately become the talk of the town and the nation. Presidential shenanigans have made it likely that every mother's daughter and son will have something to say about the difference between crime and sin, or the definition of true repentance. Whatever regrets and dismay we may feel at the present crisis, we can at least see an opportunity here: people are asking the hard and important questions about morality and ethics. One of those questions, simply put, is this: Can you teach someone to do the right thing? In such a question, schools have a natural interest.

The answer to this question depends a great deal on what one means by doing the right thing. Even in our pluralistic society, where diverse moral visions compete and contentious issues abound, there is still a reasonably large plot of common moral ground. Take, for example, the following list of ethical goals promoted by a public school district in Ohio:

- Achieving self-discipline, defined as the strength to do what we believe we should do, even when we would rather not do it.
- Being trustworthy, so that when we say we will or will not do something, we can be believed.
- Telling the truth, especially when it hurts us to do so.
- Having the courage to resist group pressures to do what we believe, when alone, that we should not do.
- Using honorable means, those that respect the rights of others, in seeking our individual and collective ends.
- Conducting ourselves, where significant moral behavior is involved, in a manner which does not fear exposure.
- Having the courage to say, "I'm sorry, I was wrong."
- Treating others as we would wish to be treated; recognizing that this principle applies to persons of every class, race, nationality, and religion.
- Doing work well, whatever that work may be.
- Respecting the democratic values of free speech, a free press, freedom of assembly, freedom of religion, and due process of law. Recognizing that this principle applies to speech we abhor, groups we dislike, persons we despise.

As Christians at Trinity, we would certainly want to add to this list, but it seems to me unobjectionable in its maxims and (to be honest) quite challenging for any community, Christian or otherwise. At Trinity, we will be addressing larger ethical issues about which there may be significant disagreement in our society; but we need to recognize that, as a school for the entire community, we will be joined by some who do not go all the way with our Christian moral vision yet still respect the individual and social aspects of our moral education.

In moral education, as elsewhere, it makes sense to start close to home—with the individual and close relationships. Eight-year-olds understand "no stealing" better than they understand "no idolatry." What is more, if you start with "no stealing" and you do your ethical training well, you will, eventually, get to "no idolatry." The various levels or stages of morality are all interconnected, and one room leads to another. Honesty with ourselves affects whether we tell the truth to our neighbor; and one who deceives himself and his friends will not find it any easier to be honest with his God. Our own ethical actions are like stones thrown into a pool, driving ripples out further than we might at first think. Long ago, Confucius pointed out this ripple effect in one of his maxims:

> If there is harmony in the heart, there will be harmony in the character. If there is harmony in the character, there will be harmony in the family. If there is harmony in the family, there will be harmony in the nation. If there is harmony in the nation, there will be harmony in the world.[1]

The question before us is whether we can teach students to do the right thing, to have such "harmony in the heart." And if we can, how? In one sense, it is clear that morality can be taught. In the elementary years at Trinity, during the grammar stage of their education, they can be told what to do. They can memorize Proverbs and the Ten Commandments, and they can learn the classroom rules. They can also be shown how to act through stories of noble and virtuous characters. As they grow older and move into the logic stage in the middle grades, we can reinforce these lessons by teaching them to think about what is right. We can explain to these students, for example, that they should tell the truth even when it hurts. We can appeal to their reason (this is the way you would demand that someone treated you, were you on the other side); to their experience (remember what happened last year when we were trying to find out who scratched the car?); and to authority (Psalm 15:4). We could test them on it to see if they've "got it."

---

1. Confucius, "Righteousness in the Heart." In *The Book of Rites: Great Learning,* sec. 2.

6 – MORAL EDUCATION

For all of this good work, however, we know that there is work to be done before they have mastered this lesson. No one understood this difficult moral task better than the apostle Paul, who described his own moral struggle thus: "What I do is not the good I want to do; no, the evil I do not want to do—this I keep on doing" (Rom. 7:19). The problem with teaching morality, as Paul's confession makes clear, is that there is a serious civil war among the faculties of the human person. Effective teaching can replace ignorance or error with understanding, but such understanding, alone, cannot bring about a "harmony in the heart." Something else is needed.

What is lacking is a third thing between our reason (which can be taught morality), and our appetites or desires (which cannot). This third thing has been described in the classical tradition as the formation of habits of right desire, and in the Jewish and Christian traditions as training (Prov. 22:6; 1 Tim. 4:7,8). Children "learn" kindness or truthfulness by practicing it, by being corrected when they fail, by being held accountable for trying again, by being expected to learn the disciplines of these virtues. As with any habit, consistent practice and repeated use are essential, and one of the exciting things about a school like Trinity is that parents can expect that the same habits that are being formed at home are being reinforced at school. I hope that teachers and parents will be talking to each other about progress in these sorts of habits, even as we talk about progress in math or spelling. By attending to both the intellectual and the moral growth of our children, we will be giving them the best education we can, an education in truth and goodness and beauty.

A Jewish Book for a Christian School

MAY 3, 2002

> *I think that it was Pat Bassett, then president of the National Association of Independent Schools, who first told me about Dr. Wendy Mogel's book,* The Blessing of a Skinned Knee. *Pat would regularly come to the January conference of the North Carolina Association of Independent Schools, and among the many gems he brought us was his reading list. I got myself a copy of the book right away, and in Mogel I found an interlocutor for Trinity's distinctive educational vision, an ally who was different enough to keep us honest. Back in 2002, it was really helpful to find someone like this, someone the larger independent school world was listening to, who made me think, "We are not crazy at Trinity, with our distinctive mission. We might just be onto something important." I've since heard Mogel speak several times (most recently in Durham, when a consortium of schools brought her here to speak to parents). I've referenced her many times in Education Committee meetings or faculty workshops. We asked the entire faculty and parent body to read her book in the summer of 2002, and I think it did us all much good. One subtle but important message I was trying to send to the Trinity community: common grace means that wisdom abounds in the culture at large and, as Justin Martyr said, all that has been well said belongs to us Christians (*Second Apology *13.4).*

I want to recommend a book to the entire Trinity community. It's not the sort of book you'd expect me to endorse. It's a new book, and I like old ones. It's written by a psychologist and I prefer poets and philosophers. It's full of practical suggestions and I have a bias against how-to manuals. Its author is Jewish, and I'm a Christian.

But for all this, I can heartily recommend *The Blessing of a Skinned Knee* to every parent at Trinity. It's a book I am going to require all our teachers to read over the summer. Why?

6 — MORAL EDUCATION

First, because it's a vision-driven book, and that vision is religious. Its subtitle is "Using Jewish Teachings to Raise Self-Reliant Children." Wendy Mogel, the author, is not only a clinical psychologist, but a woman who is serious about her Jewish faith. Every chapter is informed by the transcendent, time-tested principles of Judaism: in particular, the trio of celebration, moderation, and sanctification. I'm sure that we Christian readers will quibble with her here or there, but I can assure you that you will find here a vision for childrearing that is infused with a reverence and wisdom that could only come from being in touch with the truth that is found in scripture and in religious tradition at its best.

Second, because it's a culturally suspicious book. Too much of what we read and hear today promises too much. Naively, we are urged to buy this or download that, and all will be well. At Trinity, we have always had a sense that these cultural wonders around us might be something like a Trojan horse—we fear the psychologists, even bearing gifts. Dr. Mogel shares our concerns. In the first chapter, she describes "how [she] lost one faith and found another." It was her rediscovery of her Jewish faith that gave her answers and a vision just at a time when she was losing confidence in her psychological certainties. This book is the fruit of that change. Here is an expert who has regained some common sense (Proverbs would call it wisdom). Here is a successful professional who has learned the dangers of success. Here is a modern who has learned from the rabbis of the past. Here is a Californian who is willing to move a little more slowly and go against the flow.

Thirdly, because it's eminently practical. This is not an overly simplistic how-to with lots of checklists, but it is full of good stuff you can start doing tonight. Listen to some of the headings: "Making Chores Matter: Lessons from the Farm"; "An Action Plan for Assigning Chores"; "Changes You Can Make at Mealtime"; "The Proper Rebuke: Expressing Displeasure without Humiliating Your Child"; "Homework: The Time Bandit." Each of these sections lays out a reasonable plan for action based on timeless principles from Jewish tradition.

Finally, I recommend this book because it was written by a Jewish psychologist from California—not the profile of the sort of person you'd expect to come lead a workshop for our teachers at Trinity. But Mogel provides a valuable touchstone for us, someone very different from us, who is discovering something very much like what we are learning about children and education. All truth is God's truth, and when people from very different backgrounds and perspectives see something that corresponds, they may well be onto something. We talk about an unhurried education; Mogel talks about "hurried parents" and "holy downtime." We talk about children as "glorious ruins" and "angel-beasts"; *The Blessing of a Skinned Knee* has a section on "Recognizing Your Child's Worst Behavior as Her Greatest Strength." We talk about balancing grace and law as we raise our children; this book espouses the rabbinic formula for effective parenting: one-third love, one-third law, and one-third sitting on our hands.

I do hope you enjoy and benefit from this book as much as I have. I'd love to hear your reactions once you've had a chance to read it.

The Gift of *Non Nobis*

September 9, 2005

During the 2004–2005 school year, we attempted to send out a monthly Column *and jettisoned the more frequent and newsy* Parent News. *Parents missed the familiar newsletter, and with this piece we relaunched the old format in the fall of 2005. The* Column *morphed into a quarterly magazine format, and now it is a digital flipbook. Jeremiah's proclamation still hangs in the Blue Gym, and* Non nobis *("Not to us," from Psalm 115:1) has worked its way solidly into the core values of the school. I am often pleased to be in a staff meeting and hear someone evaluate a proposal by giving it the* Non nobis *test. I hope that when our graduates return in ten or twenty years, they will remember* Non nobis *and be able say how they have taken that with them through their lives.*

Parents today are more anxious than parents a half century ago. I think my own parents had one or two serious conversations about where I was to go to school and then they were done. But I meet parents every week for whom this conversation about the right school is like the song that never ends.

David Brooks may have told us why this is so. In his perceptive and comical account of the new generation of the ruling class, *Bobos in Paradise*, Brooks chronicles a major shift in American culture from the 1950s until the present. In the middle of the last century, a typical *New York Times* wedding announcement would introduce the couple by highlighting *whom they knew*—their associations. Clubs, relatives, connections, ancestry, alma maters—these were the currency of the day. Today the couple is introduced by their résumés. College majors, graduate degrees, nonprofit volunteerism, honors and awards—today the currency of success is *what you've done*.

THE GIFT OF NON NOBIS

It's true that almost anyone can succeed now. If you work hard and excel, you can be what you want to be. The difficulty is that we have created a generation of young people who know that they must always perform at their very best, and even better if possible. They must be smart and strong and quick and clever. Such a life can be exhausting. Even by the time they've graduated from high school, most of our children could sing along with Bruce Cockburn: "I've proven who I am so many times, the magnetic strip's worn thin."[1] No wonder anxiety is on the rise. You may be at the top, but someone younger and more energetic, with the burst of ambition that you used to have, is yapping at your heels. There is an inverse relationship between opportunity and peace of mind.

Trinity School began in 1995, when the buds of this meritocracy were beginning to bloom. At first, we were largely immune to this cultural trend, for we were so young that people expected little from us and allowed us the freedom to do our own quirky thing. But we have come of age. With ten years under our belts, we are something of a success. More and more people expect us to enter the fray of this rat race, to do our part in producing this next generation of wunderkinds. We're starting to get bills for our dues to the cultural club.

Before we start paying those bills, I think it's worth asking whether a countercultural school might turn out to be a blessing, a liberation from the intense expectations of this new formula for success. And that is exactly what we hope Trinity School will be. We can't ignore the world we live in, and we need to prepare our children to navigate the best they can; but we can teach them to stand up in the middle of the show and shout, now and then, "Who do you think you're kidding?" The good news of the Gospel is that neither our connections nor our accomplishments will win us any favor with the One who counts; against

---

1. Bruce Cockburn, "Pacing the Cage." Produced by Bruce Cockburn and Colin Linda and recorded in 1996 on *The Charity of Night*, Phantom Sound: Vision-B000093FSA, compact disc.

6 – MORAL EDUCATION

these cultural pressures is the simple, outrageous love of God in Christ, and this is what matters.

This year's theme verse captures this truth eloquently. It comes from the prophet Jeremiah, who also lived in a time of much cultural upheaval and strain. Into that world he proclaimed,

> Let not the wise boast of their wisdom
>   or the strong boast of their strength
>   or the rich boast of their riches,
> but let the one who boasts, boast about this:
>   that they have the understanding to know me,
>   that I am the Lord, who exercises kindness,
>   justice, and righteousness on earth,
>   for in these I delight," declares the Lord.[2]

The wise, the strong, the rich—we don't disparage these folks, the kinds of people independent schools are always looking for. You could marshal our accreditation standards under those three rubrics. They are good gifts from God, and we hope to teach our children to recognize and celebrate God's gifting without boasting. We don't want to be misunderstood—these gifts are not evil, but they are not what really matters, either. And when they become the focus of our lives, they become pernicious.

The knowledge of God is the only boast that will not puff us up, for it begins with the recognition that our best is a gift and our accomplishments are incomplete. Jeremiah's proclamation of good news starts with "not" and "nor." That's where I'd like to see our students this year. I want Trinity to be a school where knowledge of God is the focus, where the smart kids, the athletic kids, the talented kids, and the popular kids all lay their best down on the altar, because they know that there is Someone better than even their best. Of course, before you lay down your best, you have to know what your best is; you have to do your best. That's when you can find your voice to sing, "Not to us,

---
2. Jer. 9:23-24.

Lord, not to us, but to your name be the glory." *Non nobis, Domine* is not just a quaint Latin phrase our students memorize—it's the most wonderful gift we can ever give them.

True Grit

December 2, 2011

My friend Bill Haslam sent me a text one day in the fall of 2011: "Have you read Paul Tripp's piece in the NYT?" I had not, but as soon as I did I recognized that the matter the KIPP schools were wrestling with was spot-on for Trinity as well. Since that time, I have become even more convinced that the trait (or constellation of traits) we call grit is a true difference-maker in the lives of students. Sadly, I've also become convinced that our culture increasingly coddles and protects youth from things that could hurt them but teach them important lessons. Independent school parents probably have even more of this temptation: they are used to "taking care of" things, and they may think that their investment in education is too great to allow for failure. I think an honest conversation between school and home about when and how much to allow students to fail is an important one.

If you picked 100 American eighth graders at random, how many would graduate from college within ten years? Thirty-one. If that number seems low to you, try not to lose your sense of surprise, because it is low and it's not a number we as a nation can afford to settle for. For eighth graders who come from low-income homes, the number is eight. In a world where the jobs are increasingly going to people all over the world whose thinking and communication skills are critical and creative ("knowledge workers"), this is a real problem.

And the problem might be more complicated than you think. Just ask David Levin, founder of KIPP charter schools (Knowledge Is Power Program), made famous by the documentary *Waiting for Superman*. Levin learned something important in his early years of KIPP. The first group of students to enter KIPP blew expectations out of the water: They were the fifth-highest performing class in all of New York City, with 90 percent of their middle school graduates entering private or parochial schools. Of those, 80 percent enrolled in college (quite a bit higher than the national statistic for eighth graders). But then the mountain got steeper. Ten years out from middle school, only 33 percent of KIPP graduates had finished four years of college, beating the national average but far below KIPP's stated goal of 75 percent.

Education writer Paul Tough wrote about Levin's experience in *The New York Times Magazine*, "What If the Secret to Success Is Failure?"[1] As Levin watched the progress of those KIPP alumni, he noticed something curious: the students who persisted in college were not necessarily the ones who had excelled academically at KIPP. They were the ones with exceptional character strengths, like optimism and persistence and social intelligence. They were the ones who were able to recover from a bad grade and resolve to do better next time, to bounce back from a fight with their parents, to resist the urge to go out to the movies and stay home and study instead, to persuade professors to give them extra help after class. Those skills weren't enough on their own to earn students a BA, Levin knew. But for young people without the benefit of a lot of family resources, without the kind of safety net that their wealthier peers enjoyed, these skills seemed an indispensable part of making it to graduation day.

This account agrees with Walter Mischel's Marshmallow Test.[2] In 1970 at Stanford, Mischel set four-year-olds in a room and put a marshmallow in front of them. He told them they could eat the marshmallow if they wanted, but that he was going to leave the room and if the marshmallow was still there when he returned, he would give them two marshmallows. Mischel followed his four-year-olds for many years, and what he discovered was astounding: Kids who waited to eat the marshmallow did better in school and had fewer behavioral

---

1. Paul Tough, "What If the Secret to Success Is Failure?" *New York Times Magazine*, September 14, 2011, http://www.nytimes.com/2011/09/18/magazine/what-if-the-secret-to-success-is-failure.html. Reprinted on September 11, 2011, MM38, under the headline "The Character Test."

2. Walter Mischel and Ebbe B. Ebbesen, "Attention in Delay of Gratification," *Journal of Personality and Social Psychology* 16, no. 2 (1970), 329–37.

problems; they also had better social skills in middle school. Those children who could wait a full fifteen minutes scored on average 210 points higher on their SATs—the marshmallow test turned out to be a better predictor of SAT scores than an IQ test. Twenty years out, these students had higher college completion rates. Thirty years later, they had much higher income levels. In contrast, the kids who didn't wait to eat their marshmallows had higher incarceration rates and were much more likely to suffer drug and alcohol abuse. The children who waited for the two marshmallows usually had grown up in organized homes—places where they had learned from early on the connection between actions and consequences, where they had learned strategies for mastering immediate temptations and delaying gratification.

It turns out that character development—what Charlotte Mason called the training of the will by the formation of habits—is some of the most important work parents and teachers can do. And, as Mason knew so well, the home is more important in this work than the school. Still, a strong partnership between home and school can be a powerful influence in a child's life. Self-control, perseverance, grit, stick-to-it-ness, resilience, toughness, courage—these are the real difference makers.

How are we developing these traits at Trinity School?

First, by holding students to high expectations and giving them strong support to reach that high bar. "Easy to please, hard to satisfy"—that's a good description of a Trinity teacher, I hope. Our persuasive writing rubric in the Upper School is a great example: the same rubric applies to freshmen and to seniors, but as the students improve in their writing, the expectations for their competency rise. Everyone must master the basics of persuasive writing, but true excellence is rare. Students are urged to keep at it. There is no such thing as good writing, as a mentor of mine said—only good rewriting.

Second, by encouraging students to take risks and to make failure a part of the story. I worry for students who graduate from high school never having failed at something. Sooner or later, that failure will come, and woe to him who stares down the mouth of that dark monster for the first time at twenty-one, when the stakes are so high and the supports so low. Our robotics program is an excellent way for students to experience this kind of failure. I've been amazed to see how often those robots malfunction, just when they ought to be functioning optimally. And I've been equally amazed at the resilience of our students to dive into the mess and not lose heart.

Third, by pushing students to sacrifice regularly. Athletics might be the best place this kind of thing happens, day in and day out. On an athletic team, one is constantly sacrificing: the sacrifice of painful physical training, the sacrifice of putting team before self, the sacrifice of sportsmanship over selfishness, the sacrifice of submission to the coach. I'm told that the Duke of Wellington probably didn't actually utter his most famous line; still, I know it could have been true: "The Battle of Waterloo was won on the playing fields of Eton." Guts and grit come from training yourself to gut it out and grit it out; and nowhere does a young person have the chance for that more regularly than on the athletic field.

This is the kind of work that small independent schools do so well. And this is the kind of work that small independent Christian schools can do exceptionally well. *Non nobis.*

On Habit and Character

February 28, 2014

This is the youngest of the essays in this volume, but it has been a long time in the making. We have been talking about the formation of habit for a very long time at Trinity, and one of the first things we all learned about Charlotte Mason was her wisdom about habit. Early in the school's life, Mason educator Jack Beckman came to Trinity to share with us about habits as one very practical outworking of what Mason meant by saying that "Education is a discipline." As I was putting this volume together, I realized that I didn't have a proper article on habit, and so this is the one essay that was written with this book in mind. What is fascinating to me, and gratifying as well, is the way that Mason's hundred-year-old ideas and Aristotle's even more ancient thinking are being explored and largely vindicated by the work of modern brain scientists.

Parents choose independent schools for a host of reasons, but research by the National Association of Independent Schools shows that the number one reason is that they care about character. If this is true of independent schools in general, how much more for a Christian school, where parents know that the fruit of the Spirit (Gal. 5:22-23) has greater long-term benefit than a good GPA. Character matters.

For the formation of character, habit is essential. Aristotle claimed that we become virtuous by practicing the sort of acts that the good person would choose. Habits are the path to *arete* (which can be translated as either "excellence" or "virtue").[1] Some will ask what Aristotle has to teach us Christians about how to develop character. Granted, grace is supernatural, and without the Spirit lasting character is not possible; but God works his wonders through very ordinary means,

---

1. Aristotle, *Nicomachean Ethics* 2.4.

and Christians learn virtues like patience just as everyone else does: by practicing.

Christian educator Charlotte Mason held much the same idea in her book *A Philosophy of Education*. Character is formed by repeated acts. Acts that are repeated so often that they become automatic we call habits. The formation of habits can serve to strengthen the will, to create what Mason calls a "good will," by which she does not mean benevolence (as the phrase is often taken) but a will that is what a will should be: strong.[2] A good will can act on its own, which is the very heart of moral action. The one who does the right thing even when it hurts is the one who has practiced, over and over, doing the right thing when it hurts. He who is faithful in little will be faithful in much.

There are many admirable habits. Some are intellectual (attentiveness, thoroughness, curiosity, wonder); some are moral (truthfulness, responsibility, hospitality, humility). A liberal education will educate students liberally in many exemplars of all these habits and more. The younger we begin this work, the stronger the foundation. The teachers of our youngest children do a great work for the rest of us, laying down the rails of habit early on. At Trinity we focus on three in particular: attentiveness, respect, and responsibility. Of course we want more than these three virtues for our children, but this is a fine start, a foundation upon which the rest of their schooling can be built. Students who can attend will make better scientists and better close readers when they grow up; students who respect others and know that there is a real value to aiming outside themselves will value the wisdom in a book, in a teacher, in a dialogue partner; and students who take responsibility for their own actions and learning will complete their lessons and do the work for themselves.

Modern brain science has confirmed and clarified what the philosophers and educators have told us. Jeremy Dean set out to discover what science could teach us about how long it takes to form habits and how

---

2. Charlotte Mason, *Philosophy of Education*, 99–104.

to make them stick. His book, *Making Habits, Breaking Habits* explores the plasticity of the brain and the neurological foundations of habit-making.[3] Dean discovered that habits are formed on an inverted curve, so that early gains are easier than later ones. He also discovered that the popular psychological wisdom that it takes twenty-one days to form a new habit is far too simple and, in the case of most habits, far too short. Maria Popova has reviewed Dean's book on her blog, *Brainpickings* (one of the best blogs I can recommend, by the way).[4]

Psychologist and philosopher William James wrote a book on habit a century ago, and his practical suggestions are still worth considering today. I close with his advice from Chapter 8:

> [In] the acquisition of a new habit, or the leaving off of an old one, we must take care to launch ourselves with as strong and decided an initiative as possible. Accumulate all the possible circumstances which shall reinforce the right motives; put yourself assiduously in conditions that encourage the new way; make engagements incompatible with the old; take a public pledge, if the case allows; in short, envelop your resolution with every aid you know. This will give your new beginning such a momentum that the temptation to break down will not occur as soon as it otherwise might; and every day during which a breakdown is postponed adds to the chances of its not occurring at all...
>
> Never suffer an exception to occur till the new habit is securely rooted in your life. Each lapse is like the letting fall of a ball of string which one is carefully winding up; a single slip undoes more than a great many turns will wind again. Continuity of training is the great means of making the nervous system act infal-

---

3. Jeremy Dean, *Making Habits, Breaking Habits: Why We Do Things, Why We Don't, and How to Make Any Change Stick* (Boston: Da Capo Lifelong, 2013).

4. www.brainpickings.org/index.php/2014/01/02/how-long-it-takes-to-form-a-new-habit.

libly right...It is surprising how soon a desire will die of inanition if it be never fed.

Seize the very first possible opportunity to act on every resolution you make, and on every emotional prompting you may experience in the direction of the habits you aspire to gain. It is not in the moment of their forming, but in the moment of their producing motor effects, that resolves and aspirations communicate the new 'set' to the brain.[5]

One of the great values of a school like Trinity is that we can partner with parents to create a learning culture that reinforces the same good habits you are practicing at home, so that our children can follow James's advice and form the sorts of habits that will serve them well for the rest of their lives. "The ordering of the will is not an affair of sudden resolve; it is the outcome of a slow and ordered education in which precept and example flow in from the lives and thoughts of other men, men of antiquity and men of the hour, as unconsciously and spontaneously as the air we breathe."[6]

None of this is for ourselves, as though the goal were to become paragons of good habits. All good education is outward focused, on something other than the self. Good habits are good because they shape the self to love God first and others next. We are third. May God grant us grace to form habits that serve others well and point us to Christ. *Non nobis.*

---

5. William James, *Habit* (New York: Henry Holt & Co., 1890), 55–56, 59, 60.
6. Charlotte Mason, *Philosophy of Education*, 137.

7 – The Arts

Late have I loved you, O beauty, so ancient and so new.

Augustine of Hippo, *Confessions*

Christian schools usually emphasize truth and goodness, but beauty is often extracurricular or an elective. From the start, we had a sense that a focus on beauty was indispensable to our being an excellent school, especially an excellent Christian school. Credit for this goes in large part to founding board member Nancy Brooks, whose musical experience and expertise gave us wisdom beyond our years.

De Gustibus

December 2004

I have struggled, and still do, to articulate just how we understand beauty as an objective transcendent. I do believe with all my heart that it is, and Aquinas's thinking on this (Augustine had similar understandings) has always seemed clear-headed. But in practice, it is often hard to avoid a sense of snobbery or elitism when it comes to describing the standards by which something is judged to be beautiful. Maybe the most we can say is that a good classical and Christian education will give students the wherewithal to struggle with this question. To be honest, sometimes in these Parent News *covers I have felt that the best I could do was not to offer answers so much as to demonstrate an educated and faithful way of struggling toward understanding.*

Jack Sprat could eat no fat, his wife could eat no lean. One man's meat is another man's poison. *De gustibus non est disputandum,* as the maxim goes: "About matters of taste, there is no disputing." If there is, it will go on forever, or someone will storm out angry.

Truth, goodness, and beauty abide, but the hardest to define is beauty. So why don't I write a newsletter column on something else? Because our theme for the year, taken from Philippians 4:8, is an exhortation from Paul to think about things excellent or praiseworthy.

What makes a thing beautiful? Thomas Aquinas, who might be the smartest man to have lived in the last thousand years, said that beauty is both objective and subjective. There are conditions which any beautiful thing must meet, three to be precise: *integrity, proportion, and clarity.*[1] You might want to dispute these three, but if you think about it, he makes a good point (as usual). The South Building on UNC's campus is beautiful for the integrity of its parts. The golden sunlight in

---

1. Aquinas, *Summa Theologica* 1.39.8.

7 – THE ARTS

the last hour of the day is beautiful for its clarity. And the font Perpetua, created by Eric Gill in the early part of the twentieth century is beautiful for its proportions. (Compare it, for example, to `Courier New`, which is clunky and pedestrian.) Like truth and goodness, beauty is a reflection of some standard that is, simply, *real*.

At the same time, it's clear that people differ in the degree to which they possess good perception and sound critical judgment. We are all of us, in different ways, tone deaf to the beauty in the world. I, for one, admit that I've never really enjoyed an opera. Now it's possible that all opera is kitsch, but I know it is much more likely that there's something I'm missing. I assume that Captain Corelli heard something I've never heard.

Opera we can take or leave, and live without, but there is an unworldly beauty which we must find somehow or else be miserable for all eternity. I mean the Gospel, by which the One without beauty or majesty (Isaiah 53) shows himself to be Fairest Lord Jesus. I remember what Augustine said at age thirty-two when he found that beauty: "Late have I loved you, O beauty, so ancient and so new!"[2] Early or late, there is hope for us all.

Indeed, Trinity is a school for philistines like you and me, and our children, of course. The world is too much with us, late and soon, and we walk through it—no, we run through it—blind to the beauty all around us. Have you ever been over on campus during the last hour of the day, when the sun sets over the trees behind the soccer field? If you're rushing to pick up children and hurrying home, you might have missed that fine sight. Trinity's education aims to help students *find* beauty in nature and in human culture (through nature studies, picture studies, and art and music appreciation); and *create* beauty for themselves. Lower School students are not too young to create works of art that are beautiful in their very substance, that are created not so much to be used as to be enjoyed. If you don't believe me, come tour

---

2. Augustine, *Confessions* 10.27.

the halls of the school and see what these children have drawn under the able tutelage of our art teacher Eleatta Diver. Cindy Metzger Phillips once made me a set of notecards adorned with Trinity student art, and they are some of the finest cards I've ever seen, the work of real artists—Cindy and the kids. Every time I send one I hope that someone else sees what I see.

Strange Artists

April 2005

In the spring of 1996, I had another job and still another job offer in my hometown of Knoxville, and I came very close to doing something different from Trinity. The school, I knew, was taking a big risk on me and I on the school. I had such a steep learning curve. The incident I recounted ten years later in this piece was indeed decisive—we are moved by what we love, and I loved beauty. I owe Trinity music teacher Mary McKinney and the first Grandparents Day a great debt. The beauty that Trinity students create continues to amaze me. Just this past year I wandered into the stairwell to discover the Upper School Vocal Ensemble singing "Carol of the Bells" inside that sound chamber, and the joy came over me again.

> *This creature was truly different from all other creatures, because he was a creator as well as a creature.*
>
> – G. K. Chesterton, *The Everlasting Man*

I forget, sometimes, that I work in an art gallery and a concert hall. One afternoon last week I ducked into the deserted TK classroom for a solitary moment, only to be startled by vivid paper clowns tumbling on the bulletin board. Like Dorothy, I was not in Kansas anymore—transported from a black and white day into a Technicolor moment by the handiwork of some five-year-olds. On other days I've heard Handel wafting from the music room, and I wonder why they pay me to do this job.

I'm not alone in my pleasure. Lots of people ogle the artwork in the Trinity hallways, and I hear them talk about what they like. Some people fancy these elementary art shows because they are so, well... elementary. They enjoy the rough, primitive, unpracticed lines and forms. Others find pleasure in the opposite: hints of real talent, the mimicking of greatness, art that looks almost grown-up. I can appreciate both of those tastes, but the wonder of Trinity artwork for me is something else. It looks so *human*, which is to say, it looks so strange. Strange when you compare it to the work of all God's other creatures and creations.

If we ran a school for birds, we might line the walls with birds' nests, each different in small ways but all, really the same. As G. K. Chesterton pointed out, a bird can get as far as building a nest, and will surely sing with satisfaction when he is done. But he will get no further. Birds don't experiment with seven different styles of nest architecture; they don't use twigs and leaves to express the grandeur or the sobriety of a certain kind of nest; they don't, most of all, make little statues of birds to adorn their nests. All this, and more, our students at Trinity do before they get to second grade. And that is no tribute to our art program, as good as it is. It is simply what you get when you teach human beings instead of birds.

We sons of Adam and daughters of Eve are, essentially, living mirrors. We are called in scripture the image of God (*imago Dei*)—i.e., the mirror of God—and whenever we reflect anything in creation, we somehow mirror (imperfectly, yet truly) that divine nature. If we lined the halls of Trinity with looking glasses, we might have a gallery of sorts, but not half so interesting as the hallways lined with the eighth graders' self-portraits. Not nearly so shocking as being greeted by the bright TK clowns.

When the going gets tough, some schools cut their art and music budgets. Never on my watch at Trinity School. Truth, goodness, and beauty make a stool that wobbles badly on two legs. A Christian school ought to lead the way in the arts: visual, musical, dramatic, dance.

Nine years ago this spring I was wrestling with whether to stay in pastoral ministry or take a sharp vocational turn by giving headmastering a try. On the verge of this decision, I stood at the back of the au-

7 – THE ARTS

ditorium at the Erwin Road campus, watching the first Trinity School Grandparents Day. When the students, directed by music teacher Mary McKinney, began to sing the "Tallis Canon," I knew what I wanted: "Why would I not want a job where this kind of beauty is being made every day?" Nine years later, I am still surprised and pleased by the strange and wonderful art of these little humans we call Trinity students.

Struggling Toward Originality

MAY 19, 2006

> *In 2006, Desirée and I had the chance to go on a river tour down the Danube, including a visit to Salzburg. In preparation for that trip, I read Gay's biography of Mozart, which happened to coincide with some important curriculum work on writing at Trinity. The phrase of the title still strikes me as profound, as does the irony that I try to unpack at the end, an irony that is mirrored by the Gospel ("if anyone would save his life, he must lose it"). Today, I would express myself a little differently: I would not spare originality any of the hard words here, but I would distinguish creativity from originality and work harder to find the proper place for that at every level of education. It is this human capacity to think God's thoughts after him and to create meaning out of the data of our experience that is one of the reflections of the* imago Dei. *The arts and creative writing do this in important ways, even alongside the mastery of scales and the copying of exemplars.*

If ever there was a child prodigy, surely it was the one whose 250th birthday we celebrate this year. Before he was six, Wolfgang Gottlieb Mozart[1] began his touring as a musician, amazing audiences with his photographic memory, his skill at the keyboard, and his gift for weaving variations around a theme. His proud father wrote in 1764, "Now four sonatas by Mr. Wolfgang Mozart are at the engraver's, and imagine the noise these sonatas will make in the world when it says on the title page that they are the work of a child of seven."

Nowadays, we all want to raise Mozarts. All of our children are above average. Baby Einstein sells because we dream of raising ge-

---

1. This is the German translation of the name of the composer known more commonly as Wolfgang Amadeus Mozart. His full baptismal name was Johannes Chrysostomus Wolfgangus Theophilus Mozart.

7 – THE ARTS

niuses. Wolfgang's father was hard enough to deal with in his own day; I shudder to think what it would be like if Leopold walked into the Trinity Admission Office today and demanded, "What can you do for my son?"

But Mozart was no postmodern prodigy. He was born at just the perfect time for his genius. We often say that Mozart and his ilk define the classical era in music; but we might as truly say that the classical era shaped Mozart. Classicism assumes that the role of education is to teach the young student to know and love those expressions of truth, goodness, and beauty that have gone before—even if you are a Mozart who will one day write the *Jupiter* Symphony. Peter Gay has written,

> Mozart spent invaluable hours in [his] apprentice years listening to the works of composers then in vogue, and like other novices, he diligently copied them out. His uncommonly alert absorptive capacity always awake, he freely appropriated dominant styles, and the musical ideas of his foremost contemporaries reverberated in his own. *His manner of educating himself was the manner of nearly every great artist: he struggled toward originality by studying and imitating his elders* [italics added].[2]

At Trinity we have adopted this same "manner of educating." It is the classical method, and it agrees entirely in this crucial regard with the aims and methods of Charlotte Mason. One begins by listening to classic stories, by observing master painters, by listening to the great composers. Then follows the productive phase of learning (an early form of rhetoric) in which the student tells back the story, reproduces the painting with words, reflects on the music just heard. Like Benjamin Franklin, the student learns to write, first, by mimicking his elders. Practice and imitation are the means toward great writing. Students should aim, first, to write in a way that is pleasing; later they can learn to be original. One of the ironies of education is that if we aim at

---

2. Peter Gay, *Mozart* (London: Weidenfeld & Nicolson, 1999), 14.

originality first, we will miss it; but if we aim at skillful imitation, and stick with it, we will eventually find our own voice and say that thing that God made for *us* to say. This is true for geniuses like Mozart, for would-be geniuses like Salieri, for talented amateurs, and for hacks like me who never made it beyond the first Suzuki book.

The work of the Writing Task Force this year has moved Trinity forward toward a scope and sequence that is well matched to students' developmental capacities, so that what is done at one grade is the right preparation for the next grade's objectives. And all of this is based on this fundamental principle of classical education: imitation and mastery first, originality second. In the current climate of education, in which creative writing starts in preschool, this approach will seem crazy and misguided, and we will be misunderstood. We will be said to devalue originality. Let us be precise: originality is important, but it is not the most important thing, as Adam and Eve learned with their wonderfully creative original sin. If they had obeyed first, they would have found the only true and liberating originality, in submission to the One who alone is original. In that relationship, we each have our own song of praise to sing. May each student at Trinity School find his voice and sing along with the morning stars.

The Aristocracy of Art
February 2008

Reading Gilson's The Arts of the Beautiful *was one of the most pleasurable intellectual experiences of my life. Trinity board member MaryAnn Roper and her husband Bill had offered me their Pawleys Island beach house for a week's study leave, and I nestled into their cozy place in the winter of 2008 to read what this Thomist had to say about art. We were in the middle of a subtle but important crisis over the nature of arts education—especially in music—and I wanted someone to lift me above the fray of strong opinions. What I have written here is really just a poor précis of what he says in that important book. My goal here was to raise a high bar for the beautiful, to celebrate adequately that great transcendent, to call Trinity to an unattainable goal that was worth reaching for. I realize, upon rereading this, that I may have in the process denigrated some very worthy goals that serve our students well and inform their vocations. I was hard here on all imposters because I wanted to call forth the real thing, the* pulchritudo *of our motto.*

There are many good reasons for studying the arts in school, but most of them are incidental to the nature of art itself.

Let me count the ways, with much help from Etienne Gilson's excellent monograph, *The Arts of the Beautiful*.[1]

We can study the arts (and here I mean the fine arts of music, drama, painting, sculpture, etc.) in order to understand what they *mean*. What, for example, can we learn about the Renaissance by listening to Palestrina? What can Bach teach us about Lutheranism and Pietism? This is art in the service of truth.

. 1. Etienne Gilson, *The Arts of the Beautiful* (New York: Scribner, 1965).

Or we could study the arts to inspire ourselves to live better. Victor Hugo's portrait of Jean Valjean's redemption from misery through legalism into the virtuous life powered by grace in *Les Misérables* may help us find our own way through hard times. This is art in the service of the good.

Or we could study art to enhance our creativity. This is, of course, a worthy goal. And in a world increasingly powered by creativity, such training is invaluable. The best, most secure, least fungible jobs go, more and more, to those who know how to bring creative solutions to the table. This is art in service of commerce.

Or we could study art to become artists ourselves. This is getting closer to the heart of the matter, and who among us would gainsay such a thing? Everyone's an artist these days. I've even done some painting of my own. But I am no artist, nor the son of an artist. My art is, at best, art imitating nature. At worst, it is art imitating art, trying to paint like something I saw in a gallery in Florida. This is art, but not fine art—not that which pleases of itself, for itself. I do not mean, in any way, to denigrate the fine work that many of us have done in an attempt to explore God's amazing world, but simply to admit what is surely true: that my best work is closer to that of a skilled craftsman than to a true artist. Mine is art in service of craftsmanship.

Or we could study art to imitate nature. Nature studies are this sort of thing: the faithful reproduction of a leaf, a flower, a mushroom. This too is a glory but not an art. Art is different from imitation. Imitation is the reproduction of nature. Art is the making of beauty. God allows this new creation of beauty; the artist really does create. Imitative art is more accessible and its pleasures are morally harmless. I expect that much, very much, of what we enjoy as "art" is really imitation. Most of the time it is impossible for the artist and the spectator to know how much of the pleasure in art is due to the work itself (the only truly artistic pleasure), how much is due to some meaning assigned to it, and how much is due to the object it imitates. It is because of this inevitable

7 – THE ARTS

problem and complexity that some modern artists have attempted to portray the ugly and the abstract, for by these acts they seek to isolate the pleasure of art itself. One questions, however, how successful these efforts can be. This all is art in the service of nature and the beauty of nature.

Or we could study art in order to learn how to study art. We could teach our students to discern the elements of the beautiful: unity, harmony, radiance. We could teach them to listen carefully to enough Mozart that they will be able to recognize and discuss Mozart's *style*. This art appreciation is invaluable, and a good school will teach it, but it is not itself art. This is art in the service of aesthetics.

The glory of the beautiful is that it pleases in itself, for itself. There are different kinds of beauty: the beauty of nature, the beauty of knowledge, and the beauty of art. The last of these is a beauty unlike the others. Unlike the beauty of nature, the beauty of art always presupposes the artist—he or she is always there. (This will sound heretical, I know, but I believe that in whatever sense God is the "artist" of nature, he is an artist very unlike a Picasso or a Haydn.) Unlike the beauty of knowledge, the beauty of art is not primarily concerned with truth. The difference between our experience of these two sorts of beauty is evident to anyone who has pondered the difference, say, between discovering the meaning of Newton's laws and discovering Bach's Cantata 140. The former, once discovered, can never really be discovered again. The latter can be discovered time and time again. Though you may tire of it, after a little while you will love it again, as for the first time, or better.

Since this is the nature of art and the beautiful, there are two other important reasons for studying art, both of which strike closer to the heart of the matter for us.

We could study art in order to know that we are not artists ourselves. We are all talented, but there are few geniuses. Knowing the difference is, I think, quite important. Talented artists achieve *from the outside* that unity which is of the essence of the beautiful, achieving it from an artificial form, by imitation (though the best talents are creative and not slavish); genius, however, generates the unity *from within*, while conceiving the form which will become the work. I suppose that there is no more important lesson we can teach our children than that they are not geniuses. (That is, unless they *are* geniuses, which is quite unlikely, and which is not a secret that the world will be able to keep from them for long anyway.)

And finally, we could study art in order to learn that we are philistines. This too is an essential lesson and one not easily learned. We are all tone-deaf to some fine art—or most of us are. And as we go about in the world we learn that all manner of numbskulls and ruffians hear sounds and see tones we cannot see. Training can help in this pursuit, but the truth is that the beautiful is not a mountain easily climbed, and those who ascend are not always the brightest or the best among us. Who dares think that he can see what Cézanne saw or hear what Beethoven heard? "It takes a great deal of modesty to become familiar with great works. Like the world of nature, the world of art is an aristocracy; every man must accept his place, for if its access can be democratized to a certain extent, it cannot itself undergo the same process without being annihilated."[2]

Of the three transcendents—truth, goodness, and beauty—beauty is the humblest. She attends the others without making much of a fuss about herself. Some have even recommended, "Tend to truth and goodness, and beauty will take care of herself." I don't know about that. But I do know that she will not complain if we abuse her, and that we can live without her, but if we find her, we will spend the rest of our lives trying to find her again.

---

2. Gilson, *Arts*, 39.

8 – Diversity

I have a dream that one day...the sons of former slaves and the sons of former slave owners will be able to sit down together at the table of brotherhood.

– Martin Luther King, Jr.

The history of diversity and inclusion at Trinity is rich, and the road to where we are in our twentieth year has been steep at times, winding back upon itself. Still, I do think and hope that we are moving forward. I remember the courage of a few African-American families in those early years—Earnest and Cameron Smith were our first pioneers, followed by Nelson and Vickie Turner. I remember the reading and prayer group that Betsy Poole and Rick Adams gathered together. Then there was the task force, headed by faculty member Deidra Coles and John Sharon, our division director at that time. The task force produced a strategic plan, out of which came the board's establishment of a permanent committee, which we called the Koinonia Committee. Alicia Ramos and Perrianne Davis were instrumental in crafting a statement on diversity (which we still proudly publish on our website). And the vision of board member Hubert Davis has spurred us on as well. Now Adrienne Davis is doing excellent work as Trinity's first diversity coordinator.

8 – DIVERSITY

We're not where we want to be, but we're not where we were, either. To God be the glory for our successes; the faults are ours. Let us press on toward the goals of making Trinity School accessible to as many as possible and of shaping the student body to look as much like the kingdom of God as possible.

Everybody's Doing Diversity—But Not Like This

AUGUST 2009

This piece and the next go together, and they are set here in their rightful place at the head of this section. In 2006, the board made the important decision to establish a permanent Diversity Committee, which we called our Koinonia Committee, after the biblical word for shared community and partnership. That committee set out to write the school's first Diversity Policy, which was approved by the board in the spring of 2008. It was published that year with the following introduction. It should be noted in a book of essays that the policy itself is not mine, but the work of many minds, and especially of Alicia Ramos and Perrianne Davis. But in a book aimed at passing along the school's mission to a new generation, I would want this seminal and exemplary policy to be included. I am always proud to share it with others, for I think it captures the mission of Trinity as it works itself into the life of the school in this vitally important area.

Diversity is all the rage. Everybody's doing it. This would seem to make Trinity School's new Diversity Statement quite unremarkable. We might as well feature the school's Personnel Handbook in the next issue of the *Column*. But Trinity's Diversity Statement is remarkable, and we've enclosed a copy in this issue, so that you can see for yourself. And while some may be yawning, others may be bristling. Some of us will be skeptical at the very mention of a diversity statement. "Everybody's Doing It" is not a particularly biblical slogan. Whatever happened to not conforming to the world? Read for yourself and see whether you think the school has managed to chart a vision for diversity which is distinctively Trinity—and Trinitarian.

8 – DIVERSITY

I think we have. This is Trinity at its best: engaging the culture (if everybody's talking about diversity, shouldn't we have something to say about it?), but challenging it too by taking captive every thought to make it obedient to Christ (2 Cor. 10:5). The statement is a sort of exegesis of Trinity's mission—the mission is dominant. We have not changed the school's motto to "Truth, Goodness, Beauty, and Diversity." Rather, we have asked ourselves, "If truth, goodness, and beauty are our transcendent vision, what does this mean for diversity at Trinity?" I hope that you will be as excited as we are by some of the answers this statement begins to imagine.

It is fitting that we should launch this statement in a year when we have dedicated ourselves to living out the biblical injunction to "show hospitality" (1 Peter 4:9). The hospitality of God is profound: in Christ we who were God's enemies have been made sons and daughters. This journey from hostility to hospitality is a steep climb, impossible apart from the Incarnation of God, and everything in our baser nature wants to go the other way. The stranger is one to be feared, not welcomed. He threatens my world, my peace, my comfort, my tidy worldview. If I open the front door and invite him in, what will this stranger bring? What will he ask of me? Will he take my silverware? Will he take, somehow, my very self away from me? Do these questions seem over the top? When we've asked our students to speak and write about these things, they sometimes reflect attitudes and fears which show that we have a lot of work to do in this area. The hospitality of God is a hard act to follow, but that is what 1 Peter 4:9 calls us to. It is that hospitality which this statement praises. "The earth is the Lord's, and everything in it," but he opened his front door and invited us in, despite all the mud we track in and the fact that we are inclined to steal his candlesticks. And around the hearth of God we find people who are different from us in all sorts of ways. And if the Lord has accepted them, how ought we to live? Our Upper Schoolers aren't the only ones who need to ask themselves this question. This Diversity Statement is for us all.

The statement has been a long time in the making. By my count there have been three diversity task forces or committees of the school. The first, going back at least to 2001, did a lot of reading and praying, under the guidance of former board member Rick Adams and our own Betsy Poole. The second, under the leadership of former teacher Deidra Coles and former director John Sharon, wrote a strategic plan for diversity. The board received that plan in 2006 and put the first recommendation into effect: to establish a board committee for diversity, which they named the Koinonia Committee. It went right to work on this statement. Many thanks go to chair Alicia Ramos and committee member Perrianne Davis, who were the Jefferson and Adams of this project. The entire board approved this resolution last spring at its April meeting.

We are proud to show this statement to our prospective parents, to colleges who are now visiting our Upper School and checking us out, to candidates who apply to teach here, to our accrediting organization, and most of all to you, our parents, grandparents, and friends. Please join us in celebrating this vision and in doing all we can this year to practice hospitality and thus enhance the diversity which we already enjoy here at Trinity.

Trinity's Diversity Policy

May 2008

> *This board policy was the child of much good discussion at the Koinonia Committee. Seven years out, it is still a strong and relevant piece.*

In seeking to reflect the kingdom of God, Trinity School encourages diversity in its student body, staff, faculty, and community. The vision of diversity at Trinity is uniquely Christian and flows out of our mission.[1] The image of a diverse Trinity community is scripturally based and is already implicit in each of the five core distinctives, mentioned below, in the Expanded Mission Statement.

The Framework of Christian Faith: Diversity in the Trinity community enhances Christian faith and conviction in crucial ways. Exposure to diverse students, teachers, and leaders can demonstrate to children that people can have a perspective that is thoroughly Christian and transcends differences. Diversity in the body of Christ is also essential for the cultivation of Christian character. Exposure to those who are different in race, ethnicity, physical ability, socioeconomics, religious traditions, talents, and learning styles serves to enhance the teaching of habits of fairness, humility, truthfulness, courage, compassion, and interdependence.

Truth, Goodness, and Beauty: Trinity strives to prepare students for "benevolent engagement" with the culture at large. Exposure to various cultures, life experiences, and perspectives serves to train young people to see goodness in the variety of God's human creation and virtue in every culture, despite our universal fallenness. Such a perspective leads to a deeper and richer appreciation for beauty, an ap-

---

1. See "Explaining the Mission Statement of Trinity School" on the Trinity School website, www.trinityschoolnc.org.

preciation encompassing the full spectrum of color, rather than being monochromatic.

Classical Tools of Learning: Trinity's philosophy is not focused on memorizing content, but rather on teaching students how to learn for themselves. Through the classical tools of learning, Trinity strives to encourage children to ask all questions, discuss ideas, and analyze concepts. All of these tasks require exposure to various points of view. A diverse student body brings a variety of thought and experience that stimulate students to think more critically. In this way Trinity prepares students for benevolent engagement with today's increasingly globalized society.

A Rich and Unhurried Curriculum: Our culture often embraces diversity in a superficial sense, promoting a vision of tolerance among autonomous individuals rather than reconciliation between people in communities. In contrast, the educational mission at Trinity emphasizes going deep rather than going broad. Time is taken to appreciate the richness of God's gifts. We encourage relationships with ideas and deep discourse as opposed to the larger culture's consumption of superficial experiences without meaning. In this same way, embracing diversity at Trinity is in alignment with its principles of dipping profoundly into a story and drinking of the greater meaning. We encourage going deeply into the narratives of various groups not merely for tolerance, but for true understanding and reconciliation and insight into how these stories fit into The Great Story.

At Trinity, diversity has a distinctly Christian underpinning. We believe that embracing a diverse student body flows out of the framework of Christian faith and conviction. Living harmoniously, within the body of Christ alongside those who are of various diverse backgrounds, is implicit in the Christian mission and enhances the distinctives of our school.

8 – DIVERSITY

The body is a unit, though it is made up of many parts; and though all its parts are many, they form one body. So it is with Christ. For we were all baptized by one Spirit into one body—whether Jews or Greeks, slave or free—and we are all given the one Spirit to drink. (1 Cor. 12:12-13)

Do We Still Have a Dream?

JANUARY 14, 2000

This piece, written relatively early in Trinity's journey down the road of diversity, sounds themes that I would still want to uphold. It was (shame to say) perhaps a little riskier then than now to fall in behind Dr. King and the Martin Luther King Jr. Day, but we did from early on and I am glad of it. This was the first, I believe, of several reflections on important themes on the occasion of King's birthday. There was surely enough fodder there for a book full of reflections. I count it a great progress that in our nineteenth year I was able to hand that important task off to our first diversity coordinator, Adrienne Davis, who has carried the banner forward brilliantly.

On this, the first Martin Luther King Jr. Day of the new millennium, I would like to pose a question to the Trinity community: Would people be interested in, not to mention moved by, Dr. King's rhetoric and activism today? Sometimes I wonder.

I wonder because we have tried so many things—like busing and affirmative action—that have left some of us confused and others cynical and all of us a little less inclined to dream his dream. I wonder whether our increasingly secular culture could even grasp, much less embrace, King's eloquent appeals for justice, laced as they were with biblical metaphors and erected upon sacred notions. And I wonder whether the high moral ground of liberty and justice has been seriously leveled into a lot of talk about diversity and tolerance.

I wonder...but I still choose to believe that Dr. King's dream is worthy and (what is harder) viable for us today. Whatever the force and direction of the political winds, it seems to me that a Christian school ought to be steadily and decidedly supportive of his dreams. Martin Luther King Jr. Day is a good time for us to pause and ask what kind of progress Trinity School is making toward the dream that Dr. King envisioned.

Let Justice Roll Down

Dr. King cared deeply about justice. "Let justice roll down like waters, and righteousness like an ever-flowing stream."[1] These words from the prophet Amos capture the heart of King's passion. Justice is a fundamental virtue in the classical Christian tradition. A Christian is committed to doing what is fair—what accords with the truth—even when it hurts. Even when it means ignoring one's own self-interest. To bring this lofty discussion down to earth and close to home: It is not fair that the kind of education we are seeking to offer at Trinity School be accessible and available only to a small network of people who inhabit the same neighborhoods, attend the same churches, and earn the same salary ranges. Trinity is not for everyone, but it ought to be for many who cannot now imagine that they could come. I am thinking of people who share our faith and a desire for an unhurried but rich education, yet who might look at our tuition and never get further. If we as a school are to be and remain committed to this kind of justice, we have some hard decisions ahead of us, particularly in the way we allocate our precious resources. Trinity parents should know that these are matters the board wrestles with regularly.

To Sit Down Together at the Table of Brotherhood

Reconciliation is at the heart of God's redeeming work in the world. "God was in Christ, reconciling the world to himself," writes Paul (2 Cor. 5:19). Consequently, even the most formidable barriers of enmity between peoples are no match for the power of the One who is himself our peace (Eph. 2:14-18). King was not naïve about the height of these barriers, and I doubt he would be surprised to know that there are still walls to be torn down. In our own community, racial tension and division have been much in the news, and the Durham council mem-

---

1. Amos 5:24 (ESV).

bers emerged from their recent retreat with the goal of improved race relations high on their list. There is a crucial role for Trinity School in addressing this community need. Education is a common concern for every citizen, and Trinity can become a place where people from different traditions, races, and churches unite in the exciting shared goal of creating a school of excellence for our community. Here, again, we face important challenges. We need to get the word out to people in African-American and Hispanic communities (to name just two), but the real challenge is more than a marketing job. It is one thing (hard enough, to be sure) to attract people of color to become consumers of our services; it is quite another to invite, recruit, and persuade a diverse group of people to partner with us. The ministry of reconciliation (2 Cor. 5:18) calls us to the latter, harder task. Harder, I might add, on both sides, for it means working together in real partnership that requires us all to move out of our comfort zones.

All of God's Children

Diversity is part of God's exquisite portrait of redemption. Diversity for diversity's sake is, to my mind, a weak argument for social change. The moral horsepower of Dr. King's cause came from the classical notions of justice and freedom, not from some vague and sentimental notion that all the colors of the rainbow ought to be represented in the picture. Still, the picture of "black men and white men, Jews and Gentiles, Protestants and Catholics" joining hands reminds us of John's vision of the redeemed in Revelation: "from every tribe and language and people and nation." The quilt that God is weaving is a colored one, rich and varied. The portraits of the student body that line the halls of our school ought to be dappled, not so that we can retain our tax-exempt status or keep in step with the political trends (which are likely to shift as soon as we get in step), but so that the picture of Trinity looks as much like God's kingdom as is possible.

The better you know Trinity School, the better you know two things about the sort of dreams that Dr. King gave us: how far we have to go,

8 – DIVERSITY

and how much we care about getting there. A school that is starting from scratch has many challenges before it, and all of them vie for attention and investment. On this national holiday, let us remember that this is one challenge that we cannot ignore.

Picture Trinity School

January 23, 2004

The school photos are no longer just inside the door. I miss them—with their remembrances of our first pioneer classes, beloved faculty now gone, alumni in their student personae, and a much younger me; but they were faded by the sun and incomplete. When the student body got too big to fit into one frame, we stopped taking them. And, as this piece shows, they were always incomplete in another way. We have made some progress since 2004 when this article was penned; Trinity's students of color represent close to twenty percent of our student body now. Our pictures would look different now, but not different enough. What is our goal? That all prospective students can see themselves at Trinity, when they look at our classes, our faculty, our curriculum.

The school photos just inside the front door tell our story. I like to glance at them whenever I walk in, as they remind me how far we've come. But they also remind me of how far we have to go: There are not many faces of color in those photographs.

Trinity is still a very white school. African-American, Hispanic, Native American, and mixed-race children make up about five percent of our student population. Add in children of Asian descent and we're at seven percent. Of these, about two percent have been adopted into Caucasian families, so that we're back down to about five percent families of color. The calculus of race is as complicated as the politics, but let not the difficulties of definition obscure this truth: When the third graders color their "Guess Which One I Am?" self-portrait for Parent Night, the child with the brown crayon is likely to feel a little alone. Maybe a lot.

8 – DIVERSITY

The Summer 2003 issue of *Independent School* magazine featured several articles on the experience of students of color in typical independent schools. Listen to the voices of those students:

> I wasn't sure how the white kids would react to me. I wasn't sure if I would be able to make friends. I wasn't sure if I'd be able to compete academically.
>
> I've been leading two lives since I was fourteen: the person I am at home, and the person I am at school. In the classroom, I've become accustomed to the way every single person turns and looks at me whenever anyone mentions China, Taiwan, or the rest of Asia.
>
> Sometimes they're racist without even knowing it. Today, a friend told me, "You're my favorite black person." She didn't even realize she was being racist.[1]

Social loneliness, tokenism, cultural misunderstandings, the burden of having to explain oneself to white people, and the burden of being grateful for the opportunity of school—these are some of the particular struggles that minorities face at independent schools. And these testimonies come from schools where the numbers are stronger than at Trinity. The latest statistics (2000) from the National Association of Independent Schools (NAIS) indicate that eighty-two percent of its students are white, five percent are black, and twelve percent are other students of color. The faculty and administration of these schools are predominantly white as well.

I am being blunt about the realities not because I want to engage in what someone has called "deficit discourse"—that supposedly cathartic bloodletting which white people often do when it comes time to talk about race. I suppose that such honest assessment is better than

---

1. Patrick F. Bassett, "Listening to Students of Color," *Independent School Magazine* (Summer 2003). www.nais.org/Magazines-Newsletters/ISMagazine/Pages/Listening-to-Students-of-Color.aspx.

denial, certainly better than blatant racism. But often this confessional approach leaves us too weak and discouraged to do something about the problem.

Something, indeed, needs to be done. But what? One approach, suggested by Pat Bassett, the president of NAIS, is to discover what things a school is already doing well and then ask, how can we bring this strength to bear on the intractable problem of racism and diversity recruitment? That we can do. Here are some of Trinity's strengths, which we bring to bear on this challenge.

Trinity defines academic excellence broadly. Our mission has always pushed us toward a balanced and holistic view of education. The family and the school are both important, and when push comes to shove, the family is more important. Our unhurried philosophy means that we affirm setting limits on the demands of school. Interestingly, this way of being a school (it's not the most common way) aligns us more with the values of black and Latino cultures. In 1999, psychologist Patricia Romney and her colleagues conducted a study of achievement among black and Latino high school students in high-achieving independent schools. They found that these students, while valuing academic success, also stressed the importance of family connection, of community service, of happiness, of learning about other cultures. "They were less likely than their white and Asian-American classmates to stress high income or Ivy League colleges as desired outcomes, preferring instead to maintain a balance in their lives."[2] Sounds like the minutes from our latest Education Committee meeting.

Trinity is an output school. At least we're not a purely input school. By this I mean we don't do rigorous ability or even achievement testing at our young grades, trying to shape our student body by the input of children with a certain intellectual profile. Instead, we focus on developmental readiness and trust our educational process to *build into*

---

2. Patricia Romney, "Closing the Achievement Gap?" *Independent School Magazine* (Summer 2003). www.nais.org/Magazines-Newsletters/ISMagazine/Pages/Closing-Achievement-Gap.aspx.

the students good habits and the tools of learning. This philosophy has the potential to discover diamonds in the rough and encourage some average children to do above-average work. It has great potential for helping to close that infamous "achievement gap" between white and black students which has been the bane of public discourse about education for decades.

Trinity takes the spiritual dimension seriously. Our Christian mission is, of course, central to all that we do. We study the scriptures, we pray together, we speak openly and comfortably about our involvement in church. Romney's study also found that black and Latino students brought a greater concern for spirituality, broadly defined, than the average independent school student. Not surprising, when we think of the role that the church has played in the civil rights movement and in African-American culture. If minority families are looking for a school that supports their own family religious values, they may like what they find at Trinity School.[3]

Finally, Trinity is committed to the truth. The pursuit of truth is one of our stated goals. We aspire to an education in truth, goodness, and beauty. Our students follow a curriculum in the liberal arts that is designed to give them the skills they need to hear, understand, discern, and speak the truth. We believe that all truth is God's truth, and we are prepared to hear it, regardless of whether it reflects well on us or makes us feel good. This commitment to truth is essential for real work in the area of race and diversity. The road to reconciliation is a steep one, no safe passage for anyone who wants superficiality or pretense. The self-discovery that comes from really wrestling with the issues of race is strong tonic. Minority families know, very quickly, whether a school is really committed to working through issues.

---

3. When I wrote this, I was focused on African-American and Latino families; Lynn Hand has justly pointed out that Muslim families might not be so pleased (though we have some anecdotal evidence to the contrary). And, again, I continue to note how few Jewish families are interested in Trinity. So on balance, I think our strong Christian stance can cut both ways.

I am sure that there are other strengths that our Trinity community brings to this task of increasing our diversity. Many of you see things I don't, and I'd love to hear your thoughts. I invite us all to ask ourselves how we can change not only the pictures of our student body, but more importantly, the experiences of those minorities who join us in this work.

The Birthright of Freedom

January 13, 2012

> On the occasion of this, our sixteenth year, our celebration of MLK Day was highlighted by a visit from Vic Carter of Baltimore, who had served as committee chair for the group that constructed the MLK Memorial in Washington, DC, dedicated in October 2011. A childhood friend of Trinity teacher Rita Davis, Mr. Carter spoke to our different divisions about this important work.

Martin Luther King will be justly celebrated and remembered next week, and we will do our part at Trinity School. We celebrate this holiday every year because we believe that his ideas and his life marked a significant moment in our nation's history.

Dr. King's message showed us how powerful a simple truth can be. He was a bright man, exceedingly well educated, eminently eloquent, but his profundity came from the simplicity of the truth he came back to, over and over. As he wrote from a jail in Birmingham about the struggle of "the Negro," he said, "Something within has reminded him of his birthright of freedom."[1]

Something within—King's words, for all their amazing eloquence, would have been but decorative rhetorical flourishes had they not resonated deep *within* the hearts and minds of his hearers, black and white. He called forth *from within* a hearty assent to the proposition that all people are created equal. Freedom and dignity are not *given* to people by others or by the state, but by God. They are *birthrights*. King would have liked Charlotte Mason's notion that "children are born persons."[2]

---

1. Martin Luther King, Jr., *Letter from Birmingham Jail*, www.uscrossier.org/pullias/wp-content/uploads/2012/06/King.pdf. Originally published as "The Negro Is Your Brother," *The Atlantic Monthly* 212, no. 2 (August 1963): 78–88.
2. Charlotte Mason, *Philosophy of Education*, xxix, 18, 23.

THE BIRTHRIGHT OF FREEDOM

One way of talking about Dr. King's legacy is to say that he reminded us, simply, of what it means to be *human*. That is a fearful and wonderful thing, and the people who have memorials on the mall in Washington, DC, are people who found a way to reconnect us to this profound truth: Thomas Jefferson earned his place when he penned the Declaration of Independence; Lincoln when he wrote the Gettysburg Address; and King when he spoke of his dream from the steps of the Lincoln Memorial. These three men found a way to say the most important thing that needed to be said. And what they said was that it is a glory to be human.

It's a truth that needs to be re-said in each generation. It never grows old, but our understanding of it sometimes gets clouded. And when someone calls us back to this great truth, we sit up straight and call him a Great One.

Good schools are places that manage to stay focused on this simple but profound truth: that the students who enter their doors are "born persons," with a birthright to the freedom of a liberal education. It is a glory to be human; it is a glory to understand. Everything else is gravy. If we can hang on to this simple truth, Trinity will always be an extraordinary place to learn.

9 – Technology

Modern technology has become a total phenomenon for civilization, the defining force of a new social order in which efficiency is no longer an option but a necessity imposed on all human activity.

Jacques Ellul, *The Technological Society*

The Holy Spirit alone can establish this link with one's neighbor.

Jacques Ellul, *The Presence of the Kingdom*

Technological changes provide mile markers for the history of Trinity. We were born in 1995, when the Internet was on the periphery of our attention; when cell phones were expensive, huge, and rare (I had a pager for the first several years of the school); when laptops and tablets were futuristic dreams. Board member Dick Wolfe set me up with my first AOL account sometime in the late 1990s. Email became the predominant way of communication for us in the early 2000s—in fact, I have often said that with our lean administrative staff (especially in those days), we could never have kept the trains running on time without email. We added computer classes to the curriculum about this same time. In 2010 all of our teachers got laptops and iPads, and we began to use online resources of all sorts in new ways: virtual classes, blended classes, Virtual High School, VISnet. And now, in 2014, the

9 – TECHNOLOGY

board has approved a 1:1 learning initiative to be launched in the fall of 2015. *My, haven't you grown!*

The Once and Future School

November 2, 2012

> *Although this piece is dated 2012, its genesis goes back to 2005, when my thinking took an important turn. I read Tom Friedman's* The World Is Flat, *and I attended for the first time the Southern Association of Independent Schools Heads Conference. At that conference, radical change was all the buzz: globalization and technological advances. I returned home and wrote a piece called "A Janus-Faced School." It started an important conversation with Trinity parent and soon-to-be board member Jeff Lloyd, who works for Apple. And years later, when I thought the school was ready to move ahead in a strong way to adopt new technologies for learning and teaching, I reprised that piece and expanded it. The copyright on this piece was probably overkill. At the time, the tag "Once and Future School" was getting some traction in email threads and I didn't want Trinity to lose its chance to claim that for our own purposes.*

Which direction should a school face? Backward toward the past, or forward toward the future? Should a school be primarily conservative, guarding the repository of wisdom from our elders? Or should it be more progressive, looking ahead to the challenges that will face the generation leading the world in forty years? Should the core values of a school be shaped more by the humanities, with their attention to the great conversations of the past, or by the sciences, which are driven by new paradigms and the frontiers of knowledge? Should it guard the analog culture of learning that it inherited from the past or adopt the ways of the new digital world?

You can imagine that a school like Trinity, whose mission invokes a Christian, classical, and unhurried education, would attend to the voices from the past. Our guiding lights, from Socrates to Charlotte Mason, are all dead. We think that there is something our parents and grand-

9 — TECHNOLOGY

parents knew that is worth discovering. Dorothy Sayers, whose essay "The Lost Tools of Learning" has inspired and influenced our school since the beginning, proposed going back to the *medieval* Trivium for a better way of education. We are prone to believe, prima facie, that an old book might be better than a new one.

But in this brave new world an old computer is never better than a new one. Whether we boomer digital immigrants like it or not, all students at Trinity School are, by virtue of age, digital natives. They will work, read, play, shop, give, and worship in a world that is foreign to us: more connected and faster than we would like. We can slow it down and unplug it some, for their benefit, but we cannot turn the clock back. The question is not whether they will be digital and global citizens. The question is what kind of digital and global citizens they will be.

I refuse for Trinity School to be skewered on the horns of this dilemma. I feel enormous pressure to choose one side or the other—in one direction when I attend the annual conference of the Southern Association of Independent Schools, entitled "Leaders of the Future," or in the other when I talk to parents or teachers who want Trinity to be a sanctuary from our digital culture. But this is not what we set out to establish when we founded Trinity. We set forth, in our bylaws, the goal to "promote thoughtful and responsible engagement with the culture at large, to the end that our students will answer God's call to transform society for the common good and the glory of God." This means that we engage with culture; and it means that we do so thoughtfully. This is a third way: neither once, nor future, but once *and* future.

Remembering the past is essential to any future worth having. Some things do not change, like our humanness. Belief in a constant human nature is one of the presuppositions of a classical education. We think it wise to look back to Socrates and Charlotte Mason for guidance about education because we believe that *personhood* is something constant. Attention spans may have changed, but the need for attentiveness has not. Word-processing is a lot easier, but finding the right word is not, to say nothing of matching word and deed. Even with their smartphones and iPads, our students are still angel-beasts, glorious ruins, in need of education and redemption.

Moving into the future, Trinity students will be well prepared because they have been given the tools of learning. These gifts from the past are essential for the future. The tools of learning, the liberal arts, are those skills that teach us *how* to learn. Students who have mastered these will have the capacity to approach any learning challenge with competence and confidence. For the challenges of a knowledge-based future, knowing how to listen and speak, how to read and write, how to think clearly and speak persuasively will be more valuable by far than an encyclopedic knowledge of something that Google can uncover in a nanosecond.

In 1982 *Christianity Today* published an essay by author and scholar Tom Howard entitled, "What My Children Won't Learn in School." Howard asked himself just what he wanted schooling to do for his children:

> I want them to be civilized and articulate members of their generation. I want them to be able to live intelligently in this epoch and to bring to the choices they make the judgments formed by eons of human experience. I do not want them to be trapped inside the airless hutch of modernity. They will be assisted here by reading history and poetry and philosophy. I do not want them to be ignorant as to the sort of conditions under which all mortal life must be lived. They will get light on this from physics, astronomy, chemistry, biology, botany, anatomy, and so forth. I want their capacity to apprehend beauty to be awakened and nourished and regaled. Hence, I want them to know about Praxiteles and Virgil and Giotto and Mozart. I do not want them to be traduced by the bestial view of mankind that is the specialty of our own century. I would like them to have Ulysses and Aeneas and Roland and Lear looming in their imaginations so that they will have images against

9 – TECHNOLOGY

which to test figures like Arthur Miller's salesman, or Andy Warhol, or Charlie's Angels.[1]

What *I* want for our children, the ones who attend Trinity School now and the ones who will attend it twenty-five years from now, is a Once and Future School. I want a school that is conversant with the past and attentive to the future. I want a school that knows when to use an old tool and when to use a new one. I want a school that teaches and trains students in the ancient habits and virtues so that they will be wise and self-controlled when they face temptations I cannot yet imagine. I want a school where the technologies of the future are embraced with thoughtfulness and moderation. I want a school where the creativity and innovation that emerge remind us of Leonardo or Pascal or Jefferson. I want a school that remembers. And a school that, like the wise woman of Proverbs 31, smiles at the future.

---

1. Tom Howard, "What My Children Won't Learn in School," *Christianity Today* (September 3, 1982), 26–27.

It's Complicated
September 2010

This piece was written in the early fall of the year that we gave our teachers two new digital devices: MacBooks and iPads. We took two full days in October for professional development, and we held a parent night on technology in the fall. We also launched a steering committee to plan out the student phase of this digital learning initiative (DLI). That committee gave birth to a DLI proposal that came before the board in 2012, but the time was not right for its launch. (Technology is not only complicated; it is expensive.) In January 2014, the board did approve the DLI, to be launched in 2015—not because we think it now uncomplicated, but because we understand that our mission is to live well "as if not" (I Cor. 7:31).

Trinity is a complicated school. I'm not bragging, and I'm not complaining. I'm just telling it like it is.

One way to describe this complexity is to say that we are welcoming but wise in the way we do education. On the one hand, we want to welcome the good things the world and our culture have to offer—like four-year colleges, organized sports, differentiated instruction, the Internet, the National Association of Independent Schools, the FIRST Robotics competition, ERBs, and iPads—just to name a few cultural phenomena with which we are significantly engaged at Trinity School. On the other hand, we must be wise and even a little suspicious of the commitments that all of these engagements demand of us. Louis Armstrong was right—it is indeed a "wonderful world" we live in. But it is a fallen one, and there are always strings attached to any culture's goods. This is why Christians are called "aliens and strangers on earth" (Heb. 11:13), why the early Christians were accused of turning the world upside down (Acts. 17:6), and why Paul makes the bizarre suggestion to the Corinthians that they try living "as if not" (1 Cor. 7). It's complicated.

Choose one side of this tension and you can have yourself a simpler school. We could decide to be, simply, a best-practices school of excellence, adopting whatever research and the culture (especially the elites) are saying about how to run a school. If we were still interested in being a Christian school, we would be following what H. Richard Niebuhr called "the Christ of Culture."[1] Our Christian faith and conviction would be synonymous with the best our culture has to offer. There are schools like this, and they are very good schools. But that is not Trinity.

Quite differently, we could simplify our schooling by deciding to shun completely all the godless nonsense out there. We might say that we want only Christians at this school; we would have lots of rules and build lots of fences; and we might make sure that all our textbooks were published by card-carrying evangelicals. We would then be a poster school for what Niebuhr called "Christ Against Culture." There are schools like this, and they have an important angle on the truth—for Christ is indeed Lord over and against all. When Jesus said that the world hated him, he was dead serious. He also said the world would hate us, but he left us in it and so here we are, in the middle of the world at Trinity School, trying to live as if not at home here. It's complicated.

We decided from the very beginning that we wanted Trinity to be a place that is thoroughgoing in its Christian commitments yet hospitable toward the world and those who don't share our faith. We welcome non-Christian parents and students, but we never try to disguise or tone down our Christian convictions. We believe that the model of culture-making that Niebuhr called "Christ Transforming Culture" is one fruitful way to live as Christians in this world.

---

1. H. Richard Niebuhr, *Christ and Culture* (New York: HarperCollins, 2001). First published in 1951 by Harper & Row.

IT'S COMPLICATED

This technology initiative is just one more instance of the complexity of Trinity. We are seriously interested in these new technologies and the ways they are changing teaching and learning. We welcome them and the new possibilities they hold. We also want to be wise and cautious about the ways that technological changes shape our culture and about the unintended consequences of these new tools. Even as we are holding professional development sessions on how to teach for the 21st century using emerging technologies, we will be reading books like Nicholas Carr's *The Shadows: What the Internet Is Doing to Our Brains*.[2] Some of us parents and teachers will want to push ahead with these changes; others will want to slow down and be thoughtful. I want us to do both, which is, alas, complicated.

---

2. Nicolas Carr, *The Shadows: What the Internet Is Doing to Our Brains* (New York: W.W. Norton & Company, 2010).

What Technology Affords
March 18, 2011

I continue to find that the notion of affordance generates good thinking about technology and learning. There is a lot of bling and flash in technological advances, and some of it is just the latest form of what Charlotte Mason would call twaddle. But there are real advances. It is hard, I think, to tell the gold from the dross in the moment, but questions like the ones raised here are essential to making wise choices. Nothing ventured to try out new affordances, nothing gained.

The turn I took in the use of my blog at the time of this article has been largely sustained, with some fits and starts. The commenting never took off—which is a great example of how easy it is to get it wrong when we are trying to figure out what good this new technology is. Still, the blog has proved a serviceable way to communicate with a growing school. Many thanks to Laura Sayre for her technical help and to Holley Broughton, who keeps me supplied with lots of great pictures and tweets.

I'm at that stage of life where my children are a lot smarter than I am. They are sitting at the feet of college professors, following blogs, camping out at gateways of the cultural elites. They have a lot to teach me.

My daughter, at Duke, is taking a class on emerging technologies of learning. Her professor, Cathy Davidson, talks a lot about the idea of affordance. That was a new one for me, but the sort of new one that makes all kinds of old sense as soon as it is explained. Affordance is the latent possibility for action and interaction that is inherent (but not necessarily obvious) in an environment. Twenty years ago, I had to make it to the bank by 6:00 p.m. on Friday if I wanted cash for the weekend. But new technologies (ATM machines, debit cards, online banking) afford me new possibilities for action.

As an educator, I'm fascinated with the possibilities for teaching and learning that new technologies afford teachers. This is the sort of exploration we're making this year as we've launched a new wave of technology. I wish you could see what the first graders did for their fairy tale project. We've done a unit on fairy tales for years now, but this year Megan Wright's first grade class wrote, illustrated, recorded, viewed, and shared a fairy tale of their own making. It was clever, delightful, coherent, and instructive. Students recorded their own creations and then listened to themselves and their classmates reading. They had the chance to make the story come alive, through tone, inflection, and emphasis. All of this is what new technologies have afforded us. And the best thing, as Mrs. Wright says, is that these new affordances have come without diminishing the learning that was already there in the old project.

Technologies afford headmasters new possibilities too. I've been playing around lately with my blog, something I've maintained for about four years now, but only in occasional and episodic ways. It's occurred to me that this new medium of exchange affords me a way to be present and reflect on small things that are worthy of sustained attention, and to share Trinity and my experience of it with the wider community.

Take a look, and let me know what you think. You can comment on the blog if you like. That, by the way, is a whole new angle I haven't explored. Over four years of blogging, I have gotten about six comments. I don't know that I can (or want to) respond to everyone's thoughts, but it would be interesting to see what new possibilities such feedback affords. We're all learning together.

Here's the link to my blog, *Pedagogblog*:

http://www.pedagogblog.blogspot.com/

Our Digital *Minhag*

March 21, 2014

In January of 2014, after two intense years of discussion, debate, and learning, the Trinity board approved the Digital Learning Initiative, which funded the combination of missional pedagogies with new technologies for student learning. Two years earlier the board had approved a policy on technology and learning, and this DLI was one important and groundbreaking implementation of that policy. In the fall of 2015, after an eighteen-month runway of preparation, the school will provide digital learning devices for students in grades 6–12 and will enhance the learning technologies available to teachers and students in the Lower School.

There are those who say, "It's about time!" And there are those who say, "Please, don't do this!" Like all schools, Trinity will have its challenges in implementation. The essay below gives a window into the kind of conversation and engagement that I believe will help us implement these tools wisely. We are not Luddites, and we are not drinking the techno Kool-Aid either. We are trying to chart a wise course, one with savvy balance. I have begun the conversations I mention here, but they must be ongoing to be effective. There is no wave of the Headmaster Wand that will effect wise use of technology, but only the thoughtful embrace of these tools. I do continue to believe that we are stronger together for this challenge, and I am hopeful that we can do this well.

If you could have dinner with Wendy Mogel, what would you ask her?

(Not, I hope, "Who is Wendy Mogel?" Answer: well-known author of *The Blessing of a Skinned Knee* and *The Blessing of a B Minus*.)

I asked her about a *minhag*. It was during dessert, just before her lecture to area independent school parents on March 5. TPO President Kimberley Kaestner and I were representing Trinity at the pre-lecture dinner, and the good Dr. Mogel moved over to our table for the last course. I seized that opportunity to ask her about a passage from her first book, in a section called "Learn the *Minhag* of Your Community."

"*Minhag*," says Mogel, "is a useful Hebrew word meaning the local custom or practice of a community or a particular congregation."[1] In Jewish tradition, there are various levels of custom or tradition. There is the Hebrew Bible (the Tanakh); then there is the revered Talmud, which contains the teachings and opinions of thousands of rabbis; and then there is the Halakha, Jewish law based on the Talmud. *Minhagim* are distinct from these other traditions and laws: they are local and particular to individual communities. Jews in the Iberian peninsula had different *minhagim* than those of Central Europe. All traditional Jewish men wear yarmulkes; only Jews in certain places abstain from rice during Passover.

Mogel took this Jewish notion and rang the changes on it to describe her neighborhood's customs for what is right and safe for children. On her block at home, she says, the hierarchy of freedom works roughly like this:

- Seven-year-olds can walk a few blocks in pairs but need to call when they arrive.
- Eight-year-olds also go in pairs, with no call necessary.
- Nine-year-olds can walk alone to each other's houses but must still walk in pairs or threesomes to the local shopping street.
- Eleven-year-olds can go alone to the boulevard.
- After dark, children go no farther than a scamper home from a friend's house on their own block.

"Your neighborhood will have different customs than mine," says Mogel, "but it's useful to spend some time determining what those customs are and push yourself, if necessary, to give your child appropriate, sensible freedom. In general, physical protectiveness means

---

1. Wendy Mogel, *The Blessing of a Skinned Knee: Using Jewish Teachings to Raise Self-Reliant Children* (New York: Penguin Compass, 2001), 105.

9 – TECHNOLOGY

you are safeguarding your child from serious threat or injury. Physical overprotectiveness means you are guarding your child against life. It's worthwhile to talk to friends and neighbors whose opinions on such things you respect and to figure out the distinction between the two."[2]

I mentioned to Dr. Mogel that I had often thought of this passage as we have wrestled with what the boundaries should be for technology in our families and in our school. She seemed to resonate with this idea and affirmed that the articulation of community rules around this might be one of the most important things we need to do. This led to some interesting conversation with other heads at the table, and it soon became clear that none of us had a school we could point to that had done this successfully. We asked Dr. Mogel what schools she had seen that had done this well. She thought for a while and then admitted that she couldn't think of one.

I came away from this conversation wondering anew if this was something that Trinity could do well for the sake of our students. I have approached the leaders of the TPO and asked, "Could we set up a process whereby our parents and teachers together come to an understanding of what our community standards are around these issues?" It will not be easy: the technology shifts constantly, and our families will have a wide range of ideas about what is the right kind of protection for students. Further, we may run the risk of legalism. (Are you a bad Christian parent if you give your child a cell phone before everyone else?—Oy vey!) But I still think this could be worth a good ol' college try. What if we could come up with our own *minhag*? What if all Trinity parents understood what that was, even if they decided to exercise a more lax or a stricter standard? I can imagine us wrestling with questions like the following:

- What are the limits on screen time for each grade?
- When do students get their own cell phones?
- When do students get their own digital device?

---

2. Mogel, *Skinned Knee*, 105–6.

- When do they take school devices home?
- How do parents monitor their usage?
- When do students use their devices in a public space at home, in view of all?
- When do they take their devices to their rooms or other private places?

Community standards will be valuable, but the process of determining them will be just as important. The conversations around these difficult questions (on which we will surely disagree) just might serve to galvanize a certain community mindset that takes responsibility for the networked public spaces our students will inevitably inhabit as they grow into adulthood. We all fear the dangers that lurk in the digital streets. But as Danah Boyd points out in her book *It's Complicated: The Social Lives of Networked Teens*, "Communities aren't safe when everyone turns inward; they are only...safe when people work collectively to help one another and those around them." Boyd draws upon the work of renowned urban theorist Jane Jacobs (*The Death and Life of Great American Cities*), who claimed that the safest neighborhoods were those where people paid attention to what was happening in the public spaces. Surveillance and draconian rules won't keep streets safe: safe streets are ones where the adults notice if someone gets hurt, and come out to help.

So as we roll out Trinity's Digital Learning Initiative, let's think together about our community norms surrounding these powerful and helpful tools. For the children's sake. And maybe in a couple of years, if Dr. Mogel gets the same question at a pre-lecture dinner, she might say, "Well, there is this school in Durham called Trinity..."

10 – Athletics

Non nobis, Domine, non nobis, sed nomini tuo da gloriam.
Psalm 115:1

Trinity's athletic history goes way back, not to the very beginning (we started with grades K–4), but to the years before we had a campus. I still remember standing at the gate of our brand-new, undeveloped property, giving a tour to a family who cared a lot about athletics. My wife, Desirée, had the brilliant idea to ask them for a donation to launch an athletic program. At first our efforts were modest: a simple blacktop outside the modular on the Pickett campus, UNC track star Hubert West as part-time P.E. teacher and athletic director, and our inaugural teams (cross-country and track, because they needed no facilities and could accommodate a small group of students). When we built Phase I of the campus, a donor challenged us to add a gym, and that was a stroke of brilliance—we still use the Blue Gym for all manner of athletic and school events. Sue Eckstein came along in 2001 and soon became our first full-time athletic director, to whom we owe a great debt of gratitude.

Trinity's athletic programs have grown and blossomed in the last decade or so. With the addition of fine facilities (a baseball field, two soccer fields, and our larger Gold Gym) and the expansion into high school athletics starting in 2006–2007, we moved into a full program with Middle School, JV, and Varsity athletics. As a Division I program, we did exceptionally well; now, as a relatively small Division II program, we are having more uneven successes. But through all this the focus of the program on character and virtue has remained strong. The challenges of playing against schools whose goals are different—where winning, state titles, and NCAA recruitment reign—are real and vexing, but we continue to consider athletics a cocurricular program that teaches lessons vital to the mission of a school dedicated to truth, goodness, and beauty.

The Race That Three Girls Won

OCTOBER 4, 2002

This piece tells the story well enough, so that there is really little need for introduction. Our athletic program was still quite young—I think we had added basketball, soccer, and golf to the running sports. But the cross-country meets were a major fall event. I remember watching this unfold at the edge of the woods, piecing it all together later over the days that followed. I remember calling the head of Duke School to tell about their magnanimous runner. Over the years, when I've been asked what Non nobis *means, I often go to this story. And it's gratifying to me to know that the two Trinity girls in this story are still finding ways to live their lives for others. That is the real measure of Trinity's success.*

This is a true story about two schools and three girls who gave their best.

On Tuesday, September 24, Trinity's cross-country team traveled down the road to Duke Middle School for a three-way meet, the first of our season. Cross-country teams need a minimum of five runners to finish in order to score as a team, and our girls were one shy of the five. At the last minute, the team convinced a fifth girl, MaryMac, to run. This sixth grader had practiced with the team some, but because of her club soccer team had decided not to compete.

One of my favorite things is to sidle up inconspicuously to the huddle and listen in as Coach Hubert West gets the athletes ready to run. That day, down on their level, eye to eye, with the intensity of a preacher, he said to them, "What I'm asking for is your best. You give that and no one can ask for more." And then, as is his custom, he led them in a prayer.

10 – ATHLETICS

The Duke School track circles three times through the woods, so all the moms and dads stand around for several minutes after the start not knowing who was in front. When the girls come out of the woods, there were two Trinity girls out in front. One was the novice, the sixth grader, running stride for stride with Taylor, last year's front runner. I said to someone nearby, "MaryMac has gone out too fast. She'll never keep up." The second time they emerged from the woods, still the two were running strong, in front with a Duke School runner, Emily, close behind. Imagine our surprise and puzzlement when, three minutes later, MaryMac emerged from the woods in the lead, with the Duke School girl in pursuit, and Taylor nowhere in sight. The girls took one final lap around the soccer field and MaryMac finished first. That victory, for a sixth grader, was itself a tale, but soon I learned that it was only half the story, and maybe not even the best part of it.

When two other Duke School runners emerged from the woods, they shouted that a runner was down and needed help. Coach West ran down the trail to find Taylor. I saw him, minutes later, coming out of the woods, carrying Taylor, whose knee has been banged up pretty badly.

It was actually a couple of days before I heard the full story. Taylor, in the lead, had twisted her knee and fallen. Emily, the Duke School runner, stopped to help, and so did our own MaryMac. Emily, obviously concerned about her opponent, looked to MaryMac and said, "You got her?"

MaryMac assured her she did and Emily ran on. Then Taylor, looking up through tears and pain, said to MaryMac, "Go! Finish!"

So MaryMac took off through the woods to the finish line and Taylor lay motioning all the runners on past her until help came.

Three girls won that race. The one who fell, who swallowed her disappointment, pain, and fear and told the others to go on. The one on the other team, who gave up seconds and a sure advantage to show compassion on a worthy opponent. And the one who gave up her lead for the sake of her teammate, and then found the kick to overtake the lead again.

Non nobis, Domine, non nobis, sed nomini tuo da gloriam. Not to us, Lord, not to us, but to your name be the glory. First place goes to the one who has learned that she is third: God first, then neighbor, then self. There is truth and goodness and beauty in that order. This is an eternal glory which no Nietzschean, trash-talking superstar can ever reflect. This is the pattern of the One who ran the race and finished, who stopped to pick us up and carry us along, who was, simply, the Best There Ever Was.

Speaking of Sports

OCTOBER 2003

> *Lewis's short essay is worth reading. Lewis himself was no athlete (far from it), but he fought in the first World War and he knew what he was talking about here, both from personal experience and from his deep reading in medieval and Renaissance literature. There are many things that athletics develops in students, but the double-sided virtue of courage-and-gentleness seems to me to be one of the best. Other activities can build team spirit and cooperativeness, and honesty can be learned in many fields without balls and goals. But the grit and courage to dig deep and battle fiercely, and somehow to maintain what Lewis called meekness (which our Lord called "blessed") is nowhere tested as in athletic competition.*

Let us speak of sports in school.

Our culture asks for no justification of school athletics. Over the course of eight years, in probably three dozen open houses for prospective parents asking hundreds of questions, I do not recall ever having to acquit the school with an answer to the question "Why do you have sports at Trinity?" Here at the beginning of the 21st century in America, we hold this truth to be self-evident: young people should play sports. Boy, do we ever! The athletic industry is one of the top ten industries in the nation, generating business in the hundreds of billions of dollars each year. Sports psychologist Shane Murphy points out that *competition, teamwork,* and *winning the game* are dominant metaphors in the corporate world.[1] When I recently cancelled cable TV for a season (defined not by weather or months but playoffs), guess which channel the Denton children said they couldn't live without?

---

1. Shane Murphy, *The Cheers and the Tears: A Healthy Alternative to the Dark Side of Youth Sports Today* (San Francisco: Jossey-Bass, 1999), 33.

It would be wrong to speak of the necessity of sports. We can, you know, live without them. But there is a human *ideal* which education cannot ignore, which classical education in particular must not ignore. That ideal might be actualized in the computer lab or in the debate club, as on the basketball court. Still, it has to be said that sports provide a unique opportunity for the practice of such excellence as a classical Christian education espouses. I speak of the excellence of character that combines the virtues of courage and meekness.

Courage to venture out in spite of one's fears is rare enough; and the meekness that Jesus commended in the Beatitudes is perhaps rarer still. How much more precious, then, to find these two combined in one person. Not a second-choice compromise between two extremes, but one person who is fully courageous and fully meek. I am speaking of the person who is able to go to the mat or to the boards with all the fierceness and abandon of a warrior, but also able to admit defeat with humility or give a hand up to a fallen, obnoxious opponent.

Such a person was the medieval knight. It was said of Lancelot that he was "the meekest man that ever ate in hall among ladies" and "the sternest knight to thy mortal foe."[2] In an essay entitled "The Necessity of Chivalry," C. S. Lewis argues that however unrealistic we may feel this ideal to be, it is, nevertheless, a necessary one.[3] The future of civilization depends on men and women who have the capacity to be both brave and gentle. We want leaders who can fight well; we also want them to know which fights to pick and to know how to avoid a quarrel and win friends through diplomacy. The history of the Ottoman Empire shows the failure of the warrior to learn meekness in court; the history of the British between the two World Wars shows the failure of the meek to be bold when danger lurked.

It may seem a long way from the medieval lists to the ball field, but the challenges are much the same. At the end of practice, the coach

---

2. Thomas Mallory, *Le Morte d'Arthur*, 21.13.
3. C. S. Lewis, "The Necessity of Chivalry." In *Present Concerns* (San Diego: Harcourt Brace Jovanovich, 1986), 13.

says, "Let's run one more suicide" and the kid thinks, "I'm going to die." That is the chance to forge courage. The team shows up at school the day after the big win (or the big loss). That is the chance to forge true meekness, which is never proud—neither vain nor falsely humble. Two memorable scenes from *Chariots of Fire* capture this double demand. The speed coach says to Eric Liddell, just after he recovered from a nasty fall to come from behind and win the grueling race, "Not the prettiest quarter, Mr. Liddell, but certainly the bravest." Balancing that is the moment when the American runner slips Liddell a note before his race, "He who honors me I will honor." This was no meekness from weakness, but the gentleness of one who was strong. Like our Lord, whose feat on the cross was, at once, the bravest and the meekest of deeds.

What does all this mean for our athletic policy?

- Our athletic program must be intentional. A team of Launcelots does not just happen. It takes a trained coach, a strategy, a dedicated team, and much more. Virtue is a work of art and not of nature.

- We want an athletic program for the many and not for the few. Our goal is to push as many of our students as we can to develop these virtues. It does not serve our mission to produce athletic superstars and few (if any) people of character.

- We recognize that each student has unique gifts and unique challenges. This one needs to be pushed to compete; that one needs to be pushed to be humble.

- Sports are only as good as they are hard. Lessons are learned through the crucibles of tough situations. Being cut, sitting on the bench, making the wrong play—these can sometimes yield the most important lessons.

- Parents usually get in the way of the best lessons our children can learn when we get between the coach and the player. Let them be. Let them struggle through it. If there is a problem, send the child to the coach.

- We aim to win. How are we going to teach these students true courage if they do not face a real test and push themselves to the limit?

- We recognize that there are, in God's redemptive providence, defeats that rival victories. The crucifixion is exhibit A.

The great irony is that our culture, which is so often too serious about sports, is too lax about that which gives sport its purpose: the cultivation of virtue. Absent that, excellence on the court is just a tiny thing. It is the court of the human heart where the real victory is won or lost.

Respect the Game
April 17, 2009

The parent who recommended Heclo's book was Duke Divinity professor Kavin Rowe, who has kept me well-stocked with book recommendations. The Sandberg story caught my attention and imagination immediately, and I have referenced it many times in my work as headmaster.

One of the things I like about this piece is that, while being a column on athletics, it is not really about athletics. It might as well be about teaching, with an athletic illustration. Essentially, it is about excellence in education, which is accomplished on the court and in the classroom.

I think that this case for institutional excellence, for respecting the game of education (and of sport), is the strongest one to be made for schools' exercising caution against allowing athletics to drive the school train. I doubt there is a school in America that hasn't been accused of allowing its athletic program to wag the educational dog. The trick is to see that athletics takes its proper place in the institutional pursuit of excellence. Insofar as it promotes that kind of excellence, it is part of the dog and not the tail. But such a vision takes constant vigilance in our culture. It begins with the coaches and leadership; it requires parental support and strong institutional backing. We have to talk about and think about what we are doing, and why we are doing it. If our academic program needs athletics to round out the Trinity education, our athletic program also needs an intellectual perspective, a certain thoughtfulness, to ensure that athletics serves the school's larger goals. The athletic director and the academic leaders of a school have to be partners in thought.

All teachers and coaches get frustrated sometimes. Most of them get over it, and the way they get over it is, usually, to remember the kids.

RESPECT THE GAME

Maybe the headmaster or some unreasonable parent (it happens) or the bureaucracy of a school just about does them in. Then they happen upon a group of students collaborating on a science project or cheering each other on at the track meet and they remember why they are working at this job that doesn't pay a lot and gets little respect. It's the kids.

But it's not the kids, exactly. It's not that they are working *for* the kids. It's not that they are giving the kids what they want, as though the job of a teacher or coach was student happiness. The job of a teacher or a coach is often to get out there and disappoint a kid—one who wanted an A but got a C, one who wanted to start on the team but didn't. So when we say it's for the kids, we mean something that goes beyond the kids themselves.

The best teachers and coaches are ones who work hard, every day, because they respect their profession of teaching and coaching. They are dedicated to doing education right. They are committed to the *idea* of education. To the *institution* of education.

Institution is not a good word for most of us. Think of institutional food. I've been challenged recently, however, to reevaluate my prejudices in this direction by a book a Trinity parent recommended, *On Thinking Institutionally* by Hugh Heclo. Heclo summons former Chicago Cub Ryne Sandberg's 2005 Baseball Hall of Fame induction speech to reclaim some positive ground for the notion of institution. It's a speech worth reading and quoting.

> It was all about doing things right. If you played the game the right way, played the game for the team, good things would happen. That's what I loved most about the game, how a ground-out to second with a man on second and nobody out was a great thing. Respect.[1]

---

1. Ryne Sandburg, "Respect the Game above All Else." Baseball Hall of Fame Induction Speech, delivered July 31, 2005, Cooperstown, NY, http://www.americanrhetoric.com/speeches/rynesandbergbaseballhalloffame.htm.

Sandberg (whom I used to watch at Wrigley Field when I was in seminary) is saying that the game of baseball is something worthy of his best efforts and his devotion—his respect. His is a deep regard for the history of the game, and those who have gone before; it is also a commitment to a community of living players who embody the essence of the game. The game is not a mechanism by which Sandberg can show off his prowess; it is a tradition and an ideal which call forth excellence.

Frustrated teachers recenter themselves by remembering that they are part of an *institution* of education. Before there was ever a Trinity School, and long after we are gone, there exists this noble idea: to transform young people by instilling virtuous habits, to awaken their logical faculties, and to produce right sentiments by which their reason can hold sway over their passions; and to do this especially by steeping young students in the literature, both sacred and secular, on which the culture of the community is based.[2] This is the game of education, which is worthy of our respect.

A teacher respects the game of education when she enrolls in a summer training course to learn a new pedagogical skill; or revises a lesson plan she has taught for years because the last time it didn't go the way she wanted it to; or seeks out a colleague to talk about new strategies for a struggling student; or goes the extra mile to research for her lesson even though she knows that only eighteen fifth graders will ever know what she has done; or benches a star player whose attitude disrespects the opponent.

This way of "thinking institutionally" fits hand in glove with our distinctively Christian aspiration to live *non nobis*. It's not about us.

---

2. I owe this definition of education to C. S. Lewis's article "Our English Syllabus," in *Rehabilitations and Other Essays* (London: Oxford University Press, 1939), 81.

Sportsmanship

January 27, 2012

This piece has a sad and interesting story behind it. When I wrote it, I was in the middle of a fascinating dialogue (debate?) with Trinity board member and fierce Duke and Trinity fan Peter Feaver. I published this article knowing that not everyone would agree with me, and I included in the original an invitation to disagree with me on my blog. Peter was set, I think, to do some disagreeing in his own persuasive way. On the day after the article was published, I was with Peter at the Duke–St. John's basketball game, continuing our conversation. About two hours after the game was over, I got the call that Trinity ninth grader Blake Hubbard had been killed in a tragic accident that afternoon. Understandably, I don't think anyone (including myself) paid any attention to this article.

Nevertheless, it continues to embody some of the things I think should be true of a Christian school with a strong athletic program and Non Nobis *over its gym door, and I offer it here again, since parents and fans are an essential part of the athletic program at any school.*

It's not easy being a fan. Two weeks ago I sat in the stands at Durham Academy, with two Trinity board members, watching a varsity boys basketball game. Between cheers and fist pumps we managed to have a rather interesting conversation about being good fans. I think we were all aware that we were walking that elusive line between passionate and obnoxious.

Then, last week, I went down to Southern Pines for a meeting of independent school heads across the state, the North Carolina Independent School Athletic Association winter meeting. NCISAA had enlisted sports psychologist and Trinity parent Greg Dale to lead the group in a discussion of the "R-Word"—that is, recruiting, which is verboten

10 – ATHLETICS

but often alleged among private schools. We talked a lot about sportsmanship at that meeting—mainly because Greg was trying to keep the group focused on its stated purposes, which include things like sportsmanship and fair play. It's against these stated goals that anything like recruitment needs to be evaluated.

All this has gotten me thinking about sportsmanship and fair play. For our players, but also for our fans. I'd like to venture some opinions, and I'd be glad to hear your thoughts.

- Trinity does athletics well. Our players play hard and play fairly. Our fans are, generally, more civil and generous-spirited than you would expect at a high school athletic contest. Our coaches are not screamers and don't throw chairs. I am very proud to be a part of Trinity athletics.

- I'm going to talk about being a fan, even though I know that there are many other things that we are attending to in the world of athletics and beyond. The way we cheer is not the most important thing, but it is something. And it's something that many others in our community, especially from other schools, notice.

- The way we coach and cheer teaches our children more about what it means to follow Christ than our lectures and our *Parent News* columns. Christianity is caught as much as it is taught. Maybe more than it is taught.

- Wanting to win is essential to excellence in sport; but wanting to win more than anything else will spoil the best things that sports can bring us. This is the line that recruiting (in the bad sense) crosses. It puts winning games above the more important things that a school like Trinity values in its athletic programs.

- Passion for sports is a good thing, in players and in fans; but passion thrives on discipline. Players must channel their passion through rigorous discipline, and fans need to think about how they express their passionate loyalty and enthusiasm.

- The things most worthy of our cheers and applause are the things that last: courage, perseverance, grit, hustle, striving, humility, service, kindness, and honesty. Most Trinity students aren't planning to make a life out of playing basketball; but they should all be planning to make a life that thrives on these virtues.

- The Cameron Crazies are not, for all their fame and appeal, our role models (this from a Duke alum and parent of a Duke senior currently residing in Krzyzewskiville). For a young school like Trinity, the temptation to imitate larger and more mature institutions is almost irresistible and often constructive. But this is one area where we would do well to forge our own path. My challenge to the Trinity community: let's use our creativity to find ways of cheering that are our own, true to who we are, not slavishly imitative of a model that is powered by rudeness, taunting, mockery, and bombast. Do we really want to end up cheering "Go to hell, DA"?

- Cheer for our teams; never against the other team; and rarely against the refs. This last prohibition will be controversial. It is a national pastime to deride the refs—sometimes the show in the stands is more interesting than the game on the court. But I wonder what it teaches our children when we blame the bad call. Life is full of bad calls. I don't want our students to walk around mad, hoping for a review and a reversal. I want them to get up, take their lumps, and play on, harder than before. I want them to channel the passion of their anger at a bad call into the triumph over their own worst tendencies. And to drive the lane and make the next shot. I don't want to hear, "Are you blind?" I want to hear Trinity fans urging our players on, "Forget about it! Play on!"

- Christian schools often earn a bad reputation at secular schools. It's not fair—or is it?—that we are judged by a higher standard.

10 – ATHLETICS

We expect to find jerks in every crowd, but when they have the name of the Triune God on their sweatshirt, it's not interesting, or funny, or even annoying—it's unconscionable.

One of the best experiences of this year was a soccer tournament game last fall between Trinity School and Hickory Christian. Trinity won, but that's not the best story. The best story was told by one of our parents, Rick Hove, when he wrote, on his own initiative, a letter to the head of Hickory Christian, praising the play of both teams and the sportsmanship of the game. Rick wrote, "Your team played with such class and intensity. Their character and the chemistry of your team were evident from the onset. We play in some rough games, as I'm sure you do...So when a team plays this way, it not only reflects on the players, but the coaches and ultimately the headmaster and parents. Actually it reflects Christ." That's the kind of play we want to cheer. And that's the kind of cheering we want to lead.

Non nobis.

11 – Occasional Pieces

> *Each mortal thing does one thing and the same:*
> *Deals out that being indoors each one dwells;*
> *Selves—goes itself; myself it speaks and spells,*
> *Crying What I do is me: for that I came.*
> GERARD MANLEY HOPKINS, *"AS KING FISHERS CATCH FIRE"*

This final section comprises a few pieces that were born of specific occasions and events, both in the life of Trinity and in my own experience. I include them because they are of some historical interest; they also embody what Hopkins called "inscape," that particularity of shape that a person or object (or institution) has that reveals not only its uniqueness but something of the spiritual import of its being in the world. So it is with Trinity. Every little thing matters, and sometimes the little things matter the most, or show the most what it is that we are all about.

A Second Year of Growth

January 1996

This piece was part of a newsletter the board sent out to parents and interested people. Trinity School opened in the fall of 1995, with three teachers, a part-time administrative assistant, and a board that ran the school in ways boards ought not to do. But we knew that, and we went in search of a director, and in search of land. This article gives credit to many of the principal people who made those two things happen.

The year 1995 marked Trinity School's birth. Our infancy has been marked by some major changes, and the educational pediatricians would probably chart our growth with a steep curve.

As we enter our second year of existence, we can expect a more gradual development. The changes in 1996 may be less remarkable, but they will be no less important to the health of Trinity.

Efforts are already underway to hire the school's first director. The board has appointed a search committee of people well experienced in executive, academic, and professional searches: Fred Brooks (Chair), Jane Adams, Bob Byrd, Bill Cobey, Chip Denton, and David Spence. The director will lead the school, manage its operation, and promote its interests in the community. The committee is now gathering the names of potential candidates, and we welcome suggestions. Please contact Bob Byrd via the school to provide your recommendations.

The board has also commissioned a land search committee composed of Mark Hunt, Jim Lamont, Ralph Mason, John McAdams, Lee Murphy, and John Sanders. This talented and ambitious group of people will help the board address the most important questions that must be dealt with if we are to move toward our goal of having our own facility in the near future.

All of this is in the service of educational excellence within the classical Christian tradition. Our director will embody and articulate the school's vision; our facility will enable us to offer the best education possible. These areas of growth will affect the shape and character of Trinity School for years to come, and we invite all who can to support us with your prayers, your counsel, and commitment.

For the board,

Chip Denton

A Second Year of Growth (Revisited)

October 1996

> *The value of this piece is that it gives us a picture of the school in the middle of its second year, my first as headmaster. There is a window into the different classes and the daily life of the school. And one gets a sense of the early trajectory of growth. In what other year has the school nearly doubled its enrollment and added an entire grade, too?*

I have chuckled a little to read over a newsletter from early in 1996, where I prophesied that in our second year of existence we could "expect a more gradual development." It seems I am a poor prophet. Our second academic year has brought 72 students (nearly doubling last year's student body), three new classrooms and two offices, two new teachers, and a new headmaster (I assumed my duties in August).

We'd love to give you a tour of Trinity, and we invite anyone to stop by and see our growing school. What would I want you to see if you stopped by?

I'd want you to see the fourth graders presenting their projects on the solar system, all excited because they spotted Jupiter in the southeastern sky the night before.

I'd want you to hear the third graders sounding off the states and capitals.

I'd want you to sit in my office and hear the euphonious syllables of the Pledge of Allegiance in Latin tripping off the tongues of the fourth graders next door.

11 – OCCASIONAL PIECES

I'd want you to go along with Mrs. Messer's second graders as they visit the Museum of History in Raleigh and handle some actual Native American artifacts, having studied several North Carolinian tribes.

I'd want you to listen in as grandmother and amateur ornithologist Jane Stam teaches the first graders the different calls of birds.

I'd want you to observe the fifth graders debating among themselves the question of whether Theseus or Hercules was the greater hero.

Until you can manage to stop by the school, take a few minutes to "look around" Trinity by reading over this newsletter. We thank you for your interest in our school and appreciate your support.

A School for Our Community
OCTOBER 5, 2001

The occasion for this piece was the dedication of the first permanent facility of Trinity School. We bought the land on Pickett Road in 1998 and erected the first modular unit here in 1999. In the fall of 2001, we moved into what is now the Lower School (then the only school, grades K–8—we had no TK yet). The Blue Gym was also part of this first permanent phase. On a beautiful Sunday in October of that year (the same day the US invaded Afghanistan—I will never forget!), we gathered on the front porch of the building and flowed out into the parking lot for a public dedication, as described in this article. We were privileged to hear from the late Doris Betts, writer and UNC professor, whose address captured beautifully Trinity's aspirations and possibilities. Later that year we buried a time capsule under the front porch, to be opened in fifty years.

The first brochure Trinity School ever published in 1995 stated plainly that it was our desire to be a school "for our community." In those early days of the school's life, such language was admittedly idealistic and perhaps even a little comical: After all, what could thirty-nine children under the age of ten do for the mighty Triangle? When several of us first appeared before the city commissioners to request special permission to open up a school at rented space at Hope Creek Church on Erwin Road, the real question in all our minds was not whether we were for our community but whether our community would be for us. Thankfully, their answer was affirmative, and the rest, as they say, is history.

In the seventh year of that history, on this October weekend, the community will come to us for what may well be the most public event Trinity has ever held: our building dedication. We expect to welcome several hundred people, both insiders and guests, to this exciting and gratifying event. And the occasion of such a public event gives us a chance to say, again and with perhaps a little more credibility, that we aspire to be a school "for our community." And this newsletter gives us a chance to say what we mean by such an important prepositional phrase.

The object of that preposition is the community we call Durham and Chapel Hill. The original steering committee and board were drawn from both communities, and our student body has always balanced pretty evenly between the two. It is poetic justice indeed that the line dividing Durham and Orange Counties runs through the land that now hosts our campus. We are gratified that both Rosemary Waldorf and Nick Tennyson, mayors of Chapel Hill and Durham, respectively, will honor us with their presence at Sunday's dedication.

Trinity aspires to be for our community, first, by identifying with it. As our families mirror the social, economic, religious, racial, political, and ethnic diversity of the Triangle, we sense that we are fulfilling our mission. We have a long way to go before we can say with confidence that we are where we want to be (does any school really ever get there?). We are especially aware of the challenges of identifying Trinity with the African-American and Hispanic communities that are so vital to this place we call home. Still, we rejoice in some real progress: Our families hail from about forty different churches in the Durham-Chapel Hill area; our sixth through eighth graders spend an afternoon each month in the community doing service projects; we have begun a Spanish program for our youngest students; and we have been able to attract gifted people of color to some important positions of leadership in our school.

There is more, however, to our vocation in this community. We serve Durham and Chapel Hill best as we honor our distinctive calling as a Christian school of excellence. At the first gathering of the steering committee of the school, in early February of 1995, the question was asked, "Describe the sort of school you could be excited to help build."

What was remarkable about that conversation was the unity of vision that was there at the beginning and has continued ever since: our calling is to be both a confessional (not denominational) Christian school and a school of serious intellectual pursuit. Our own short history and the longer history of Christian schools and colleges in our country show us that the marriage of thoroughgoing Christian faith and the pursuit of academic excellence has not always been an easy one. But between the Scylla of anti-intellectual religiosity and the Charybdis of a postmodern secularism lies a way: the life of the mind in submission to the One who is Life and Truth, our Lord Christ.

We recognize that this is a distinctive calling that sets us apart from our community at large—a community that is either united by secularism or divided by sectarianism. The best thing we can do for our community is to be different from our community, to be a school that refuses to compromise on its commitment to "mere Christianity," that focuses on the bedrock truths that have united Christians across time and tradition. The Head of our school taught us this: "You are the salt of the earth. But if the salt loses its saltiness, how can it be made salty again?" And so it is our deep conviction that if our school ever becomes something different than a Christian school of excellence, we will have failed not only ourselves and our founders, but also the Durham–Chapel Hill community.

The prospect of building this school is exhilarating. As we dedicate this, our first permanent facility, may we rededicate ourselves to the dream that kept us going long before we had a school building of our own, the same dream that will keep this beautiful building from becoming a haunted schoolhouse one day: Trinity School, where serious-minded and generous-spirited Christians of different traditions gather to learn and pray together, to welcome people of different faiths and of none who want to share in our quest, all to the glory of God.

My Chronicle of Narnia

December 9, 2005

I remember where I was when I wrote this: in the den at our home on Hulon Drive. The movie was coming out, and I had a strong sense that our entire culture was about to take over something that was very precious to me. This article was an attempt to claim something and also an attempt to testify. I sent it to the Durham paper and they published it in the OpEd section. And we did take a crowd of older Trinity students to the show that Christmas.

I was once a king in Narnia, and always will be now. This week Hollywood gives me an excuse to tell the story of how I first came through the wardrobe into the snowy wood with the lamppost and met Mr. Tumnus with his parcels. And, eventually, Aslan. Trinity School, too, comes into this story.

I was eighteen, home from my first year of college, home for Christmas. My parents' house on Yosemite Trail was not the Professor's English country estate, but for this sort of adventure, really, any house will do. Lucy wandered into the spare room and found the wardrobe; I, somehow, wandered into a bookstore and found a boxed set of books I had never heard of. I cannot tell you why I bought *The Chronicles of Narnia* (deep magic?), but I did and then retired to my bedroom where I discovered a portal to a world I had not known before. If any man is in Christ, he is a new creation, and I shall never be the same again.

The wardrobe door does not always open into Narnia, and only Aslan knows why it opened for me that Christmas in 1976. I was surely not trying to get in. I had skirted Narnian woods all my life: my parents took me to church every Sunday, for Sunday School and worship and youth group to boot. But by the time I headed off to college I was bored with religion and uncommitted to the most basic truths. Some things had happened that first fall at Emory that piqued my interest—a fraternity Bible study in Mark's Gospel, for instance—but I was merely *interested.* It took me another six months, the rest of my freshman year, to come to a settled Christian conviction, but I know now, looking back, that I passed into another world when I read *The Lion, the Witch and the Wardrobe.*

Lewis says somewhere that before he became a Christian, his imagination was baptized by reading the fiction of George MacDonald. Exactly! Narnia baptized my imagination and prepared the way for my conversion, which is a change not of the mind alone, but of the heart and the will. Through reading the Narnian Chronicles, I found myself *wanting* to find that other world, *wanting* to meet Aslan. And I began to think that, given the chance, I would *choose* just such a life.

With stout and grateful heart, I raise my glass to you, my Virgil, donned in rumpled tweed.

You can see that I care a little too much about this movie coming out on Friday. It will never be good enough, so I really don't want to see it. I am wondering who this director is, Mr. Adamson, who lays hands on the Narnian tale. Has he been to Narnia before? (I'm not likely to find that out—Aslan tells each one his own story, and not another's.) Will Disney manage to make its bucks and keep the Christian fabric of the tale whole? Can a movie baptize the imagination the way I know a book can, or do surround sound and special effects cauterize that faculty?

But I will see the film. In fact, we are planning to take the sixth, seventh, and eighth graders for a school-wide viewing, and then return to talk about it in classes and smaller groups. For in the end I know that he is not a tame Lion, and I wonder if maybe, just maybe, this will be the Christmas that some Trinity student hears the crunch of Narnia snow beneath her feet and feels the warm breath of the Lion who speaks "Peace, child."

Boundary Lines in Pleasant Places
December 12, 2008

The economic downturn of 2008 hit us all hard. Schools everywhere were pivoting and plotting new strategies to deal with the financial challenges facing them. As this article reveals, Trinity had providentially entered into a strategic planning project under the guidance of Independent School Management. Veteran consultant Walker Buckalew showed up just in time. The rigorous standards of ISM's Stability Rating and their disciplined and inflexible template for planning were good tonic for us. Wendell Berry's piece in Harper's *went along with this hand in glove. By God's grace Trinity has continued to grow through these tough times. The message of this piece continues to be relevant, I think, even as the economy has improved. Hitching aspirations to outlays continues to be a necessary boundary, especially as we struggle to keep a Trinity education accessible.*

It is a helpful exercise to say what one is not. A school's excellence is bounded by its calling, its mission, its resources. A school cannot be all things, else it will end up being too many things, and none of them particularly remarkable. We have long said that that most curious word in our mission, *unhurried*, means at least this: to do a few things well. What are those few things? And what are the many which one has chosen not to do—or, if you believe in God's calling, which do not fall within God's good and perfect will for this school?

Such a pruning of the wish lists would have been almost heretical even a year ago. But the times they are a-changin', and have changed in fact. Limits are coming back in vogue. Saving, reducing debt, planning cautiously, budgeting—these are all at the top of the agenda now, like it or not. The current climate has forced us all to learn how to hitch appetites to outlays (in the words of George Will) and not the other way around. It seems to me that every institution I know—certainly every school I know—is being forced to exercise thrift, moderation, and prudent self-governance. I do not want to make light of the pain which many are feeling in this present economic climate, but such virtues are worth fighting for, and if we can come out of this with more temperance and less greed, we will have gained something valuable.

Trinity is not immune from the leveraging and hopeful optimism that attended this cultural journey, now interrupted by such a precipitous fall in the general economy. We've grown every year in our enrollment. We've built new buildings before we had the students to fill them, on the hopeful premise that if we build it they will come. And we've birthed a new Upper School, which has been like starting the school all over again.

Recently the school leaders gathered on a Saturday for a marathon session of strategic planning. Six months ago, long before we had a whiff of this downturn, we invited a seasoned consultant from Independent School Management to come and lead us through this process, which would end in a five-year plan to guide the school in its growth and allocation of resources. I think every board member and senior staffer would agree with me that the timing of this planning could not have been more providential. With the economy in a tailspin, it was the perfect time for us to ask hard questions about where we wanted to take the school and what resources we would need to get there. Much of our time was spent in facing the reality that there were many things on our wish lists which were simply not possible in the next few years.

This may sound dismal, but it is not. Limits are good, not bad. As Wendell Berry has pointed out in a recent essay in *Harper's*,[1] hell is the place where there are no boundaries (like Lewis's sprawling purgatory in *The Great Divorce*), and it was Milton's Satan who could not abide the necessarily limiting nature of being a creature. The saints think and speak differently: "The boundary lines have fallen for me in pleasant places" (Ps. 16:6).

---

1. Wendell Berry, "Faustian Economics," *Harper's* (May 2008), 35–42.

In pleasant places indeed. On the cusp of this Thanksgiving season, let us give thanks for the wonderful land we enjoy as a school. And for the mission, still healthy and intact after fourteen years of being an orthodox (talk about boundaries!) Christian school which cares deeply about good education. We may not be able to offer the bells and whistles which would be ours if our boundaries were different, but that is not simply OK—it's good. There are some resources which, though bounded and limited, are inexhaustible. Like faith, hope, and love. And the joy of learning the truth.

So in this season when we tighten our belts and learn to do without, let us do so with the confidence that God, who has been very good to Trinity School, will continue to guide us. And in a few months, when we publish our strategic plan for the next five years, don't expect everything you could imagine. But do expect something worth investing in: a Trinity School that is striving to offer an excellent Christian education.

What I Learned in Africa

November 12, 2010

> *In 2010 my daughter took six months off from her Duke studies to live in Moshi, Tanzania, and explore African culture. In October of that year, Desirée and I went to visit her, and at the end of our time we visited South Africa, where we witnessed first-hand the work of Mukhanyo Christian Academy (MCA), a school that friends of Trinity had started. Trinity's connection to MCA has only grown stronger over the years, with a band of our students taking leadership to sponsor what is now our annual Run for Mukhanyo. Several of those students recently made a trip to MCA to get to know the students, do some student teaching, and help with the construction of a field and playground. It is gratifying to see this relationship strengthen. The challenge of sustainable and dignifying help continues to be a real one, and my hope is that the creativity of these students may bring to light new paradigms for helping these poor brothers and sisters.*

Many of you have asked about my trip to Africa. Some of you have even said remarkable things like, "When will we get to hear more about it?" Visions of an interminable Trinity family slide show darted through my head for just a few moments, but this column is probably a much more merciful way to subject you to my remembrances. Here are some of the lessons I brought back. None of it is groundbreaking, but I learned it for myself and I expect it will stick to me in new ways. I hope so.

That joy and generosity are often inversely proportional to prosperity

I am picturing ninety-year-old GoGo, the grandmother of one of the students at Mukhanyo Christian Academy in South Africa. When we visited her at her squalid home, we found at least a dozen children around her. I don't know how many of them she has to feed. I do know that she is the only adult in her grandson's life and that every Thursday night she leaves him alone in the ramshackle home so she can travel to the big city of Pretoria to beg on Fridays. When we arrived at her home, escorted by two teachers and an administrator from the school, she fell all over herself to say "Thank you" for the school, which is a light in her darkness. So thankful was she that she fetched a beautiful grass sleeping mat (*icansi* in Zulu), which she had made herself, and presented it to Desirée. It was far and away the nicest thing in her house, and every part of us wanted to scream "There's been a terrible mistake! Please take this back." Our hosts shot us silent, meaningful glances, and we understood immediately to keep our unworthiness to ourselves and simply accept the gift. GoGo's smile and pride and joy almost made my American guilt vanish. I am still amazed by this gift. You'll find it hanging on the wall in the Great Room.

That the gulf between rich and poor is almost unimaginable

I knew this before I got to Africa. Our latest US Census confirmed this. Former President Jimmy Carter has been sounding this concern for some time. But the disparity hits home hard when one travels to Africa. Poignant moment for me: on our last night near Jo'burg the fledgling Mukhanyo Christian School was burglarized for the second time in two weeks. They stole all the tables and chairs and the students' artwork. Driving us to the airport, one of the teachers was lamenting this tragedy and the fact that the school simply couldn't afford an alarm system. I asked how much an alarm system cost. The answer: about the same amount we paid to go on a one-day safari.

That education matters

I visited four schools on my trip. Of the four, the ones that caught my imagination were three schools that are educating the African poor. One was Amani Centre for Street Children in Moshi. They send social workers out onto the streets and fill buses with AIDS orphans, whom they bring to their boarding school, where the children receive food, medical care, and an education. The school does all it can to reunite these orphans with extended family or village neighbors. The second school was the School of St. Jude in Arusha, whose tagline is "Fighting Poverty through Education." It's an amazing place, started by an Australian. They educate about 1,400 of the brightest and poorest Tanzanian children. Their goal is to graduate generations of Tanzanians who have the skills and education to make their own lives better and to invest themselves in Tanzania's future. It's an exciting vision, which many in Australia and beyond have caught onto. The third school was the fledgling Mukhanyo Christian Academy I've mentioned already. Trinity has strong unofficial ties to this school, and it was a joy to see that the original vision has come to fruition. These children are receiving an education, modeled on Trinity's curriculum, which is far superior to what they would be getting otherwise.

That English is the key

Signs placarded across St. Jude's read, simply, "Speak English." My daughter has had no trouble forming an English class from the local girls she has met in the marketplace in Moshi. Students at Mukhanyo speak a half dozen tribal languages, but MCA classes are all held in English. This is such a valuable skill for the students, as their standard exams will be given in English. It's almost unimaginable, but students from rural and impoverished schools across Africa are educated in their native tongues and then asked to take exams in English, exams which determine whether they can advance in school. English is the lingua franca of Africa, and those who master it will be the leaders of the future.

That aid is a problem

So I admit to having picked up Dambisa Moyo's *Dead Aid* in the Jo'burg airport; and I admit further that I haven't read the counterpoint to her provocative and incendiary thesis that aid is the problem in Africa. But the reason I picked up the book is that the more time I spent in Africa the less certain I became that Western aid had really benefited the African continent. There's more here than I can explore right now, but I'd be very interested to have Trinity students explore this subject and to see what new paradigms (microfinancing, entrepreneurial solutions, etc.) might help Africa, honor Africans' dignity, and create a sustainable model by which non-Western generosity can be channeled for long-term good. One of the good stories I saw was Jenny's friend Sinead, who has started a business with African women. They crochet purses, beautiful purses, and sell them in Chicago and New York. Sinead used to be a buyer for Ralph Lauren, so when you combine the painstaking craftsmanship of the African mamas with the discerning taste of a Western fashionista, you can create something really special. The women are making money, opening bank accounts, and plowing profits back into the business. The purse I bought for Desirée was one of the best gifts I've bought her in a long time, and all the more since we got to give the money directly to Mama Abel, who made the purse.

That I love my wife and daughter

I told you that my lessons weren't groundbreaking, just true and powerful. You husbands and parents will know what a blessing it is to have some unhurried time with the people we love. And for you parents of younger children, let me add that it's a joy to have your children grow up. I know we often cry and lament the fact that their childhoods are passing, but there is a new joy in seeing them grow into the people God has made them to be and to discover his calling on their lives. My prayer is that we're setting you all up for that kind of joy in the future.

Thanks for listening, and if anyone really wants the slideshow, I'd be glad to oblige!

Our Given Christmas Story

December 16, 2010

I close with this piece. Its occasion was Christmas, but more personally my mother-in-law's declining health. When I wrote this I had no idea that she would die within two months, and that this would be the last Christmas we had with her. She had lived in our home for her last years, and I learned a great deal from that experience.

I think this article is a fitting ending to this volume, because it is really about the Gospel, which is at the center of all that Trinity is and does. I have learned so much about the truth of the Gospel through my time at Trinity. I can't imagine caring for my mother-in-law without Trinity: its community, its support, its reminders of the most important things. One day Trinity will go on without me. And one day, perhaps, I will go on without Trinity. But I pray that neither goes on without this Gospel story at the center. Soli Deo gloria.

My mother-in-law, who lives with us, has dementia. When I come home at the end of the day and greet her, she is likely to say something bizarre like, "How many chickens did you sell?" And if I leave and come back in five minutes, I might as well have been gone for three days. We start all over, and probably not with chickens. In our family we laugh about this. I think it is the laugh of love, which knows that comedy is a humane way of handling tragedy.

Just the other night, my son came bounding downstairs with a copy of Oliver Sacks's *The Man Who Mistook His Wife for a Hat*. Sacks is a clinical neurologist who writes sympathetically observant essays about patients with neurological disorders. "Read this page," Teddy exclaimed. "Doesn't this remind you of Beannie [his grandmother]?" Sacks was speaking about Mr. Thompson, a patient with Korsakoff syndrome, who was continually disoriented. "Abysses of amnesia would open constantly before him, and he would bridge them, nimbly, by fluent confabulations and fictions of all kinds."[1] Sacks points out that he had literally to make himself and his world up every moment. This is quite different from most of us: "We have, each of us, a life-story, an inner narrative—whose continuity, whose sense, *is* our lives. It might be said that each of us constructs and lives a 'narrative,' and that this narrative *is* us, our identities."[2]

My mother-in-law doesn't have Korsakoff syndrome, but my son was still seeing something. She has to make herself and her world up every moment. Her narrative is no longer cohesive and dependable. It's not that she doesn't need a narrative; in fact, to be with her is to watch her struggling to find or invent a life story. Most of us enjoy, without recognizing it, a *given* story, which we assume without much effort. Not my mother-in-law. Dementia must be exhausting.

It occurs to me that I suffer from a sort of spiritual dementia. I forget who I am and contradict my real story. I live in this world as though it were my home. I act like a slave and not a son. I am motivated more by guilt and fear than by love. I try over and over to justify myself, to prove who I am by what I accomplish. I work the angles so that I can please as many people as possible. I think that if I throw one more sacrifice in the fire I will be happy and God will be pleased. A man who lives like this is really quite disoriented. It's not that he doesn't need a narrative; in fact, to be with him is to watch him struggling to find or invent a story that works. All this flailing about is just a sign that he has not possessed a *given* story. Spiritual dementia is exhausting.

Every Christmas I am *given* a story that starts like this:

> "In those days, a decree went out from Caesar Augustus that all the world should be registered..."[3]

---

1. Oliver Sacks, *The Man Who Mistook His Wife for a Hat* (New York: Simon & Schuster, 1985), 109.
2. Sacks, *Man Who Mistook*, 110.
3. Luke 2:1 (ESV).

It is a familiar story. Sometimes I have thought it too familiar and have wished that I could hear it now for the first time, fresh and unaffected by many hearings. But this Christmas, with dementias on my mind, it occurs to me that the familiarity is a good thing. This story about a Savior and God's glory is our given story, the one whose continuity is our life. My spiritual maturity is directly proportional to the likelihood that in any given interaction I will assume this narrative as mine. When Luke tells us that Mary "treasured up all these things and pondered them in her heart,"[4] she is modeling for us the life of faith.

One of the things you can count on from Trinity School is that we will tell this story to our students over and over and over again. Just as we want their multiplication facts to become automatic, so we want this story to be their given narrative: I am not my own; God is first; God rescued me in Christ so that I might live for him. *Non nobis, Domine*. Glory to God in the highest.

I love the story of the demon-possessed man in Mark's Gospel. Jesus met him and rescued him, showing in a powerful way what it meant for him to be his Savior. And when his friends and neighbors came looking for him, they were astonished to find him "clothed and in his right mind." No more spiritual dementia for this man. He had a story, about a Savior and about God's glory.

So do we. Merry Christmas.

---

4. Luke 2:19.

Bibliography

Aquinas, Thomas. *Summa Theologica.* Vols. 19–20 of *Great Books of the Western World.* Edited by Robert Maynard Hutchins. Chicago: Encyclopaedia Britannica, 1952.

———. "Whether the Will Is a Higher Power Than the Intellect." In *Summa Theologica. Great Books of the Western World*, vol. 19, 434. Chicago: Encyclopaedia Britannica, 1952.

Aristotle. "Moral Goodness." In *The Nicomachean Ethics.* Translated by J. A. K. Thomson and Hugh Tredennick. Harmondsworth: Penguin, 1976.

Athanasius. *On the Incarnation.* Translated and edited by a Religious of CSMV, with an introduction by C. S. Lewis. Crestwood, NY: St. Vladimir's Seminary Press, 1993. Original edition published in 1944 by Centenary Press.

Auchincloss, Louis. *The Rector of Justin.* Boston: Houghton Mifflin, 1964.

Augustine. *The City of God.* Translated by Marcus Dods, DD, with an introduction by Thomas Merton. New York: Modern Library (Random House), 1978.

———. *The Confessions.* Translated by Philip Burton, with an introduction by Robin Lane Fox. New York: A. A. Knopf, 2001.

———. *On Christian Doctrine.* Translated by D. W. Robertson. New York: Macmillan, 1986.

Barbour, Ian G. "Ways of Relating Science and Religion." Chap. 4 in *Religion and Science: Historical and Contemporary Issues.* San Francisco: HarperSanFrancisco, 1997.

Barnard, Chester I. *The Functions of the Executive.* Cambridge, MA: Harvard University Press, 1971. First published 1938.

Bassett, Patrick F. "Listening to Students of Color." *Independent School Magazine*, Summer 2003. www.nais.org/Magazines-Newsletters/ISMagazine/Pages/Listening-to-Students-of-Color.aspx.

Bennett, Arthur, ed. *The Valley of Vision: A Collection of Puritan Prayers and Devotions.* Edinburgh: Banner of Truth Trust, 2002.

Berry, Wendell. "Faustian Economics." *Harper's*, May 2008: 35–42.

Blair, Kristen. "When Homework Becomes Overwork." *Carolina Journal Online*, May 8, 2014. http://www.carolinajournal.com/opinions/display_story.html?id=11055.

Boreiko, Karla. Opinion article in *The Chapel Hill Herald* (local edition of *The Herald-Sun*, Durham, NC), February 13, 1997.

Boswell, James. *The Life of Samuel Johnson*, vol. 4. Oxford English Classics. London: Talboys and Wheeler, and William Pickering, 1826. https://books.google.com/books?id=GXVwaQsnAOwC.

Boyd, Danah. *It's Complicated: The Social Lives of Networked Teens*. New Haven: Yale University Press, 2014.

Brooks, David. *Bobos in Paradise: The New Upper Class and How They Got There*. New York: Simon & Schuster, 2001.

———. "The Organization Kid." *The Atlantic Monthly* 287, no. 4 (April 2001): 40–54. http://www.theatlantic.com/magazine/archive/2001/04/the-organization-kid/302164/.

Bruce Cockburn. *The Charity of Night*. Produced by Bruce Cockburn and Colin Linden. Phantom Sound & Vision, B000093FSA, 1996, compact disc.

———. *Dart to the Heart*. Produced by T. Bone Burnett. Columbia Records, B00000295H, 1994, compact disc.

Carr, Nicholas G. *The Shallows: What the Internet Is Doing to Our Brains*. New York: W. W. Norton & Company, 2010.

Chesterton, G. K. "The Ethics of Elfland." Chap. 4 in *Orthodoxy*. San Francisco: Ignatius Press, 1995. First published 1908 by John Lane Company.

———. *The Everlasting Man*. San Francisco: Ignatius Press, 1993. First published in 1923 by Dodd, Mead & Co.

———. *What's Wrong with the World*. New York: Dodd, Mead & Company, 1910.

Christensen, Clayton M., Michael B. Horn, and Curtis W. Johnson. *Disrupting Class: How Disruptive Innovation Will Change the Way the World Learns*. New York: McGraw-Hill, 2008.

Cicero. *De Officiis*, book 1. Loeb Classical Library. Cambridge: Harvard University Press, 1913.

———. *De Oratore*, books 1 and 2. Translated by E. W. Sutton, with an introduction by H. Rackham. London: W. Heinemann, 1967. First published in 1944.

Collins, Billy. "On Slowing Down." Choate Rosemary Hall graduation address, June 3, 2001. Reprinted in *Independent School Magazine*, Summer 2003. http://www.nais.org/Magazines-Newsletters/ISMagazine/Pages/On-Slowing-Down.aspx.

BIBLIOGRAPHY

Collins, Francis S. *The Language of God: A Scientist Presents Evidence for Belief.* New York: Free Press, 2006.

Comenius, John Amos. *The Great Didactic of John Amos Comenius.* With an introduction by M. W. Keatinge. London: A. and C. Black, 1910. Facsimile of the second edition, reprinted by Kessinger Publishing.

Cooper, Elaine. *When Children Love to Learn: A Practical Application of Charlotte Mason's Philosophy for Today.* Wheaton, IL: Crossway Books, 2004.

Cooper, Harris. "Does Homework Improve Academic Achievement?" *Duke Today*, September 23, 2006. http://today.duke.edu/2006/09/homework_oped.html.

Csikszentmihaly, Mihaly. *Flow: The Psychology of Optimal Experience.* New York: Harper & Row, 1990.

Darley, John M., and C. Daniel Batson. " 'From Jerusalem to Jericho': A Study of Situational and Dispositional Variables in Helping Behavior." *Journal of Personality and Social Psychology* 27:1 (1973), 100–108.

Davidson, Cathy N. *Now You See It: How Technology and Brain Science Will Transform Schools and Business for the 21st Century.* New York: Penguin, 2011.

Dean, Jeremy. *Making Habits, Breaking Habits: Why We Do Things, Why We Don't, and How to Make Any Change Stick.* Boston: Da Capo Lifelong, 2013.

Delbanco, Andrew. *College: What It Was, Is, and Should Be.* Princeton, NJ: Princeton University Press, 2012.

———. *The Real American Dream: A Meditation on Hope.* Cambridge: Harvard University Press, 1999.

Dobell, Brian. "The Rejection of Platonic Ascent." In *Augustine's Intellectual Conversion: The Journey from Platonism to Christianity*, New York: Cambridge University Press, 2009.

Eliot, T. S. "The Idea of a Christian Society." In *Christianity and Culture.* Orlando, FL: Harcourt Brace & Company, 1976.

———. "Notes Towards the Definition of Culture." In *Christianity and Culture.* Orlando, FL: Harcourt Brace & Company, 1976.

Ellul, Jacques. *The Presence of the Kingdom.* 2nd ed. Colorado Springs, CO: Belmers & Howard, 1989.

———. *The Technological Society.* New York: Vintage Books (Alfred A. Knopf), 1964.

Emerson, Ralph Waldo. "An Address." In *The Essential Writings of Ralph Waldo Emerson.* Edited by Brooks Atkinson. New York: Modern Library, 2000.

Finkel, Donald L. *Teaching with Your Mouth Shut.* Portsmouth, NH: Boynton/Cook Publishers, 2000.

Friedman, Thomas L. *The World Is Flat: A Brief History of the Twenty-First Century*. New York: Farrar, Straus and Giroux, 2005.

Gaebelein, Frank E. *The Pattern of God's Truth: Problems of Integration in Christian Education*. Winona Lake, IN: BMH Books, 2009.

Galilei, Galileo. *The Assayer*. Abridged and translated by Stillman Drake. First published in 1623. web.stanford.edu/~jsabol/certainty/readings/Galileo-Assayer.pdf.

Galloway, Mollie, Jerusha Conner, and Denise Pope. "Nonacademic Effects of Homework in Privileged, High-Performing Schools." *Journal of Experimental Education* 81, no. 4 (2013), 490–510.

Gay, Peter. *Mozart*. London: Weidenfeld & Nicolson, 1999.

Gilson, Etienne. *The Arts of the Beautiful*. Normal, IL: Dalkey Archive Press, 2000. First published in 1965 by Scribner.

Goldsmith, Barbara. *Obsessive Genius: The Inner World of Marie Curie*. New York: W. W. Norton, 2005.

Greenfeld, Karl Taro. "My Daughter's Homework Is Killing Me." *The Atlantic Monthly*, September 18, 2013. http://www.theatlantic.com/magazine/archive/2013/10/my-daughters-homework-is-killing-me/309514/.

Hamilton, Alexander. *The Federalist*. Cambridge, MA: Belknap Press of Harvard University Press, 1961.

Hanson, Victor Davis, and John Heath. *Who Killed Homer? The Demise of Classical Education and the Recovery of Greek Wisdom*. New York: Free Press, 1998.

Hart, Betty, and Todd R. Risley. *Meaningful Differences in the Everyday Experience of Young American Children*. Baltimore: P.H. Brookes, 1995.

Heclo, Hugh. *On Thinking Institutionally*. Boulder, CO: Paradigm Publishers, 2008.

Hirsch, E. D. *The Schools We Need and Why We Don't Have Them*. New York: Doubleday, 1996.

———, ed. *What Your Second Grader Needs to Know: Fundamentals of a Good Second-Grade Education*. New York: Dell, 1993.

Hoffmann, Roald. "Research Strategy: Teach." *American Scientist* 84 (January 1996): 20-22.

Homer. *The Odyssey*. Translated by Robert Fagles, with introduction and notes by Bernard Knox. New York: Penguin, 1996.

Hopkins, Gerard Manley. "As King Fishers Catch Fire." In *Poems and Prose*. New York: Penguin Classics, 1985.

Howard, Thomas. "What My Children Won't Learn in School." *Christianity Today*, September 3, 1982: 26–27.

Hugo, Victor. *Les Miserables*. New York: Penguin Group, 1987.

Jacobs, Jane. *The Death and Life of Great American Cities*. New York: Random House, 1961.

James, William. *Habit*. New York: Henry Holt and Company, 1890.

John Coltrane. *A Love Supreme*. Performed by John Coltrane's Quartet. Recorded December 1964. Impulse Records, B000063IZQ, 1965, LP 33-1/3 rpm.

Jones, L. Gregory. *Embodying Forgiveness: A Theological Analysis*. Grand Rapids, MI: Wm. B. Eerdmans, 1995.

Jordan, David Starr. "Agassiz at Penikese." *Popular Science Monthly* 40 (April 1892): 721–28. Reprinted as a monograph by Marine Biological Laboratory, 1907. http://en.wikisource.org/wiki/Popular_Science_Monthly/Volume_40/April_1892/Agassiz_at_Penikese.

———. "With Agassiz at Penikese." *The Independent* 62 (1907): 1179.

Justin Martyr. *Second Apology*. In *Fathers of the Church: Saint Justin Martyr*. Translated by Thomas B. Falls. New York: Christian Heritage, 1949.

Kahneman, Daniel. *Thinking, Fast and Slow*. New York: Farrar, Straus and Giroux, 2011.

Keller, Helen. *The Story of My Life*. New York: Bantam Dell, 2005.

King, Martin Luther, Jr. "Letter from Birmingham Jail." www.uscrossier.org/pullias/wp-content/uploads/2012/06/King.pdf. Originally published as "The Negro Is Your Brother," *The Atlantic Monthly* 212, no.2 (August 1963), 78–88.

Kirk, Russell. *Prospects for Conservatives*, rev. ed. Washington, DC: Regnery Gateway, 1989. Previously published as *A Program for Conservatives*. Chicago: Henry Regnery, 1962.

Kuyper, Abraham. "Sphere Sovereignty." In *Abraham Kuyper: A Centennial Reader*. Edited by James D. Bratt. Grand Rapids, MI: Wm. B. Eerdmans, 1998.

Lewis, C. S. "The Christian in the World." Chap. 3 in *C. S. Lewis: Essay Collection and Other Short Pieces*. Edited by Lesley Walmsley. London: HarperCollins, 2000.

———. *The Chronicles of Narnia*. 7 vols. New York: HarperCollins Publishers, 2001.

———. *The Great Divorce*. New York: Macmillan Company, 1946.

———. Introduction to *On the Incarnation*, by Athanasius. Translated by a Religious of CSMV. Crestwood, NY: St. Vladimir's Seminary Press, 1993. First published in 1944 by Centenary Press.

———. *The Magician's Nephew*. Vol. 6 of The Chronicles of Narnia. New York: HarperCollins, 1994.

———. "The Necessity of Chivalry." In *Present Concerns*. Edited by Walter Hooper. San Diego: Harcourt Brace Jovanovich, 1986.

———. "On a Theme from Nicholas of Cusa (*De Docta Ignorantia*, III, ix)." In *Poems*. Edited by Walter Hooper. New York: Harcourt Brace Jovanovich, 1977.

———. "Our English Syllabus." In *Rehabilitations and Other Essays*. London: Oxford University Press, 1939.

———. *Present Concerns*. Edited by Walter Hooper. San Diego: Harcourt, 1986.

———. *Surprised by Joy: The Shape of My Early Life*. New York: Harcourt, Brace, 1956.

Louv, Richard. *Last Child in the Woods: Saving Our Children from Nature-Deficit Disorder*. Chapel Hill, NC: Algonquin Books, 2008.

Macaulay, Susan Schaeffer. *For the Children's Sake: Foundations of Education for Home and School*. Westchester, IL: Crossway Books, 1984.

Marcou, Jules. *Life, Letters, and Works of Louis Agassiz*, vol. 1. New York: Macmillan & Co., 1896.

Maritain, Jacques. "The Nature of Man and Education; The Christian Idea of Man." In *Education at the Crossroads*. New Haven: Yale University Press, 1943.

Mason, Charlotte M. *Home Education*. The Original Home Schooling Series, vol. 1. Rockland, ME: Charlotte Mason Research & Supply, 1989. First published by Kegan Paul, Trench, Trubner and Co. in 1925.

———. *A Philosophy of Education*. The Original Home Schooling Series, vol. 6. Rockland, ME: Charlotte Mason Research & Supply, 1989. First published by Kegan Paul, Trench, Trubner and Co. in 1925.

———. *School Education*. The Original Home Schooling Series, vol. 3. Rockland, ME: Charlotte Mason Research & Supply, 1989. First published by Kegan Paul, Trench, Trubner and Co. in 1925.

Medina, John. *Brain Rules: Twelve Principles for Surviving and Thriving at Work, Home, and School*. Seattle: Pear Press, 2008.

Merton, Thomas. *The Seven Storey Mountain*. Orlando, FL: Harcourt Brace, 1998.

Mischel, Walter, and Ebbe B. Ebbesen. "Attention in Delay of Gratification." *Journal of Personality and Social Psychology* 16, no. 2 (1970), 329–37.

Mogel, Wendy. *The Blessing of a B Minus: Using Jewish Teachings to Raise Resilient Teenagers*. New York: Scribner, 2010.

BIBLIOGRAPHY

———. *The Blessing of a Skinned Knee: Using Jewish Teachings to Raise Self-Reliant Children.* New York: Penguin Compass, 2001.

Moyo, Dambisa. *Dead Aid: Why Aid Is Not Working and How There Is a Better Way for Africa.* New York: Farrar, Straus and Giroux, 2009.

Murphy, Shane M. *The Cheers and the Tears: A Healthy Alternative to the Dark Side of Youth Sports Today.* San Francisco: Jossey-Bass Publishers, 1999.

National Endowment for the Arts. "Reading at Risk: A Survey of Literary Reading in America." Research Division Report #46. Washington, DC: National Endowment for the Arts, 2004. http://arts.gov/sites/default/files/ReadingAtRisk.pdf.

Neely, Jack. *Knoxville's Secret History.* Knoxville, TN: Scruffy City Publishing, 1995.

Newton, Isaac. *Newton's Principia: The Mathematical Principles of Natural Philosophy.* Translated by Andrew Motte. New York: Daniel Adee, 1846. http://archive.org/stream/newtonspmathema00newtrich.

Niebuhr, H. Richard. *Christ and Culture.* New York: HarperCollins, 2001. First published in 1951 by Harper & Row.

Niebuhr, Reinhold. *The Irony of American History.* Chicago: University of Chicago Press, 2008. First published in 1952 by Charles Scribner's Sons.

Nietzsche, Friedrich. "Maxims and Arrows." In *Twilight of the Idols.* Oxford: Oxford University Press, 1998.

Noll, Mark A. *The Scandal of the Evangelical Mind.* Grand Rapids, MI: Wm. B. Eerdmans, 1994.

Parvin, Paige P. "The Vanishing Bookworm." *Emory Magazine*, Spring 2005. http://www.emory.edu/EMORY_MAGAZINE/spring_2005/reading_at_risk.html.

Pink, Daniel H. *A Whole New Mind: Why Right-Brainers Will Rule the Future.* New York: Riverhead Books, 2006.

Plato. *The Republic.* Translated by Benjamin Jowett. New York: Modern Library, 1982.

———. *Symposium.* Translated, with introduction and notes, by Alexander Nehamas and Paul Woodruff. Indianapolis, IN: Hackett Publishing Company, 1989.

Plummer, Ken. "Life Stories and the Narrative Turn." In *Documents of Life 2: An Invitation to a Critical Humanism*, vol. 2. Gateshead: Athenaeum Press, 2001.

Polkinghorne, John C. *Belief in God in an Age of Science.* New Haven, CT: Yale University Press, 1998.

BIBLIOGRAPHY

Postman, Neil. "Education." In *Building a Bridge to the 18th Century: How the Past Can Improve Our Future*. New York: Alfred A. Knopf, 1999.

———. *The End of Education: Redefining the Value of School*. New York: Knopf, 1995.

Powers, William. *Hamlet's Blackberry: A Practical Philosophy for Building a Good Life in the Digital Age*. New York: Harper, 2010.

Ptolemy. *The Almagest*. Translated by R. Catesby Taliaferro and Charles Glenn Wallis. Chicago: Encyclopædia Britannica, 1955.

Ripley, Amanda. *The Smartest Kids in the World: And How They Got That Way*. New York: Simon & Schuster, 2013.

Romney, Patricia. "Closing the Achievement Gap? Five Questions Every School Should Ask." *Independent School Magazine* 62, no. 4 (Summer 2003): 30–35.

Rousseau, Jean-Jacques. *Emile: Selections*. Translated by William Boyd. New York: Bureau of Publications, Teachers College, Columbia University, 1962.

Sacks, Oliver W. *The Man Who Mistook His Wife for a Hat and Other Clinical Tales*. New York: Simon & Schuster, 1998.

Sayers, Dorothy. "The Lost Tools of Learning." Paper presented at a Vacation Course in Education, Oxford, 1947, and published in revised form in *Hibbert Journal: A Quarterly Review of Religion, Theology, and Philosophy* 46 (October 1947–July 1948). http://www.accsedu.org/filerequest/2552.

Smith, Nora Archibald. "The Book of Nature." In *The Child Welfare Manual: A Handbook of Child Nature and Nurture for Parents and Teachers*, vol. 2. New York: The University Society, 1915.

Taylor, James S. *Poetic Knowledge: The Recovery of Education*. Albany, NY: State University of New York Press, 1998.

———. "Something Like Perfection: The Recovery of Education." *Classical Homeschooling* 2. http://classicalhomeschooling.com/classical-homeschooling-second-issue/something-like-perfection.

Tolstoy, Leo. *Anna Karenina*. Translated by Constance Garnett, with an introduction by Thomas Mann. New York: Random House, 1939.

———. *Two Old Men*. Burke, VA: Trinity Forum, 2010.

Tough, Paul. "The Character Test: What If the Secret to Success Is Failure?" *The New York Times Magazine* online September 14, 2011. http://www.nytimes.com/2011/09/18/magazine/what-if-the-secret-to-success-is-failure.html. Reprinted September 18, 2011, MM38, under the headline "The Character Test."

Whitney, Gleaves. "Recovering Rhetoric: How Ideas, Language and Leadership Can Triumph in Postmodern Politics." The Heritage Foundation. http://www.heritage.org/research/lecture/recovering-rhetoric.

BIBLIOGRAPHY

Wilson, Douglas. *Recovering the Lost Tools of Learning: An Approach to Distinctively Christian Education.* Wheaton, IL: Crossway Books, 1991.

Wolfe, Alan. "The Opening of the Evangelical Mind." *The Atlantic Monthly*, October 1, 2000. http://www.theatlantic.com/past/docs/issues/2000/10/wolfe4.htm.

Index

aesthetics, 200
affordance, 232–33
Africa, 269–72
Agassiz, Louis, 141–42
age, developmental, 109. *See also* education, unhurried
aid, international, 271–72
all truth is God's truth, 39, 51, 62–63, 173, 218
"angel-beast," 110, 173, 227
Aquinas, Thomas, 40, 53, 54–55, 164, 189
architecture, classical, 127–28
arete, 182
Aristotle, 128, 155, 182
art
    aristocracy of, 198–201
    and human creativity, 195–97
    study of, 19, 105, 129, 196–97
    of teaching, 143–46
    of Trinity students, 196–97
    See also liberal arts
Aslan, 264–65
aspirations, for Trinity, 229–30. *See also* students, goals and aspirations for
assessments
    developmental, 109–10

assessments (*continued*)
    and Programme for International Student Assessment (PISA), 36–37
Athanasius, 11
athletics, 239–54
    and character development, 181
    cross-country, 241–43
    sacrifice in, 181
    Trinity's goals for, 246–47
    Trinity's history of, 239–40
attention, 107, 147–50, 226
Augustine, 40, 61, 87, 187
    conversion of, 48–49
    and the great transcendents, 40
    wanderers analogy, 33
authority
    delegated to school, 4
    of teachers and adults, 111
balance, 19, 127–30
Barbour, Ian, 58
Barnard, Chester, 153
Bauerlein, Mark, 101
beauty, 42–43, 128, 189–201. *See also* great transcendents; truth, goodness, beauty
Benton, Thomas Hart, 122
big ideas, relationships with, 39, 105–6

INDEX

Blair, Kristen, 155, 156
blog, the headmaster's, 233
body of Christ, 51, 208, 209
bonitas, 39. *See also* truth, goodness, beauty
bonum arduum, 164
boredom, 140–42
born persons, children as, xiv, 111–12, 220, 221
Boswell, James, 90
boundaries, in education, 20, 157, 236, 266–68
Boyd, Dana, 237
Brooks, David, 156

Canada, Geoffrey, 36
Carr, Nicholas, 231
character, development of, 180–81. *See also* education, moral; habits, and character development
Chariots of Fire, 246
Chesterton, G. K., 87, 106, 134, 192, 193
Christ, 11, 18–19, 30, 33, 49, 57, 60, 88, 123, 134, 206, 212, 252, 254, 264, 275
    body of, 5, 208, 209–10
    and culture, 230
    habits pointing us to, 185
    lordship of, 23–24, 45, 61, 63, 110, 263
    love of, xiv, 176
    virtues fulfilled in, 4, 39, 51
    the Word (*Logos*), 123
Christmas story, 273–75
Chronicles of Narnia, 264–65
Cicero, 48–49, 90, 143
clarity, and classical beauty, 189–90
classical Christian school, *see* school, Christian; school, classical; education, classical
classical ideal, 89–92
classical tradition, 4, 16, 39–43, 67–69, 90. *See also* education, classical
classics, and the ideal of humanity, 90
coaching, athletic, 181, 241, 242, 245–47, 248–49, 252, 254
Cockburn, Bruce, 110, 175
Collins, Billy, 156
columns, classical, 127–29
Comenius, John Amos, 143–45
commerce, art in service of, 199
common grace, 62, 171
communication, 33, 138, 158, 223
community
    and athletics, 252
    and classical education, 71, 146
    customs and standards of, 234–37, 250
    and diversity, 205, 208, 211–214, 219
    involvement in and service to, 18, 35–38, 47, 217
    of learners, 86, 123, 163–64
    of readers, 101, 114
    role in education, 51–52
    safety of, 237
    a school for the, 26, 38, 168, 213, 261–63
    and technology, 234–37
    Trinity as a, 3–5, 25, 51–52, 219
conflict, of codes, 153
Confucius, 169
conversion, of Augustine, 48–49
Cooper, Harris, 169
countercultural, Trinity as, xiv–xv, 12–14, 175

courage, 4, 137, 168, 180, 203, 208, 244, 245–47, 253
course, Latin vs. English, 82
craftsmanship, 199
creation
　artistic, 199
　and origins, 57–60, 62
　under Christ's lordship, 23, 60, 63, 87
　the wonder of, 19, 60
　See also nature
creativity, 195, 199, 228
　artistic, 195–97, 199
　of God, 60, 79
Csikszentmihaly, Mihaly, 148, 159
culture, 3–4, 18, 41, 70, 171, 190, 250
　African-American and Latino, 217. 218
　and athletics, 244, 247, 248
　Christ and, 230
　and common grace, 171
　educational, 156–57, 185, 225
　engagement with, 205–6, 208, 226, 229
　and *paideia*, 70–72
　shifts in American, 174, 178
　and Trinity's mission, 18–21
Curie, Marie, 119
curriculum
　classical, 89–92
　development of, 122
　liberal arts, 218
　rich and unhurried, 209
　See also pedagogy; education, classical; education, rich; education, unhurried
customs, of a community (*minhagim*), 233–36

Dan the Animal Man, 60
Dean, Jeremy, 183–84

Declaration of Independence, 221
dedication, of the Lower School Building, 261–63
De Officiis, 143
De Oratore, 90
development, of children, 83, 108–9
developmental age, 109. *See also* education, unhurried
Dewey, John, 120
differentiation, 159
Digital Learning Initiative, 229, 234, 237. *See also* learning, and technology
discipline, in athletics, 252
discovery, role of in learning, 123
diversity, 203–21
　and the kingdom of God, 213
　policy on, 208–19
doctrinal statement, 86
dream, of Dr. Martin Luther King, Jr., 106, 203, 211–14
drill, as homework, 136, 137, 138
drop-out rate, 36
Duke of Wellington, 161, 181
Duncan, Arne, 35, 36

education
　in the arts, 196
　child-centered, 81–84, 112
　Christian, 65–95, 86–88
　classical: 57–83; and diversity, 209; and the Gettysburg Address, 74–76; and mathematics, 77–80; and *paideia*, 66, 70–73; respecting children's development, 83; and sports, 245–46
　definition of, 89–92
　engagement in, 97, 103, 107, 123
　and the greatest good, 32
　the ideal, 47, 89–92
　from the inside out, 114–17
　the institution of, 249–50

education (*continued*)
- intellectual: and athletics, 248; in balance, 129, 170; at Christian schools, 86, 263; and faith, 53–56; and homework, 157; and tools of learning, 15; and truth, 39; well paced, 19
- liberal, 67–69, 71–72, 85, 183, 221. *See also* liberal arts
- "by littles," 74
- moral, 161–85
- and nature, 140–42
- as private cultivation, 7–8
- purpose of, 6–8, 9–11, 15–17, 31–34
- and relations with things, 39–40, 110
- rich: xiv, 19, 77, 97–123, 148–49; and Charlotte Mason, xiv, 97–98; definition of, 97, 209; and diversity, 209, 212; and engagement, 97, 103, 107, 122–23; and mathematics, 77; and poetic knowledge, 115–16; and truth, goodness, beauty, 39–40, 43
- role of parents in: and athletics, 246–47; and community, 3–5; and engagement, 13, 138, 141; fostering good habits, reading, and play, 105, 121, 132, 138–39, 149, 157–59, 170, 180; and homework, 138–39, 149; as primary, 3–5, 20; respecting students' minds, 88
- role of teachers in: and Christian education, 50–51, 60, 63; and differentiation, 84n1; and fostering of habits, 101, 180, 183; and homework, 137, 158–59; and pedagogical methods, 84n1, 93–95, 122, 130, 143–46, 149, 159; and respect for education, 248–50; and respect for students' personhood, 112; and student engagement, 1, 120, 141–42, 183

education (*continued*)
- of the self, 27–30
- and successful pedagogy, 93–95
- and technology, 223–37
- as transactional, 82
- unhurried: xiv, 125–59, 173, 225, 266; and diversity, 209, 212, 217; and limits, 266–68; and mathematics, 77
- as vocational and civic training, 6–8
- of the whole person, 39
- and wonder, 6–8, 112

Eliot, T. S., 40, 72
Ellul, Jacques, 223
Emerson, Ralph Waldo, 121
engagement
- with culture, 208, 209, 226
- in learning, 97, 103–6, 107, 123, 234

English language, importance of, 271
enjoyment
- of art and literature, 116
- of learning, 146
- *See also* learning, love and enjoyment of

ethics, teaching of, 167–70
evolution, and origins, 58–60
excellence
- academic, 80, 217, 263
- boundaries of, 266
- and diversity, 213
- habits as path to, 182
- institutional, 248–50
- a school of, 213, 230, 262
- and sports, 245–47, 252

expectations, importance of high, 180
experiment, education as, 9–11

INDEX

faith, xiv, 4, 87, 268, 275
   framework of, and diversity, 208, 209, 212, 263
   Jewish, 171–73
   and learning, 45, 47–49, 51, 52, 53–56, 86–87, 92, 143, 229–31
   and politics, 22–25
family, role of in education, 3–5, 19–20, 149–50, 157–59. *See also* education, role of parents in
Family and Student Time Policy, 157
fans, athletic, 251–54
field trips, 100, 103–6, 163–66
"flow," 148, 150, 159
founders, of Trinity School, xvii–xix, 257
framework, of Christian faith and conviction, 51, 52, 208, 209. *See also* faith; education, Christian
freedom, birthright of, 220–21
Frost, Robert, 125

Gaebelein, Frank, 41, 51
Galileo, 79
generosity
   and prosperity, 269–70
   unhurried, 151–54
   See also virtue
genius, 62, 79
   and art, 200–201
   of classical education, 81–84
   Mozart as a, 195–97
   See also intellect
Gesell Institute, 107, 108–9
Gettysburg Address, 75–76, 104, 106, 221
gift, of *Non nobis*, 174–77
Gilson, Etienne, 36, 198–201
glory
   of the beautiful, 200
   to be human, 221

glory (*continued*)
   of God, 19, 33, 60, 92, 123, 179, 226, 243, 263, 275
goals, 47, 76, 91
   age-appropriate, 133
   of athletics, 246
   ethical, 167–68
   for Trinity School, 13–14, 18–21, 204, 217–19, 224
   See also students, goals and aspirations for
God
   at the heart of Trinity School, 19
   image of, 39, 56, 60, 87, 193
   See also glory, of God
Goldsmith, Barbara, 119
Good Samaritan test, 152–53
goodness, *see* truth, goodness, beauty
grace, common, 62, 171
grammar
   and homework, 137
   stage of the Trivium, 10, 68, 69, 75, 81–84, 91, 145, 169
   See also Trivium
Great Didactic, The, 144–46
great transcendents, 39–43, 189, 201
   See also truth, goodness, beauty
Greek ideal, 16–167
Gregory the Great, 108
grit, importance of in learning, 178–81
growth
   children's, 107–9, 132, 144–46, 170
   of Trinity School, xvii–xix, 70, 257–60

habits
   of attention and patience, 91

INDEX

habits (*continued*)
  and character development, 161, 167, 170, 180–81, 182–85, 208
  formation of, 170, 180–81, 182–85, 208, 218, 228, 250
  of learning, 105, 137
  necessary in education, 105, 181, 218
  of reading, 99–102, 139
Hamilton, Alexander, 24
harmony, in the heart, 169
Hart, Betty, 121
Hirsch, E. D., 65, 83, 114
"history from the inside," 106
history, of Trinity School, xvii–xix, 223–24, 239–40, 261–62
home, *see* family, role of in education; education, role of parents in
Homer, 72–73, 81, 115
homework
  as bridge between home and school, 137
  differentiation in, 159
  excess and defects of, 135–36, 156
  limits on, 159
  purpose and goals of, 137–39
  recommendations regarding, 157–59
  and System 2 thinking, 149
  and unhurriedness, 157–59
Hopkins, Gerard Manley, 255
hospitality, 183
  and diversity, 22, 206–7
Howard, Tom, 227

ideal, 245
  classical, 89–92
  Greek, 16–17, 128–30
ideas
  and the big idea, 39, 105–6
  as currency of education, 50

ideas (*continued*)
  as food for the mind, 118–23
  engagement with, 123
  See also knowledge; intellect
image of God (*imago Dei*), 39, 56, 60, 87, 193
imitation, 196–97, 199–200
in loco parentis, 4
independent schools, public purpose of, 35–38
integration
  of faith and learning, 51
  of science and religion, 58
integrity, and classical beauty, 189
intellect, 51, 54–55, 65. *See also* education, intellectual

James, William, 184–85
Jefferson Memorial, 100, 103
Jefferson, Thomas, 24, 221
Johnson, Samuel, 90–91
journey, spiritual, 27–30
joy
  in art, 190, 192–93, 199–200
  of family, 272
  of learning, 32, 105, 116, 122–23, 146, 268
  and prosperity, 241–42
Judaism, teachings of, 65, 171–73
justice, 4, 5, 129, 163, 176, 211, 212, 213

Kahneman, Daniel, 147–48
Keller, Helen, 116
King, Martin Luther, Jr., 106, 203, 211–14, 220–21
KIPP charter schools, 178–79
Kirk, Russell, 40, 100
knowledge
  beauty of, 200

knowledge (*continued*)
  desire for, 112–13
  education and, 29, 32
  of God, 53, 55, 176
  and homework, 137–38
  mathematical, 77–80
  poetic, 114, 115–17
  pursuit and cultivation of, 53–55, 57–58, 68–69, 75, 85, 105–6
  teaching and, 144
  through relationship with ideas, 105–6
  and virtue, 49
Koinonia Committee, 205, 207, 208
Kuyper, Abraham, 23, 45, 63

"language dancing," 121
learning
  approaches to, 68–69, 93–95, 120–21, 196
  classical, 65–95, 209
  culture and community of, 86, 164, 185, 225
  developmental approach to, 107–10
  and engagement, 105, 159
  and faith, 11, 50–52, 53–56, 63
  habits of, 105, 137, 183
  lifelong, 84, 137, 140, 159
  love and enjoyment of, 32, 49, 113, 116, 122–23, 140, 159
  pace of, 129, 144–46
  purpose of, 17
  rich, 97–123
  and technology, 28, 225, 227, 231, 232–33, 234–37
  tools of, 23, 68–69, 74, 75, 209, 218
  as transactional, 82
  unhurried, 125–59
  as "unnatural," 83
  See also education

Levin, David, 178–79
Lewis, C. S.
  on beauty, 43
  on chivalry, 245
  on education, 71
  and mere Christianity, xiii, 11, 19, 45
  poetry of, 29
  on reality and the self, 40
liberal arts, 33, 68–69, 85–86, 218, 227. *See also* education, liberal
Liddell, Eric, 246
limits, in education, 217, 266–68
Lincoln, Abraham, 74–76
Lincoln Memorial, 100
logic
  in classical education, 1
  in the Gettysburg Address, 76
  as a liberal art, 76, 85–86
  stage of the Trivium, 10, 68, 69, 75, 81, 83, 83n2, 169
  See also Trivium
"Lost Tools of Learning, The," 10, 15, 81, 83, 85, 226, 227
Lower School, dedication of, 261–63

Maritain, Jacques, 65, 89
Marshmallow Test, 179–80
Mason, Charlotte
  on children as born persons, xiv, 111–13, 220
  and the classical method, 81
  on education as a life, 97, 118
  and education as the science of relations, 39–40
  on habit and the formation of character, 180, 182, 183
  on ideas, 113, 119–20, 122
  on play, 132
Mason, George, 10
mastery, 28, 69, 197

mathematics, 71, 77–80, 82, 129
Medina, John, 148–49
meekness, 245
Merton, Thomas, 93, 94–95
mind
  food for the, 105, 118–23
  life of the, 105, 118, 119, 122, 123, 263
  training and building up of the, 55–56, 85, 87, 88, 144–46, 263
  See also thinking
minhag, 234–37
minorities, in independent schools, 216–19
Mischel, Walter, 179–80
mission
  Christian, 5, 23, 45, 47, 51, 209, 218
  classical, 47, 65, 127, 225
  and diversity, 205, 208–9
  of Trinity School, 23, 206, 218, 262, 268
  unhurried, 125, 157, 266
moderation, 24, 127, 128–29, 172
Mogel, Wendy, 171–73, 234–37
moral education, 161–85
  thoughts on, 167–70
  See also virtue
motto, of Trinity School, 16, 39–43, 61, 198. See also truth, goodness, beauty; *Non nobis*
Mozart, Wolfgang Amadeus, 195–97
Mukhanyo Christian Academy, 269–70, 271
multitasking, 147–50

Narnia, 264–65
narrative
  and diversity, 209
  the Gospel, 161, 275
  personal, 274

narrative (*continued*)
  in *Two Old Men*, 151–54
  Trinity's unifying, 73, 161
National Association of Independent Schools (NAIS), 35–36
National Endowment for the Arts, 99–100
nature
  analogy to human development, 107–10
  and art, 190, 199–200
  studies, 190
  and teaching, 143–46
  and wonder, 141–42
Neely, Jack, 31
neighborhood, customs of, 235–36. See also community
Newton, Isaac, 79
Nicholas of Cusa, 29
Nicomachean Ethics, 161, 182
Niebuhr, H. Richard, 230–31
Niebuhr, Reinhold, iii
Nietzsche, Friedrich, 1
Non nobis, 174–77, 181, 185, 239, 241, 243, 250. See also glory, of God
nonpartisanship, 23

organisms, qualities of, 108–9
originality, artistic, 195–97
origins, and evolution, 57–60, 62
orthodoxy, 57, 58, 268

paideia, 16, 70–73
parents, see education: role of parents in
Pedagogblog, 233
pedagogy, 65–66, 93–95, 144–46. See also education: role of teachers in; teaching; teachers

INDEX

permanent things, the, 40–41. *See also* great transcendents; truth, goodness, beauty
perseverance, 180, 241–43, 253
personhood, sacredness of, 111–13. *See also* born persons
pert stage, 83
picture studies, 190
Programme for International Student Assessment (PISA), 36
Plato, 9, 16–17, 33, 47, 77, 78, 163
play, 131–34
poetic stage, 83
politics, 22–25
Polkinghorne, John, 42–43
poll-parrot stage, 83
Popova, Maria, 184
Postman, Neil, 15, 82
poverty, and gulf between rich and poor, 270
practice
  and the formation of good habits, 170, 183
  homework as a means of, 137, 138–39
  and mastery, 28, 197
  of virtue, 163, 166, 183, 245
  of writing, 146
proportions, classical, 127–30, 189–90
prudence, 100, 163–66. *See also* virtue; education, moral
Ptolemy, 78
public schools, 35–38
pulchritudo, 39, 198. *See also* beauty

Quadrivium, 68

reading, 7, 12, 141, 227, 233, 265

reading (*continued*)
  and classical education, 72, 90, 91
  as homework, 137, 139
  habits of, 99–102, 139
Reading at Risk, 100
reconciliation, and diversity, 209, 212–13, 218
recruitment, athletic, 251–52
redemption, 26, 49, 63, 199, 213, 227
relations, education as the science of, 39–40
religion, and science, 57–60
respect, 78, 123, 168
  in athletics, 248–50
  for authority, 91
  for children as born persons, 84, 88, 111–13, 146
  habit of, 183
  for political views, 25
  in teaching, 94, 248–50
responsibility, xv, 7, 183
rest, importance of, 125, 146, 158
revelation, general and special, 57–58
rhetoric
  in classical education, 81, 83, 83n2, 90, 91, 145, 196
  in the Gettysburg Address, 75, 76
  as a liberal art, 69, 86
  of Martin Luther King, Jr., 211, 220
  stage of the Trivium, 10, 68, 69, 75, 81, 83
  See also Trivium
rich education, *see* education, rich
risk taking, encouragement of, 180
Risley, Todd, 121
Rousseau, Jean-Jacques, 9, 82–83

Sacks, Oliver, 273–74
sacredness, of personhood, 111–13

sacrifice, in athletics, 181
Sandberg, Ryne, 249–50
Sayers, Dorothy, 10, 15, 81, 83, 85, 226
school
  and the arts, 187, 189–91
  boredom in, 140–42
  Christian, 50–52: and the arts, 193, 198; and athletics, 251, 253–54; and classical, 16, 77, 79; as a community, 51–52; and diversity, 211; and education, 9, 86–88, 229–32, 268; interdenominational, xiii, 11; and moral education, 4, 47–49, 161–62, 163–66, 182–85
  classical, xiv, 16, 89–92
  for the community, 6, 38, 146, 168, 213, 261–63
  as countercultural, xiv–xv, 12–14, 175
  of excellence, 20, 187, 213, 262–63, 266, 268
  and home, 20, 135–37, 138–39, 180, 217
  and homework, 135–39, 155–59
  independent, 35–36, 181, 182, 216–18
  and moral education, 161–85
  Mukhanyo, 269–70, 271
  and political discussion, 22–26
  problems in, 131–34
  public, 36–38, 167–68
  purpose and goals of, 4, 6–8, 13–14, 15–17, 18–20, 32–34, 47, 54, 118, 123, 221, 227–28, 248
  role of in raising children, 3–5
  safe, 20
  sports in, 244–47, 248–50
  and technology, 225–28, 233, 236
  as a "village," 3–5, 51–52
  well paced (unhurried), 19–20, 155–59, 217

science
  and the formation of habits, 183–84
  of relations, 39
  and religion, 57–60
  the subject of, 62, 82, 164
self, the way of, 27–29
service-learning, 35, 37–38
Shapiro, Judith, 119
Socrates, 143–44, 226
Socratic method, 94–95
souls, types of, 108
sports, at Trinity, 241–43, 246–47, 252–54. *See also* athletics
sportsmanship, 181, 251–54
Spring on the Missouri, 122
standards
  age-appropriate, 133
  for technology, 236–37
strategic planning, 239–40
students
  African, 269–70
  and athletics, 181, 244, 246–47, 253
  and desire for knowledge, 112–13
  and development of habits, 180–81
  and engagement with culture, 208, 209, 226
  and engagement in learning, 1, 97, 103, 107, 122–23
  goals and aspirations for: intellectual, xiv, 1, 23, 49, 62, 68–69, 79, 85–86, 105, 107, 113, 115, 118, 157–58, 180, 183, 190, 196, 209, 217–18; interpersonal and social, 13, 37, 129, 130, 150, 158–59; moral, 13, 168–70, 180–81, 182–83, 246, 250, 253; spiritual, 33, 51, 122–23, 218, 226; technological, 227, 228
  interaction of, 13–14, 51, 103–5, 164–65, 241–43
  and multitasking, 149, 150

students (*continued*)
  and technology, 226, 227, 228, 233, 236–37
  and unhurriedness, 157–59
Summa Theologica, 40, 53, 54–55, 189
summum bonum, 32–33
systems of thinking, 147–49

taste, artistic, 189
Taylor, James, 114, 115–16
teachers
  and Christian education, 50–52, 63, 87–88
  excellent, 94, 95, 130, 249, 250
  as midwives, 122, 144
  respect for and commitment to education, 248–50
  responsibilities of, 138, 158–59, 180–81
  See also education, role of teachers in
teaching
  appropriate time for, 144–46
  the art of, 143–46
  pedagogical methods in, 65–66, 93–95, 144–46
technology, 223–37
  and affordance, 232–33
  and community standards, 234–37
telos, 16–17
Temple School, 9
thinking
  critical, 83n2, 84
  as a human activity, 56, 67, 68
  independent, 86, 87, 120–21, 122
  "institutionally," 249–50
  systems of, 147–49, 159
Tolstoy, Leo, 151–54

tools of learning, 23, 68, 69, 74, 75, 209, 218, 227. *See also* "Lost Tools of Learning, The"
tourism, educational, 103–6. *See also* field trips

transcendents, *see* great transcendents
transformation
  schools as agents of, 7, 47
  spiritual, 48–49
Trinity Reads, 101, 114, 151
Trinity School
  as countercultural, xiv–xv, 12–14, 156, 175
  founders and founding of, x, xvii–xix, 17–19
  goals for, 13–14, 18–21, 204, 217–19, 226, 228
  history of, xvii–xix, 257–58
  as a school for the community, 6, 38, 146, 168, 213, 261–63
Trivium, 10, 20, 67, 68–69, 74, 83–84, 226. *See also* grammar; logic; rhetoric
truth
  as the currency of education, 50
  and diversity, 212, 218, 220, 221
  See also truth, goodness, beauty
truth, goodness, beauty, 29, 39–43, 129, 189, 193, 201
  and diversity, 206, 208, 218
twaddle, xiv, 113, 232
Two Old Men, 122, 151–54

unhurriedness
  definition of, 125, 146, 266
  and diversity, 209, 212, 217
  and education, xiv–xv, 77, 125–59
  generosity of, 151–54

unhurriedness (*continued*)
  and homework, 155–59
  as part of Trinity's mission, 65–66, 157, 209, 225
  See also education, unhurried

Van Doren, Mark, 93, 94–95
veritas, 39. *See also* truth; truth, goodness, beauty
verities, the eternal, 41–42
village, Trinity as a, 3–5
Virginia Declaration of Rights, 10
virtue, 4–5, 29, 49, 164, 167, 245, 267
  Aristotle on, 128, 137, 161
  and athletics, 244–47
  of courage, 4, 137, 244–45
  and diversity, 208, 212
  of generosity, 151–54
  and habit, 161, 170, 182–85, 228
  of justice, 4, 163, 212
  and moral education, 163–64
  of prudence, 4, 163–66, 267
  reading as a path to, 101
  of temperance, 137, 163, 267
virtues, cardinal and theological, 4, 163–64

Washington, DC, 100, 103–6
Wellesley, Arthur (Duke of Wellington), 161, 181
West, Hubert, 239, 241–42
winning, in athletics, 244, 252
wisdom, xiv, 19, 47–48, 150, 171, 172, 176, 183
  and prudence, 163–66, 172
  the way of, 28–30
  See also virtue
Wolfe, Alan, 85, 86–87

wonder, 29, 132, 144
  sense of, 8, 19, 115, 141, 183
writing
  creative, 83n2, 84, 195, 196–97
  expectations for, 180
  not multitaskable, 150
  of students, 131–33